T0202716

Progress in IS

"PROGRESS in IS" encompasses the various areas of Information Systems in theory and practice, presenting cutting-edge advances in the field. It is aimed especially at researchers, doctoral students, and advanced practitioners. The series features both research monographs that make substantial contributions to our state of knowledge and handbooks and other edited volumes, in which a team of experts is organized by one or more leading authorities to write individual chapters on various aspects of the topic. "PROGRESS in IS" is edited by a global team of leading IS experts. The editorial board expressly welcomes new members to this group. Individual volumes in this series are supported by a minimum of two members of the editorial board, and a code of conduct mandatory for all members of the board ensures the quality and cutting-edge nature of the titles published under this series.

More information about this series at http://www.springer.com/series/10440

Jan Recker

Scientific Research in Information Systems

A Beginner's Guide

Second Edition

 Springer

Jan Recker (iD)
University of Hamburg
Hamburg, Germany

ISSN 2196-8705   ISSN 2196-8713   (electronic)
Progress in IS
ISBN 978-3-030-85438-6   ISBN 978-3-030-85436-2   (eBook)
https://doi.org/10.1007/978-3-030-85436-2

This Springer imprint is published by the registered company Springer Nature Switzerland AG.
The registered company address is: Gewerbestrasse 11, 6330 Cham, Switzerland

Preface to the Second Edition

Time flies. I am writing this preface about nine years after I put the finishing touches on the first edition of this book. What happened in the years that followed was not even in my imagination at that time. I married, became a father, moved to a new continent, and changed my university affiliation (more than once!). Oh, and there has been a global pandemic as well. The world has moved on, science has moved on, the information systems field has moved on, and I have moved on. Time for the book to make progress, too.

When I look back at the first edition now, I believe it was a useful book and hope it was helpful to many. By April 2016, the book had been used by some 450 research institutions in more than 60 countries. It also turned out that a primary audience for the book included not only doctoral students and early career academics, as I thought would be the case, but also under- and postgraduate students with an interest in information systems research. For this last group, the book provided an entry point from which to learn what research is about, how they might go about entering the field, and how they could address the challenges that awaited them. Some institutions created or updated their research training courses based on this book. All this, of course, makes me proud and made writing the book worth the effort, because the monetary reward did not. Stories of vampires falling in love with high-school students sell considerably better.

Still, I wanted to be sure I was leading young scholars toward a good path and not putting the wrong expectations into their heads. The content was in need of updating, revision, and polishing. I held no illusions that the first version of this book would not deal with some matters in an insufficient way and that it would not contain omissions or deal inappropriately with certain topics that are ongoing matters of contention. Over time, my own experiences also widened, and my knowledge deepened. A second edition is an opportunity to update the content in this book and to address topics I should have addressed more thoroughly in the first edition or did not address at all.

What you will find in this second edition is the same essential scope and narrative of the first edition, the same tone and structure, and the same broad, introductory, overview level of discussion without the nitty-gritty details you can read about elsewhere. But I did make several changes in the book, from start to finish.

First, I added new parts to the *introduction*. I now spend more time introducing the field of information systems before dealing with learning of how to become a researcher. I also revised Chap. 2's discussion of the core principles and concepts of scientific research to ensure these important messages were conveyed well.

Another set of major changes is in the part of the book about conducting research. I expanded the writing on *theory development* and put more of my own spin on the topic, particularly by adding more material about theorizing processes and techniques. Next, I substantially updated and expanded the description of *research methods*, which now covers additional approaches, including computational methods. I also revised the content about matters like qualitative methods and design science because colleagues pointed me to some elements of dispute.

In the third part of the book, I substantially revised the chapter on *academic publishing* to draw on the perspective of a journal editor who handles and decides on submissions like those that new researchers will eventually make. Finally, I expanded the material on *ethics in research*. I added, for example, several cases I encountered myself for illustration.

I retained all other material from the first edition in a revised, updated, and more polished way. Even those who read the first edition should be interested in reading the second edition because of these useful additions and revisions.

Let me finish this preface with a quotation from Germaine Williams, Tyrone Gregory Fyffe, and Walter Murphy (better known as The Specials) because they have captured well what I have felt when I look back at when I wrote the first edition and now the second, and when I realize how quickly time, career, and life moves on:

> *Enjoy yourself, it's later than you think.*
> *Enjoy yourself, while you're still in the pink.*
> *The years go by, as quickly as you wink.*
> *Enjoy yourself, enjoy yourself, it's later than you think.*

Hamburg, Germany   Jan Recker
August 2021

Purpose, Structure, and Audience of this Book

Purpose and Audience

This book introduces higher-degree research students and early career academics to scientific research as occurring in the field of information systems and adjacent fields, such as computer science, management science, organization science, and software engineering. As a field of research, information systems is concerned with the *development, use, and impacts of digital information and communication technology by individuals, collectives, and organizations*. With this focus, expertise in this field includes understanding current and future business, management, societal, and individual practices that are enabled by or infused with digital technologies, from laptops and computers to mobile devices and digital wearables, among many others.

The book largely draws on my own experience in information systems research, research-level teaching, postgraduate student supervision, and mentoring of early career researchers between 2005 and 2017 at Queensland University of Technology, a leading institute for information systems research in Australia, between 2018 and 2020 at the University of Cologne, and since 2021 at the University of Hamburg in Germany. As the book is based on these experiences, it is positioned relative to the worldview and experiences that I have developed in my work, my own training, and through my own mentors and advisors. As a result, while most aspects of the book relate to experiences, challenges, and processes in scientific research in general, it is also influenced by the domain, scientific paradigm, interests, beliefs, and values with which I undertake my research. You may find that you disagree with certain views that I express, but that should not reduce the practical value of the book.

This book complements other textbooks for research students and scholars rather than replace them. Instead of focusing primarily on research methods as many other textbooks do, it covers the entire research process, from start to finish, placing particular emphasis on understanding the cognitive and behavioral aspects of research, such as motivation, modes of inquiry, theorizing, planning for research, planning for publication, and ethical challenges in research.

The book guides research students through the process of learning about the life of a researcher by explaining the essential elements, concepts, and challenges of the research journey. By directing students to useful resources, it not only provides a gateway through which the student can not only learn about becoming a researcher but also inquire deeply into particular elements the book covers.

Designed to be comprehensive but also succinct, the book focuses on key principles and challenges—the core of the research process—without delving into the many details, associated challenges, exceptions, and other issues. It is meant to guide beginning researchers in their quest to do scholarly work and to assist them in developing their own answers and strategies over the course of their studies.

Structure

This book is organized into eight chapters in three parts:

Part I: *Basic Principles of Research* introduces the journey and challenges of pursuing a research degree in information systems. Motivational components are discussed, along with key principles of scientific knowledge and scientific inquiry, forms of conduct, and reasoning. It introduces a basic vocabulary of scientific research and lays the foundation for reflecting on scientific research in information systems, whether one's own research or research one encounters.

Part II: *Conducting Research* dissects the research process in information systems as a science into the phases of planning, designing, and executing. Each of these phases then receives due attention in terms of specifying a research question, planning a research design, developing and appropriating theory in research, and choosing and executing suitable research methods. In doing so, this part of the book provides a general process model that is applicable to doctoral students in information systems and contains guidelines that can help them address the challenges they encounter along the way.

Part III: *Publishing Research* reflects on the communication of research outcomes and provides practical suggestions for managing it. Publication strategies and writing tactics are the focus of this part, along with ethical considerations pertaining to research in terms of conduct, collaboration, and publication. Part III also offers a closing reflection on the key processes and outcomes of scholarly work.

Acknowledgments

Many people have influenced my work and my life in significant ways—certainly too many to mention here. Any attempt to name all of them and give them the full credit they are surely due is sure to fail, so I will not even try to create anything close to an exhaustive list. That said, there are a few individuals that I believe deserve being named explicitly.

My own thinking is strongly inspired by these academic scholars who have guided me, with whom I work, and whom I hold in highest esteem for their professionalism, dedication, humility, and enthusiasm. I am a much better researcher than I could have ever hoped to be because I had the opportunity to work with people like Michael Rosemann, Ron Weber, Brian Pentland, Youngjin Yoo, Andrew Burton-Jones, Peter Green, Marta Indulska, Jan Mendling, Hajo Reijers, Jan vom Brocke, Stefan Seidel, Michael zur Muehlen, Nick Berente, Wil van der Aalst, and others. The advice and experiences that I offer in this book I owe to the knowledge that they and others shared with me. I also thank Nick, Jan, Hajo, Stefan, and Michael for reviewing chapter drafts and offering constructive feedback.

I also acknowledge my friends who have shared their life experiences with me and who are happy to let me indulge in my sharing mine. I know they know that I am referring to them, and I thank them for helping to make my life a wonderful and joyous experience.

My thoughts are also with my family, my children, my parents, my sisters and their children, my late grandparents, and other family members near and far. Deciding to follow an academic career has meant long separations that, while difficult, have helped me appreciate having these wonderful people as my family and what time we do have together.

Laura, you continue to inspire me always to be the best person I can be. You are my main reason for trying to do the best I can, and importantly also my main reason to come home to you and our wonderful children.

Jan Recker

Contents

Part I
Basic Principles of Research

Part I
Basic Principles of Research

Chapter 1
Introduction

1.1 Welcome to the Information Systems Field!

Welcome! You are probably reading these lines because you have just commenced your journey to becoming a researcher or perhaps because you have started a doctoral degree or contemplate doing so or you are attending a postgraduate research course. Maybe you are reading this book because you are studying information systems (IS) or you are studying some other topic but heard about information systems and wanted to know more about it. Maybe you are doing research in a field that does not have a similar book.

In any case, here we are, so let us talk about the research discipline of information systems. A formal definition of information systems research is that *it is primarily concerned with socio-technical systems that comprise individuals and collectives that deploy digital information and communication technology for tasks in business, private, or social settings.* In this sense, the information systems research discipline is concerned with examining the **development, use, and impact of digital information and communication technology**.

We call information systems a socio-technical field because information systems scholars distinguish *technical* components, like tasks and technology (e.g., digital infrastructure, systems, platforms, hardware, software, algorithms, or data), from *social* components, like individuals and collectives (e.g., networks, governments, organisations, communities, groups, teams, societies), that develop and use digital technical information and communication components in social, cultural, economic, hedonic, psychological, or economic contexts. The information systems field always emphasises both social and technical components, along with the interactions between them because it is at this intersection that many of the most interesting problems and opportunities emerge. As one example, consider augmented reality: it has technological components as we need hardware and software like video, audio, or even sensory touch technology to be able to augment our perceived reality, and we also need to understand what part of social reality we want to augment (leisure or

© Springer Nature Switzerland AG 2021

J. Recker, *Scientific Research in Information Systems*, Progress in IS,
https://doi.org/10.1007/978-3-030-85436-2_1

business, games or work?). Augmented reality really lies at the intersection of the technological and social components of reality.

The socio-technical perspective that our field encompasses differentiates it from other fields. For example, most engineering fields, including computer science, emphasise technical components like hardware and software, while many business, management, economic, and broader social sciences emphasise social components (people and collectives of people). Information systems emphasises neither side over the other and sees phenomena, problems, opportunities, and outcomes as emerging from the interaction between them. The phenomena, problems, opportunities, or outcomes we study are often instrumental, such as efficiency and productivity, because information systems research tends to be taught and practised in business schools, but these elements can just as well be humanistic, such as well-being, equality, diversity, inclusion, and freedom.

A second cornerstone of the information systems field is its focus on *digital information and communication technology* artefacts. Information systems scholars are not interested in *all* technical artefacts that are featured in socio-technical situations—bicycles and chairs are artefacts that are of little interest to these scholars; they are instead concerned about those artefacts that enable users to access, store, manipulate, distribute, display, and communicate information. Among information and communication technologies, the information systems field's interest is primarily in *digital* technologies, that is, technologies that rely on digitisation, the encoding of analogue information into digital format (essentially, bits and bytes that contain 0s and 1s). This focus may sound restrictive, but keep in mind that many artefacts today—from airplanes to cars, from kitchen scales to sound systems and toothbrushes—contain digital components. The success of brands like Google, Apple, and Amazon exemplifies how digital technology components in long-standing artefacts like books and music players have changed not only the nature of these products (from books to e-books, from cars to digital mobility solutions) but sometimes also entire markets and society. Digital technologies like Twitter have changed political processes, and 3D printers are changing the construction, engineering, design, and even food industries. Entirely, digital artefacts like autonomous robo-traders, chatbots, and autonomous vehicles change how we deal with finances, solve problems in conversations, and move from one place to another.

The information systems field is fast, broad, and multidisciplinary. Technological advancements have been rapid and are increasing at an astounding pace. A life without the Internet, smartphones, social media platforms, and microblogging seems unthinkable now, but all are developments of just the past two decades. Developments like the miniaturisation of hardware, increasingly powerful microprocessors, inexpensive and reliable memory, broadband communication networks, and the efficient power management of technological devices have led to a widespread—even ubiquitous—uptake of digital information and communication technologies in businesses and our private and social lives. We have powerful computers in our pockets or on our wrists. In fact, today's smartphones are many times more powerful than the mainframe computer that the National Aeronautics and Space

Administration (NASA) once used to send astronauts to the moon. They are faster than the computer on board the *Orion* spaceship NASA is currently testing to go to Mars.

Information systems is also a broad field of research because digital technologies are part of many first-world human experiences. We plan holidays through automated recommender systems, we choose modes of transportation using shared mobility service platforms, and we engage in physical activity in response to signals from wearable devices. We use digital technologies, like computers and laptops, frequently at work and use these and other technologies, such as smart, connected devices, online social networks, and wearable devices, in other parts of our lives. We also develop technology ourselves. Long gone are the days when computer "nerds" sat in offices and programmed software; today, almost anyone, including (and perhaps especially) children, can deal with software development personally. We learn to program robots using Lego Mindstorms and publish our own websites, blogs, and podcasts.

Because digital information and communication technology are so pervasive and have such an impact on our lives, it should not be surprising that the study of digital information and communication technology is of interest to academic scholars in many disciplines. Scholars from multiple disciplines are addressing a variety of key questions pertaining to information systems, including the following:

- How do people use digital technology?
- How does digital technology contribute to organisational performance?
- How are organisations using digital technology?
- How can societal issues be resolved through digital technology?
- Can major challenges like climate change be addressed through digital technology?
- How can healthcare be assisted through digital technology?
- How do we use digital technology for learning?
- What role does digital technology play in global markets and local governments?
- How does digital technology help organisations innovate their business processes?
- How can digital technology contribute to greening the planet?
- How do people build capabilities for dealing with digital technologies and related issues?
- How can digital technologies improve the performance of highly specialised professionals, such as athletes?
- How can digital technologies improve the diversity and inclusion of marginalised groups?
- How can nations protect themselves and others from cyberattacks?
- How can digital technology contribute to improving democracy, equality, and peace?

The search for answers to these and other questions can take many forms, and the potential pathways to these and other questions are rooted in a variety of well-established fields of scientific inquiry. The following is an incomplete list of some of the most prominent types of inquiry:

- Scholars in information technology (IT), software engineering, and computer science study the technical and computational attributes of digital technology.
- Scholars in the social, behavioural, cognitive, and psychological sciences study individuals' exposure, use, appropriation, and general behaviours in digital technology domains.
- Scholars in organisational science, management, and business study how corporate environments shape and are shaped by digital technology.
- Economists study the large-scale effects of the diffusion and innovation of digital technology on organisations, markets, regulatory policies, and societies.
- Scholars in the environmental sciences study the impact of digital technologies on natural resources and environmental changes, like climate change.

Clearly, the study of the development, use, and impacts of digital information and communication technology involves a diverse array of questions and approaches, which makes information systems research both exciting and challenging. Research in this area is multifaceted and comprehensive, yielding insights from a variety of perspectives and lenses that increase our knowledge about the role of information systems in our lives and help make positive changes in our world.

Information systems research is also challenging because scholars in this field are exposed to a wide variety of theories, methods, approaches, and research frameworks from other research traditions. Making sense of information systems research and contributing to the current state of knowledge require a scholar to learn, critique, apply, and extend multiple forms of inquiry, learn multiple theories on various levels of abstraction and complexity, and consider multiple approaches to conducting research. Information systems research addresses a fast-moving target as the artefacts that are at the core of this research change quickly and often, even over the course of a single study. Such dynamism is more difficult to accommodate than the stability that is common in other disciplines.

I hope you take from this discussion the fact that information systems research deals with exciting, challenging, and innovative aspects of human existence. We live in an age when digital information and communication technology transcends and in some cases defines many of our experiences. Digital devices are everywhere and are changing everything. Many more digital objects (about 20 billion) are connected through the World Wide Web than people (about 8 billion), and they change what we do and how we go about our lives. Information systems research seeks to unravel the complexities and problems that stem from this digital transformation of the human experience.

1.2 Understanding Your Motivation to Pursue Research

Before we delve deeper into the domain of information systems and explore the intricacies of research in this domain, it is useful to revisit the reasons you embarked on this quest in the first place. What is your motivation? Is it the thirst for knowledge? Is it the desire to develop innovative solutions and create impact? Is it to use your degree as a stepping stone to a professional career as a thought leader in a particular field or industry? Is it curiosity related to the desire to explore an intellectual challenge or opportunity?

None of these answers is right or wrong, of course. They just outline possible intrinsic motivations to embark on a journey that will take you several years to complete. To find an answer for yourself, you can ask which of the three dimensions of motivation speak to why you are considering information systems research: ambition, dedication, and commitment.

One dimension is *ambition*. The ambition to complete a research degree like a doctoral degree to progress towards an academic career is different from the ambition to pursue a research degree to focus on thought leadership in industry or corporate careers. One of the differences lies in the emphasis on publishing scientific papers from your research work, which is bread and butter for an academic but less so for an industry professional.

Dedication refers to your level of enthusiasm for working on a new and intrinsically complex challenge for a substantial amount of time—even years. If your research topic does not excite you, it will be difficult to sustain your enthusiasm for working on it over a prolonged period. In fact, many of the dropouts with whom I have spoken have shared that they lacked dedication to the topic on which they were working.

Finally, *commitment* refers to the willingness to free the necessary time and resources to work on the research. Research work is often unstructured, open-ended, and risky, so pursuing the tasks that must be completed requires commitment. Particularly noteworthy obstacles to commitment include having to work a regular job while pursuing research and raising a family at the same time. Notwithstanding high levels of ambition and/or dedication, the commitment of time and resources may simply not be high enough to complete the research to the required level of quality. Completing research work while working part- or full-time is not impossible, but smart resource management and commitment must come with such work.

Your levels of ambition, dedication, and commitment will accompany you on your research journey and will change over the course of your research program. I have assisted many students through their journeys to their doctoral degrees (and have, of course, completed this journey myself); how their lives proceed over the course of their doctoral programs and how the changes in their private contexts influence their journeys in terms of ambitions, dedication, and commitment take many forms.

Whatever your motivation is and however the context of your studies may vary, one element remains stable: the journey of scientific training and education is, at its heart, a research journey. It requires you to be a scholar in the fullest sense, one who develops the habits of mind and ability to generate new knowledge creatively, conserve valuable ideas, and transform this knowledge and these ideas responsibly through writing, teaching, and application.

What will be required of you during this journey? Completing a research degree program will demand that you demonstrate your ability to conduct research that makes a unique contribution while meeting standards of credibility and verifiability:

(1) the ability to ask and frame important questions
(2) the ability to generate knowledge and assess, critique, and defend claims of having generated new knowledge
(3) a broad and deep understanding of important phenomena in your area of research and the ability to understand and critically evaluate current knowledge and its progression in that area
(4) understanding of theoretical and methodical approaches to examining and developing current knowledge

The journey is long and the challenges manifold, and many of us start not as fully developed scholars but as apprentices who are interested but not well versed in the domain or its theories and methodologies. Some of the key challenges that surround research training programs are lessons that are not taught in method textbooks or theoretical essays but come only through experience, personal observation, and advice from fellows and academics who are more experienced.

We set out now to discuss these important lessons and examine the key principles that inform a junior scholar on his or her path to becoming a researcher. The experiences and advice I offer in this book are drawn not just from the field of information systems but also from the "reference" disciplines: tangential but influential fields of research like behavioural and organisational psychology, management, business, economics, computer science, and social science.

1.3   The PhD Challenge

From now on, I focus on research training as part of a doctoral degree program, such as a PhD. Several of the points I make are also relevant to other degrees, such as a master's degree in science, a master's degree in research, or a postgraduate honours degree, but the doctoral program is by and large the main university program that teaches how to do research.

At Queensland University of Technology, where I completed my own doctoral degree, the PhD is awarded "in recognition of a student's erudition in a broad field of learning and for notable accomplishment in that field through an original and substantial contribution to [the body of] knowledge" (Queensland University of Technology, 2007). Other universities may frame this statement differently, but the essence of the requirement tends to be consistent. What does this apparently innocuous statement mean, and why is meeting its requirements difficult?

Most people equate this statement with "doing research," although doing so is misleading because research can mean many things. For example, we do "research" when we consider buying a new car. We may also "research" follow-up information about something we learned from the news. Consultants do "research" when they try to develop a problem solution for their clients. Similarly, software developers routinely do "research" when they design new applications.

However, these examples of research generally do not contribute to the body of knowledge and meet the research requirement for a doctoral degree. Should the iPhone app developers who brought us Fruit Ninja, Angry Birds, or Cut the Rope be awarded doctoral degrees for their innovative games? No. Most research is done in the colloquial sense of gathering existing information about a subject of interest, while research that is recognised as a scholarly activity searches for fundamental concepts and new knowledge that meet two key principles of *scientific research*:

(1) It contributes to the advancement of human knowledge.
(2) It conforms to systematic principles that govern the collection, organisation, and analysis of data, which are defined and accepted by scientists.

We will examine these two principles in more detail in Chap. 2. For now, we simply acknowledge that these two principles of research distinguish scholarly research from other types of research and that confirming to principles of scholarly, scientific research is a challenging task that, on successful completion, can be recognised by the receipt of a doctoral degree.

As all doctoral students, as well as the junior and senior academic faculty that assist them, inevitably learn, research is messy, goes back and forth, speeds up and slows down, and can lead to dead ends and changes in direction. Progress is not steady, nor is it always fully transparent or explicit. Therefore, a doctoral degree will not be awarded simply because we followed a particular research process mechanically; instead, the process of research is only the mechanism by which we seek to achieve an outcome that is worthy of recognition. We learn about research from scientific papers, books, and theses that address it, but all of these works are merely "reconstructed stories" written *ex post* (after the research) about what was done and what was found by doing it. These works reconstruct the research in a simplified way, brushing over the errors, mistakes, doubts, failures, and irrelevant results. In fact, most stories read as if the researchers knew all along what the results would be: "We studied a phenomenon, we conjured a theory, and guess what? Our evaluation with data showed that our theory was right!"

In short, research that is conducted in pursuit of a doctoral degree—in fact, any scientific research—is not a mechanical process. The research "construction" process is messy and characterised by trial and error, failure, risk-taking, and serendipity, so it requires perseverance through many iterations of inductive, deductive, and abductive reasoning, ideas and trials, tests, and retests. A friend of mine spent five years setting up, executing, and analysing experiments until his results confirmed his iteratively revised and redefined theory. It took Thomas Edison 2,000 tries before he succeeded with his first innovation. Two thousand! When I say research is a challenging task, I am not exaggerating.

One of the common misconceptions is that those who start a doctoral degree will complete it. Like many other university courses, the doctoral degree program is subject to attrition rates, unplanned extensions, and failure to complete. Statistics do not paint an optimistic picture:

- Fewer than 65 percent of students who start PhD programs finish them (Bowen & Rudenstine, 1992).
- Attrition in residential doctoral programs is as high as 50 percent in face-to-face programs (de Vise, 2010) and 50–70 percent in online programs (Rigler Jr. et al., 2017). In Germany, statistics vary. Attrition rates are said to be about 15 percent of doctoral students in social science disciplines and about 25 percent in engineering disciplines (Franz, 2015).
- Ten percent of doctoral students claim to have considered suicide, and 54 percent of doctoral students have felt so depressed at various stages that they had difficulty functioning (OnlinePhDPrograms.Net).
- In one study, 43 percent of participating graduate students reported experiencing more stress than they could handle, with PhD students expressing the greatest stress. More than half listed stress or burnout as a major concern, about a quarter cited feeling like outsiders, and nearly a third listed their relationships with professors as a cause of stress (Patterson, 2016).

Despite this somewhat gloomy picture, a doctoral degree can yield enormous opportunities. It provides an entré into research as a career, as many jobs in research, such as that of a university professor, require it. Doctoral degrees are also helpful in securing positions outside academia, along with attractive salaries. The immense personal gratification of completing the degree is one of many rewards. I sometimes say that it is statistically more likely that they will succeed in completing their PhD studies than they are to succeed in their marriages. I mean it as a joke, but there is some truth to it.

I think the rewards outweigh the challenges, but you should be prepared for the complexity and challenge of this journey as the process of earning a doctoral degree differs from that of any degree that precedes it. Consider the analogy Waddington (2007) provided to illustrate this point:

> *Elementary school is like learning to ride a tricycle. High school is like learning to ride a bicycle. College is like learning to drive a car. A master's degree is like learning to drive a race car. Students often think that the next step is more of the same, like learning to fly an airplane. On the contrary, the PhD is like learning to design a new car. Instead of taking in more knowledge, you have to create knowledge. You have to discover (and then share with others) something that nobody has ever known before.*

This analogy highlights that a doctoral degree cannot be earned by repeating, memorising, and/or using the bits and pieces of knowledge someone gives you. In the PhD process, students must identify, explore, and resolve a problem that has not been solved sufficiently—or even not been addressed at all. As a result, the student becomes the world's leading expert on that particular problem. That thinking also suggests that the supervisor(s) cannot take the student all the way through that process. They can guide, they can assist, and they can criticise, but they cannot hold the answer to the particular problem because then it would not be a PhD problem to begin with.

The problem of correctly interpreting the task, coupled with the problem of the definition of what scientific research is about, can lead to "interesting" but completely inappropriate PhD ideas, proposals, and strategies. Sørensen (2005) classifies these types of inappropriate views on PhD activities, all of which share a common trait: they are not examples of scientific research that warrants a doctoral degree:

- **The great idea**: "I've just had this great idea! I don't know if anyone else has ever had the same idea, because I haven't checked, and I'm new in this field. Anyway, my idea is brilliant, so I really would like to share it with you all."
- **Other people's idea**: "I have just read this great book that I really like a lot. I'll just give you a short resume of the interesting points in the book and apply it to this situation over here."
- **The software hacker**: "I just built this great computer system/software tool/ mobile application. It is not based on previous theories or empirical findings. I am not very theoretical myself, but the system has a lot of fantastic features, and the interface is neat. Plus, people could really use it."
- **The theory hacker**: "I've come up with this theory/conceptual framework/ model/methodology. It is not related to other theories/conceptual frameworks/ models or any empirical data for that matter. Most of the concepts have been defined differently by all the big-shot scholars in the field, but I just do not like their categories so I have invented my own. I think it must be better, though I haven't checked."

To avoid these and other pitfalls, the remainder of this book guides you through the jungle that is research by giving you some background on the essential principles of scientific research, helping you find important problems to address, guiding your choices of methods and analysis, and helping you develop and publish new findings and theory.

1.4 What This Book Is About

This book offers advice and guidelines for conducting good research as part of a doctoral education in information systems. Conducting good research requires students to train their minds to act in scientific ways–to think like researchers.

To that end, the book discusses both the essential and tangential challenges that are key to learning how to perform good research. Three categories of such challenges are reflected in the three parts that constitute this book.

Part 1, *Basic Principles of Research*, contains Chaps. 1 and 2 and is concerned with the key principles and concepts of the scientific research that constitutes the key exercise of the doctoral program. Chapter 1 addresses the requirements of a doctoral education.

Chapter 2 introduces information systems research as a science and revisits scientific research and the principles of the scientific method on which it is built.

Part 2, *Conducting Research*, contains Chaps. 3, 4, and 5 and is concerned with the three key stages involved in any research project. Chapter 3 addresses theorising, examining what a theory is, why we require them in research, how theories are composed, and how theories are developed and applied.

Chapter 4 concerns research design, which refers to developing a blueprint for executing a study of a particular phenomenon or problem of interest. The chapter discusses the formulation of research questions, the development of a research plan, and the choice of an appropriate research methodology.

Chapter 5 then presents key research methods that can be elements of the research design. Broadly, it distinguishes quantitative methods of inquiry from qualitative methods of inquiry and touches on other forms of research, such as design research and mixed methods.

Part 3, *Publishing Research*, contains Chaps. 6, 7, and 8 and is concerned with the stage of the research process that follows the actual research: publishing the findings from the study. This third part of the study addresses challenges that relate to the craft of communicating effectively and efficiently your research in the form of articles, reports, theses, books, and other outlets.

Chapter 6 explains how to develop articles about studies that have been conducted. Various writing strategies are exemplified, essential parts of good papers are reviewed, and advice is offered for handling peer reviews and dealing with rejections and revisions.

Chapter 7 addresses three aspects of ethical considerations in conducting and publishing research: ethics in research conduct, ethics in research publication, and ethics in research collaboration.

Finally, Chap. 8 contains some brief reflections of mine on this book.

1.5 Further Reading

This chapter forays into several areas about which more readings are available. For example, you may want to read more about the information systems discipline and its history. A good starting point is Hirschheim and Klein's (2012) excellent article about the field's history. Wanda Orlikowski also collaborated on several good articles about research on technology and organising (Orlikowski & Barley, 2001; Orlikowski & Baroudi, 1991; Orlikowski & Iacono, 2001).

If you want to learn more about socio-technical thinking and its role in information systems scholarship, I recommend the excellent article by Suprateek Sarker et al. (2019). Bostrom and Heinen's (1977a, 1977b) articles about socio-technical systems from the early days of the information systems field in the late 1970s and a number of articles that also introduce and review the socio-technical perspective (e.g., Beath et al., 2013; Bostrom et al., 2009; Briggs et al., 2010; Lee, 2001) can also give you a good grounding in the field.

If you want to learn more about what "digital information and communication technology" artefacts interest information systems scholars, you can read about the debates about IT or IS artefacts (Akhlaghpour et al., 2013; Kallinikos et al., 2013; Lee et al., 2015; Orlikowski & Iacono, 2001; Weber, 1987) and whether these artefacts reside at the core of the information systems field (e.g., Alter, 2003; Benbasat & Zmud, 2003; Lyytinen & King, 2006; Nevo et al., 2009; Sidorova et al., 2008; Weber, 2006). A range of articles explain the particularities of digital artefacts compared to other types of technological objects (e.g., Baskerville et al., 2020; Ekbia, 2009; Faulkner & Runde, 2019; Kallinikos et al., 2013).

Other good readings deal with the research student's journey. Avison and Pries-Heje (2005) compiled and edited a volume regarding the practices of and recommendations from leading information scholars about the pursuit of a doctoral degree in information systems. In the early days of the discipline, Davis and Parker (1997) also shared their recommendations in a book for doctoral students. Several discussion papers summarise advice from senior scholars to students and early-career academics (e.g., Dean et al., 2011; Dennis et al., 2006; Klein & Lyytinen, 1985; Lyytinen et al., 2007; Van Slyke et al., 2003; Venkatesh, 2011).

References

Akhlaghpour, S., Wu, J., Lapointe, L., & Pinsonneault, A. (2013). The Ongoing Quest for the IT Artifact: Looking Back, Moving Forward. *Journal of Information Technology, 28*(2), 150–166.

Alter, S. (2003). 18 Reasons Why IT-Reliant Work Systems Should Replace "The IT Artifact" as the Core Subject Matter of the IS Field. *Communications of the Association for Information Systems, 12*(23), 366–395.

Avison, D. E., & Pries-Heje, J. (Eds.). (2005). *Research in Information Systems: A Handbook for Research Supervisors and Their Students.* Butterworth-Heinemann.

Baskerville, R., Myers, M. D., & Yoo, Y. (2020). Digital First: The Ontological Reversal and New Challenges for IS Research. *MIS Quarterly, 44*(2), 509–523. https://doi.org/10.25300/MISQ/2020/14418

Beath, C. M., Berente, N., Gallivan, M. J., & Lyytinen, K. (2013). Expanding the Frontiers of Information Systems Research: Introduction to the Special Issue. *Journal of the Association for Information Systems, 14*(4), i–xvi.

Benbasat, I., & Zmud, R. W. (2003). The Identity Crisis Within the IS Discipline: Defining and Communicating the Discipline's Core Properties. *MIS Quarterly, 27*(2), 183–194.

Bostrom, R. P., Gupta, S., & Thomas, D. M. (2009). A Meta-Theory for Understanding Information Systems Within Sociotechnical Systems. *Journal of Management Information Systems, 26*(1), 17–47.

Bostrom, R. P., & Heinen, J. S. (1977a). MIS Problems and Failures: A Socio-Technical Perspective, Part I: The Causes. *MIS Quarterly, 1*(1), 17–32.

Bostrom, R. P., & Heinen, J. S. (1977b). MIS Problems and Failures: A Socio-Technical Perspective, Part II: The Application of Socio-Technical Theory. *MIS Quarterly, 1*(4), 11–28.

Bowen, W. G., & Rudenstine, N. L. (1992). *In Pursuit of the PhD.* Princeton University Press.

Briggs, R. O., Nunamaker, J. F., Jr., & Sprague, R. H., Jr. (2010). Special Section: Social Aspects of Sociotechnical Systems. *Journal of Management Information Systems, 27*(1), 13–16.

Davis, G. B., & Parker, C. A. (1997). *Writing the Doctoral Dissertation: A Systematic Approach* (2nd ed.). Barron's Educational Series.

de Vise, D. (2010, April). Nearly Half of Doctorates Never Completed. *The Washington Post*.

Dean, D. L., Lowry, P. B., & Humpherys, S. L. (2011). Profiling the Research Productivity of Tenured Information Systems Faculty at U.S. Institutions. *MIS Quarterly, 35*(1), 1–15.

Dennis, A. R., Valacich, J. S., Fuller, M. A., & Schneider, C. (2006). Research Standards for Promotion and Tenure in Information Systems. *MIS Quarterly, 30*(1), 1–12.

Ekbia, H. R. (2009). Digital Artifacts as Quasi-Objects: Qualification, Mediation, and Materiality. *Journal of the American Society for Information Science and Technology, 60*(12), 2554–2566.

Faulkner, P., & Runde, J. (2019). Theorizing the Digital Object. *MIS Quarterly, 43*(4), 1279–1302.

Franz, A. (2015). The Social Position of Doctoral Candidates within the Academic Field: Comparative Considerations Regarding Doctoral Program Attrition in Germany and the USA. *International Dialogues on Education, 2*(2), 44–54.

Hirschheim, R., & Klein, H. K. (2012). A Glorious and Not-So-Short History of the Information Systems Field. *Journal of the Association for Information Systems, 13*(4), 188–235.

Kallinikos, J., Aaltonen, A., & Marton, A. (2013). The Ambivalent Ontology of Digital Artifacts. *MIS Quarterly, 37*(2), 357–370.

Klein, H. K., & Lyytinen, K. (1985). The Poverty of Scientism in Information Systems. In E. Mumford, R. Hirschheim, G. Fitzgerald, & A. T. Wood-Harper (Eds.), *Research Methods in Information Systems* (pp. 123–151). Elsevier Science Publishers.

Lee, A. S. (2001). Editor's Comments: Research in Information Systems: What We Haven't Learned. *MIS Quarterly, 25*(4), v–xv.

Lee, A. S., Thomas, M., & Baskerville, R. L. (2015). Going Back to Basics in Design Science: From the Information Technology Artifact to the Information Systems Artifact. *Information Systems Journal, 25*(1), 5–21.

Lyytinen, K., Baskerville, R., Iivari, J., & Te'Eni, D. (2007). Why the Old World Cannot Publish? Overcoming Challenges in Publishing High-Impact IS Research. *European Journal of Information Systems, 16*(4), 317–326.

Lyytinen, K., & King, J. L. (2006). The Theoretical Core and Academic Legitimacy: A Response to Professor Weber. *Journal of the Association for Information Systems, 7*(10), 714–721.

Nevo, S., Nevo, D., & Ein-Dor, P. (2009). Thirty Years of IS Research: Core Artifacts and Academic Identity. *Communications of the Association for Information Systems, 25*(24), 221–242.

Orlikowski, W. J., & Barley, S. R. (2001). Technology and Institutions: What Can Research on Information Technology and Research on Organizations Learn from Each Other? *MIS Quarterly, 25*(2), 145–165.

Orlikowski, W. J., & Baroudi, J. J. (1991). Studying Information Technology in Organizations: Research Approaches and Assumptions. *Information Systems Research, 2*(1), 1–28.

Orlikowski, W. J., & Iacono, C. S. (2001). Research Commentary: Desperately Seeking the 'IT' in IT Research-A Call to Theorizing the IT Artifact. *Information Systems Research, 12*(2), 121–134.

Patterson, E. (2016). Why Do So Many Graduate Students Quit? *The Atlantic*. Retrieved February 4, 2021 from https://www.theatlantic.com/education/archive/2016/07/why-do-so-many-graduate-students-quit/490094/

Queensland University of Technology. (2007). *Appendix 9: Queensland University of Technology Doctor of Philosophy Regulations (IF49)*. QUT. Retrieved November 9, 2011 from http://www.mopp.qut.edu.au/Appendix/appendix09.jsp

Rigler Jr., K. L., Bowlin, L. K., Sweat, K., Watts, S., & Throne, R. (2017). Agency, Socialization, and Support: A Critical Review of Doctoral Student Attrition. In *3rd International Conference on Doctoral Education, Orlando, Florida*.

Sarker, S., Chatterjee, S., Xiao, X., & Elbanna, A. R. (2019). The Sociotechnical Axis of Cohesion for the IS Discipline: Its Historical Legacy and its Continued Relevance. *MIS Quarterly, 43*(3), 695–719.

Sidorova, A., Evangelopoulos, N., Valacich, J. S., & Ramakrishnan, T. (2008). Uncovering the Intellectual Core of the Information Systems Discipline. *MIS Quarterly, 32*(3), 467–482.

Sørensen, C. (2005). *This is Not an Article. Just Some Thoughts on How To Write One*. mobility.lse. ac.uk/download/Sorensen2005b.pdf

Van Slyke, C., Bostrom, R. P., Courtney, J. F., & McLean, E. R. (2003). Experts' Advice to Information Systems Doctoral Students. *Communications of the Association for Information Systems, 12*(28), 469–478.

Venkatesh, V. (2011). *Road to Success: A Guide for Doctoral Students and Junior Faculty Members in the Behavioral and Social Sciences*. Dog Ear Publishing.

Waddington, T. (2007). *Lasting Contribution: How to Think, Plan, and Act to Accomplish Meaningful Work*. Agate B2.

Weber, R. (1987). Toward a Theory of Artifacts: A Paradigmatic Basis for Information Systems Research. *Journal of Information Systems, 1*(2), 3–19.

Weber, R. (2006). Reach and Grasp in the Debate over the IS Core: An Empty Hand? *Journal of the Association for Information Systems, 7*(10), 703–713.

Chapter 2
Information Systems Research as a Science

2.1 About Science

A friend once gave me a book called *What Is This Thing Called Science?* (Chalmers, 1999) to help me understand the nature of science. My immediate response was that I did not need it as I was already a tenured associate professor with a good track record in publishing and the promise of many publications to come. Clearly, I thought, I know what science is about.

I could not have been more wrong. This is not to say that all my prior efforts were fallible, misguided, and successful only by chance, but learning about the basic principles of science opened my eyes to some fundamental elements that govern much scholarly work.

Scholarly research that is worthy of a doctoral degree could be described as "scientific research" that conforms to systematic procedures, a method of "scientific inquiry." Science is the attempt to derive knowledge from facts using certain methods in a systematic and organised way.

Historically, two categories of science have evolved: natural sciences and social sciences. The **natural sciences**, which concern the study of naturally occurring phenomena and objects, include fields like chemical sciences, physical sciences, life sciences, and biological sciences. The phenomena under scrutiny are real and tangible objects like bodies, plants, and matter, although some objects, such as subatomic particles, chemical elements, and microscopic organisms, are difficult to observe.

The **social sciences** concern the study of people and collections of people. These sciences comprise fields like psychology, sociology, organisational science, and economics. All studies involving humans are part of the social sciences.

The distinction between natural science and social science is important because the modes of inquiry and research processes for the two can differ. The natural sciences are often referred to as "exact" sciences as inquiries in the natural sciences rely on precise measurements of phenomena and their properties. (This account of

© Springer Nature Switzerland AG 2021
J. Recker, *Scientific Research in Information Systems*, Progress in IS,
https://doi.org/10.1007/978-3-030-85436-2_2

the relationship between the exact sciences (mathematics) and their applications in natural sciences, like physics, is very simplistic. There are many nuances to this relationship that are not covered in this text.) Examples of such work are in any high school chemistry or physics book. In the natural science of physics, for example, properties like the speed of light and gravity have been calculated precisely, although Heisenberg's uncertainty principles state a fundamental limit on the accuracy with which certain pairs of physical properties of a particle, such as position and momentum, can be simultaneously known. Still, for the purpose of our argument here, the natural sciences are largely exact.

To illustrate this point, consider the first direct observation of gravitational waves on 14 September 2015. Scientists had tried to directly prove the existence of such waves for more than 50 years. The ripple in space-time that was finally noticed had the length of a thousandth of the width of a proton, proportionally equivalent to changing the distance to the nearest star outside the solar system by the width of a human hair. What is astonishing is that Albert Einstein predicted the existence of gravitational waves in 1916 and also predicted that events in the cosmos would cause distortions in space-time that spread outward, although they would be so minuscule that they would be nearly impossible to detect. In 2015, detection was finally possible, and the phenomenon occurred precisely as Einstein predicted.

This level of precision in prediction or proof is pretty much impossible in the social sciences, where phenomena and the measurements we use to collect data about them are more vague, imprecise, non-deterministic, and ambiguous. To illustrate this point, think about a study that examines whether happy people sleep more or less than unhappy people. You will inevitably run into problems as soon as you try to figure out how to define—let alone measure precisely—what happiness is or when you try to isolate the cause of variations in sleep length. There could be noise in the bedroom, light shining through the window, more or less wind wafting through the room, differences in what the person ate or did that day, all of which could affect sleep patterns Among these conditions, any one of them or a combination of any of them may be related to sleep and some definition of happiness!

One of the many manifestations of the issue of exactness in science in the happy-people-sleep-differently example is the challenge of *measurement error*. Measurement error is invariably present in the social sciences because the phenomena that are studied are complex, vague, ambiguous, and dynamic: happiness can mean different things to different people or at different times, and it can manifest in different ways. If the thing itself is so hard to grasp, how can an even carefully constructed measurement of it ever be precise? In the social sciences, the phenomena we study cannot be faithfully defined or isolated precisely, so there will always be imprecision in how we study our phenomena of interest and, therefore, in the findings we obtain.

We will return to this issue later in this book, but for now, be aware that, as a scholar in information systems, a discipline that is socio-technical and deals with social behaviour in the forms of individuals/organisations/economies/other collectives, you are a part of the social sciences. As soon as our investigation concerns a human element, imprecision, vagueness, and ambiguity creep into our research and you cannot definitively "prove" anything.

Another challenge of information systems as a social science is that our phenomena are dynamic, not stable. In the natural sciences, many of the phenomena are largely invariant over time. The laws of gravity do not change. The anatomical structures of beings, such as our skeletons, do not change except through evolution over eons; for most purposes, we can consider them to be invariant. In consequence, once we have figured out something about an invariant object, we "know" it and can move to the next question. Medical doctors take a long time during their education to study the anatomy of human bones, but once finished they know human anatomy.

The ability to "know" something is different in the social sciences, particularly in information systems, as our phenomena change and evolve all the time. When you study how one collective of people acts—say, during an emergency—the results will be different at a different point in time, such as when the same group experiences a second emergency. This is because people learn and adapt their behaviours and the context will be different—a different place, a different time, a different set of experiences.

In information systems, the situation is even more complicated. Not only the social elements are dynamic (people change) but also the technical elements. Digital information and communication technologies change and evolve all the time. Computers get faster, better, and cheaper, and new technology replaces the old. We could study the same thing over and over again because the setting, context, and phenomenon itself will always be different. It would be next to impossible to make an accurate prediction for a hundred years into the future like Einstein did about gravitational waves.

Personally, I like that the information systems field is inherently dynamic and ambiguous. It forces us to be as precise as possible to approximate the phenomena we want to study and measure. It also means that our problems and interests change all the time. We are in a constant chase with reality, trying to catch up with all the changes to the technical and social elements that come together when people develop or use digital technology. I like to think that in this field, we will have always have work to do and the work can never be boring.

2.2 Scientific Knowledge

Given the distinctions between natural sciences and social sciences, consider the aim of science that we mentioned in Chap. 1—that science "contributes to the advancement of human knowledge." The goal of scientific inquiry is to discover laws and propose theories that can explain the natural or social, tangential or latent phenomena that concern us. Scientific knowledge is produced as an outcome of scientific inquiry.

Given the issues of precision and dynamism, the challenge of this goal is that this scientific knowledge can be imperfect, vague, and sometimes even incorrect in the social sciences because of the measurement error that creeps into scientific studies.

The key insight here is that all scientific knowledge is by definition a set of *suggested explanations* of particular phenomena. I often illustrate this notion by reminding students that at one time, we *knew* that the earth was flat. Our theories, which were mostly inspired through western religion as well as the limited measurements of the time (look at the horizon and see how the ocean "ends" at a certain line), suggested this knowledge to be accurate. Now we presumably *know* that this theory of the earth was not correct. New evidence was obtained through sailing around the earth without dropping off the edge. Later, astronauts observed from a distance that the earth is spherical. These new data and new observations led scientists to conclude (well, suggest) that the earth is a sphere, not a flat disk. They have devised measurements, such as those taken from planes flying at elevations of more than 35,000 feet, where one can observe the curvature of the earth. The evidence, in terms of data and mathematical proof, is substantial, increasing our trust in the suggested explanation instead of "trusting our eyes" when we gaze at the horizon.

This example shows that scientific knowledge is tentative and bound to the particularities of a specific point in time. The body of scientific knowledge in a domain—that is, the outcome of all research to date—is always the *current accumulation* of suggested theories, evidence, and measurement methods in that domain.

This definition of the body of knowledge makes no statement about the quality of the body of knowledge as the theories, evidence, and measurement methods may be good or poor. We all learn about examples like Ptolemaic, geocentric, and heliocentric astronomy that show how new knowledge supersedes existing knowledge. Such new knowledge could be a new theory, such as when Newton's ideas about gravity replaced Aristotelian physics, but it could also be new evidence, like results and/or observations that may either support or refute a scientific idea. For example, John Latham discovered black swans in 1790, which forced an update to the prevalent theory that all swans are white.

Progress in scientific inquiry—that is, the advancement of general human knowledge—can be examined by comparing how well we improve the current accumulation of theories, evidence, and measurements in a certain domain. For instance, a contribution could be an improvement in the explanatory power of a theory about a certain phenomenon. We could also add to the body of knowledge by finding better evidence of a theory or making more accurate measurements.

How can one achieve such a contribution? The body of knowledge focuses essentially on two concepts—theory and evidence—and their relationship, as shown in Fig. 2.1.

Thus, we can contribute to the body of knowledge in three ways:

(1) **Improving our theories that contain explanations of phenomena**: for example, research on theories that explain why people accept or reject information technology over time has improved these theories by identifying additional, originally not considered factors like habit, emotion, and anxiety, which add to our initial understanding that we accept technology when it is useful and easy to use (Venkatesh et al., 2016). Chapter 3 returns to the question of how we arrive at better theories.

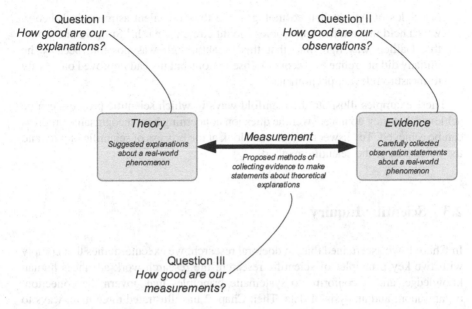

Fig. 2.1 The body of knowledge

(2) **Improving our scientific evidence**: for example, we may be able to collect data about a phenomenon for which no observations exist to date. A prime example is Darwin's voyage on *The Beagle*, when he encountered and systematically described many previously unknown species of plants and animals. This evidence allowed him, as well as other scholars, to refine theories about plants and animals and laid the groundwork for a whole new theory, the theory of evolution. Arriving at this new theory was possible only because systematic statements about observable facts were first created through careful exploration and observation. We return to methods of observation later in Chap. 5.

(3) **Improving our methods for collecting observations in relation to theory**: here is an example from the history of science. One of the most important contributions Galileo Galilei made was improvements he invented for telescopes. Starting with a telescope with about 3x magnification, Galileo designed improved versions with up to about 30x magnification. Through the Galilean telescope, observers could see magnified, upright images of the earth and sky. The new telescope yielded greatly improved measurements over those that were possible with the naked eye. It was only through these refined instruments that Galileo noted how the positions of some "stars" relative to Jupiter changed in a way counter to what was possible for stars that were "fixed," the current theory at the time. He discovered that the "fixed stars" were sometimes hidden behind Jupiter.

The improved measurements of Jupiter's satellites created a revolution in astronomy, as a planet with smaller bodies orbiting it did not conform to the principles of Aristotelian cosmology—the then prevalent astronomical theory, which held that all heavenly bodies should circle the earth.[1] Still, we know now that Galileo was right and that this breakthrough was possible because he initially did not refine the theory or observations but instead improved our ability to measure relevant phenomena.[2]

These examples illustrate the manifold ways in which scientific progress can be achieved, but they do not answer the question concerning how recognisable progress can be achieved. To answer that, we must look at the process of scientific inquiry and the postulates of the scientific method.

2.3 Scientific Inquiry

In Chap. 1, we ascertained that, in doctoral research, we execute studies that comply with two key principles of scientific research: the research work advances human knowledge, and it conforms to systematic principles that govern the collection, organisation, and analysis of data. Then Chap. 2 has illustrated three main ways to advance human knowledge: by creating scientific output in the form of contributions to theory, evidence, or measurement. Now we turn to the second principle, the process of scientific inquiry. Scientific inquiry refers to how scientists study the natural world and propose explanations based on the evidence derived from their work. It defines the process of academic work using accepted techniques and principles for investigating real-world phenomena.

A doctoral program deals with only one type of research, the class of scientific research. For research to be called scientific, scientific inquiry requires that the research process must be based on gathering empirical and measurable evidence that is subject to specific principles of reasoning. In other words, scientific research builds on principles that are accepted by scientists and that help to ensure that the outcomes meet the expectations for transparency, codification, reproducibility, and communicability. **Transparency** refers to the sources of the resulting scientific knowledge being traceable and verifiable. **Codification** means that the knowledge can be represented in some form—words, symbols, video—that enables interpretation by someone other than the originator. **Reproducibility** requires that the knowledge be possible to replicate or copy. Finally, **communicability** means that the

---

[1] Galileo initially endured significant resistance to his findings because his measurement instrument, the telescope, was not trusted as a scientific instrument. It took decades of replication, a scientific principle I explain below, before his findings were confirmed to the extent that they were trusted as valid observational evidence.

[2] Refining measurements remains relevant to this day. For example, improvements in neuroscientific measurement methods like fMRI scanners have recently been developed and provide much more precise measurements of brain activities than any other measurement instrument previously used in cognitive psychology.

knowledge must be in such a form that it can be conveyed, discussed, and challenged by others.

Although research procedures vary from one field of inquiry to another, several common features in scientific research methods distinguish scientific inquiry from other methods of obtaining knowledge. Most important is that scientific inquiry must be *as objective as possible* to reduce biased interpretations of results, maintain a neutral and (where possible) factual position on a phenomenon, and minimise the dependency and partiality of the research team or any interpreter of the findings.

To ensure as much objectivity as possible, scientific research must follow the principles of replicability, independence, precision, and falsification (I know that last one sounds counter-intuitive, but read on):

(1) **Replicability**

Replicability refers to the extent to which research procedures are repeatable such that the procedures by which research outputs are created are conducted and documented in a manner that allows others outside the research team to independently repeat the procedures and obtain similar results. The question is, "If I repeated your research based on how you conducted it and described it to me, would I get the same results?" Replicability relies to an extent on carefully detailed documentation, archival, and sharing of findings, data, measurements, and methodologies so they are available for scrutiny by other scientists such that they can verify the results by reproducing them.

Replication in the social sciences has come to the forefront of public attention in part because of the replicability crisis (Yong, 2012) that emerged around 2010, when scientists noted that many scientific studies were difficult or impossible to reproduce. A survey of 1,500 scientists in 2016 found that 70 percent of respondents had not been able to reproduce at least one experiment of other scientists and 50 percent had not been able to reproduce one of their own experiments (Nature Videos, 2016). In my own work, I made both experiences as well.

(2) **Independence**

Independence concerns the extent to which the research conduct is impartial and free of subjective judgment or other bias stemming from the researcher or researcher team. Independence can be easier to achieve when one is working with factual, objective, precise data and can be harder in interpretive research, where the researcher attempts to explain a phenomenon by interpreting participants' sentiments or statements about it. As Chap. 5 will show, different research methods are challenged by and deal with independence in different ways; for example, in some studies, teams of external coders are used so as to avoid the researchers' subjective judgment.

Independence distinguishes scientific research from other forms of problem-solving, such as consultancy, where the researcher has contractually stipulated vested interests, such as wanting to be paid for his or her work and not wanting the organisation that is paying for the work disapprove of it by arriving at an expensive or disappointing outcome.

(3) **Precision**

The precision principle states that the concepts, constructs, and measurements of scientific research should be as carefully and precisely defined as possible to allow others to use, apply, and challenge the definitions, concepts, and results in their own work. Especially in the social sciences, many concepts—happiness, satisfaction, joy, anxiety, and so forth—are difficult to define, and they carry many connotations. Precise definitions and measurements are critical to ensuring that others can comprehend, use, and even challenge the researcher's interpretation of the concept.

(4) **Falsification**

Falsification is probably the most important principle in scientific research. It originates from the thinking of philosopher Popper (1959), who argued that it is logically impossible to prove theories in scientific research. Instead, he argued that scientific theories can only be disproven or falsified. In other words, falsifiability describes the logical possibility that an assertion, hypothesis, or theory can be contradicted by an observation or another outcome of a scientific study or experiment. That a theory is "falsifiable" does not mean it is false but that if it is false, then some observation or experiment will produce a reproducible and independently created result that is in conflict with it.

The falsification argument carries two important implications. First, it draws a clear boundary around the possibilities of scientific research: our theories are sets of suggested explanations that are assumed to be true because the evidence collected to date does not state otherwise. To illustrate, Newton sat under the apple tree and apples fell on his head, which allegedly gave him inspiration about a theory of gravity. Per that theory, apples fall to the ground because of gravitational forces exerted by the earth's core that pull them toward the ground. Does the theory conclusively and irreversibly predict that all apples will always fall to the ground? No, it does not. There is no logical way to prove conclusively that all apples will continue to fall to the ground even though all apples to date have done so. If we were to find an apple that, say, scoots off into the sky, we would have found evidence that is contrary to the theoretical prediction and would have falsified Newton's theory.

The second implication of the falsification argument is that a good scientific theory is one that can be falsified. This principle suggests that theories must be stated in a way that they can, hypothetically, be disproven. If we do not define a theory in a way that allows us or others to disprove the theory, then we have not complied with the scientific inquiry process and cannot offer a scientific contribution to the body of knowledge. For example, the assertion that all swans are white is falsifiable because it is logically possible that a swan can be found that is not white. By contrast, consider the example of the Rain Dance Ceremony theory:

> *If you perform the Rain Dance Ceremony and all the participants are pure of heart, it will rain the next day.*

Proposing this theory is not a scientific undertaking because the theory is not falsifiable: if you perform the ceremony and it rains, the theory is confirmed. If you perform the ceremony and it does not rain, it contends that one of the participants was not pure of heart, so again the theory is confirmed. Unfortunately, being pure of heart is not a property that we can precisely, reliably, and independently measure, so we cannot create a scenario in which we could disprove the Rain Dance Ceremony theory.

The idea behind the principles of scientific inquiry is not to accredit or discredit research endeavours but to separate scientific research from other fields of research. A common example is that of theology, which is not a science because its research processes do not conform to the principles of scientific inquiry. For one thing, the principle of falsifiability is violated because phenomena like divine intervention cannot be tested or verified independently. Similarly, the humanities, literature, and law are not sciences in that their work relies heavily on the ability to interpret a complex material in a sense-making process, a procedure that is not independently repeatable because it is subject to the individual who performs the inquiry.[3]

The principles of scientific inquiry are themselves only a sort of theory of science in that they are not "true" in any sense; they are merely what many scientists agree to be a useful pattern for doing science, which relies on systematically testing theories, challenging evidence, and improving measurements, to see if what we think about the universe is correct. Not all scientists agree on these principles. For example, Feyerabend (2010) suggested in an analysis of substantial scientific breakthroughs that many of the great scientific discoveries were made by chance rather than by applying a rigid process of inquiry. He concluded that conforming to particular methods of "scientific inquiry" would actually limit the ability to create significant breakthroughs through science. Also, some social scientists question some notions, such as falsification or independence, as means to guarantee the quality of research. For example, Giddens (1993) argued that social science, unlike natural science, deals with phenomena that are subjects, not objects, so they are in a subject-subject relationship with a field of study, not a subject-object relationship. In this situation, he continued, social scientists inevitably deal with a pre-interpreted world in which the meanings developed by the study's subjects enter into the constitution or production of that world. In this understanding, there is not really space for objectivity and independence.

These discussions also have their place in the field of information systems, which is a *pluralistic* field, meaning that multiple positions of science are allowed to coexist. You can choose to follow the position of interpretive scholars (e.g., Walsham, 1995a), you can follow the position described through the principles of scientific inquiry, and you can even build your approach to science around Feyerabend (e.g., Hirschheim, 2019). While I like the pluralism of our field, it complicates things for those who conduct, evaluate, or apply science. Still, pluralism

---

[3] These statements do not qualify these research inquiries as good or bad; they are merely used to distinguish different types of research.

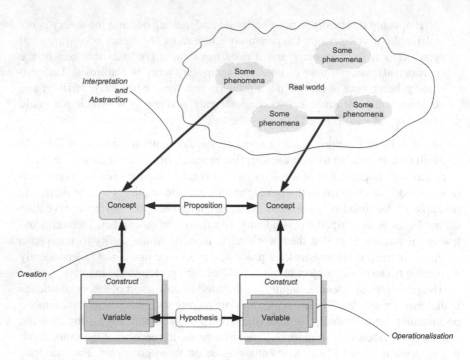

Fig. 2.2 Concepts in the scientific research process

promotes scientific progress since it allows advancements in human knowledge to be obtained from a proliferation of views rather than from the determined application of one preferred ideology. Every scientific framework can be judged on its productiveness or its efficacy in light of the goal of a research project. If a chosen approach is not effective or fruitful, it can be modified or something else can be tried.

2.4 Essential Scientific Concepts

One of the problems that I encounter frequently with doctoral students is that our conversations are hampered by our use of "standard" research concepts and terms when our definitions of terms like construct, concept, and variable may differ.

To address this problem, have a look at how I define some concepts in Fig. 2.2.

First, we need to define the term *concept*. A concept describes an abstract idea that is inferred or derived from instances that we perceive in the real world, that is, mental representations that we develop, typically based on experience. Concepts can be of real phenomena (dogs, clouds, gravity) as well as latent phenomena (truth, beauty, prejudice, usefulness, value).

We use concepts as a language mechanism to describe the general properties or characteristics that we ascribe to things or phenomena. For example, we use the concept of weight to describe the force of gravity on objects. Weight is a general property that applies to all tangible things in the real world. We can also use the same concept, weight, to illustrate the psychological state of someone who is experiencing stress, tension, and anxiety, as we do when we refer to the "weight on their shoulders." We also develop new concepts to describe a new or newly discovered property. Emotional intelligence, for example, is a concept that purports to describe our ability to identify, assess, and control our emotions and those of others. This concept has gained some prominence in a debate regarding whether it is a personality trait or form of intelligence not accounted for in current theories of personality and intelligence (which, by the way, are also concepts).

As abstract units of meaning, concepts play a key role in the development and testing of scientific theories. They give us a vocabulary with which to reason about real-world phenomena (or the link between two or more real-world phenomena, as shown in Fig. 2.2) and a way to describe the characteristics or properties of those phenomena and their relationships. Concepts can be linked to one another via propositions, which are suggested, tentative, or conjectured relationships between two or more concepts, such as that more intelligence leads to better decisions. Propositions are sometimes called conceptual hypotheses.

Note the keywords suggestion, tentativeness, and conjecture used above to explain the notion of a proposition. These terms characterise propositions as proposals for an explanation about how phenomena are related. Whether the propositions hold true is an entirely different question and typically an empirical one that we must answer using appropriate research methods.

The problem with concepts is that many of the *phenomena* we are interested in (satisfaction, empathy, intelligence, anxiety, skill, and so on) are imprecise because they are not directly observable. They are abstract and difficult to capture, define, and visualise because, in the social sciences, we are often concerned with understanding behaviours, processes, and experiences as they relate to "digital technology in use."

For example, take the simple proposition that "education increases income." The concepts of education and income are abstract, so they can have many meanings. As a result, such a proposition could be tested in potentially infinite ways, and many different results could be obtained, so a proposition cannot be tested. To testing them against data, they must be converted into operational hypotheses.

As Fig. 2.2 shows, hypotheses are suggested links between constructs. *Constructs* are operationalised concepts, where we take the abstract meaning of a concept, like education, and try to operationalise it to something in the real world that can be measured. Education, for instance, could be operationalised as the highest degree earned, which could be measured by ascertaining what degree (e.g., high school, undergraduate, graduate, postgraduate) a person had completed. The concept of income could be operationalised as annual salary in US dollars before tax (or monthly income after tax, or annual income after tax, and so on). In any case, a construct must be specified as precisely as possible.

Thus, a construct is an operationalisation of a concept in such a way that we can define it by measuring the construct against data. We use this process to describe fuzzy concepts in terms of constituent components that are defined in precise terms.

In doing so, we try to eliminate <u>vagueness</u> (how many centimetres exactly is a "tall" person?) and <u>ambiguity</u> (e.g., whether the statement "I own a bat" refers to an animal or a piece of sports equipment).

This process is mentally challenging. For instance, to operationalise the concept of prejudice, we would have to ask ourselves what prejudice means to us. Are there different kinds of prejudice (race, gender, age, religion, body type)? How can we measure them? Do we need to measure all of them?

Depending on the answers, we can create unidimensional or multidimensional constructs. *Unidimensional constructs* are composed of only one underlying dimension, such as weight, height, or speed, so they can be measured through one *variable*. A variable an the empirical indicator that allows us to approximate the underlying construct, a measurable representation or manifestation of a latent construct in the real world. For example, when we define the concept "weight" as the construct that describes the force gravity places on an object, we can define a measurement variable that specifies levels of weight using, for instance, a metric scale (in kilograms). Because weight is a relatively simple, unidimensional construct, there is typically no need to define multiple measurement variables as measuring a person's weight in kilograms and pounds would obtain the same result since the scales have a percental equivalency. Other good examples of unidimensional constructs are age, time, and income.

Gender has traditionally been used as a unidimensional construct with a simple measurement variable (male/female), but a wider range of genders is socially accepted now in many societies. Since most constructs are more complex, they are composed of a multidimensional set of underlying concepts. Intelligence, for example, cannot be measured by a single variable because the concept pertains to multiple kinds of abilities—abstract thought, communication, reasoning, learning, planning, problem-solving and emotional intelligence. Such constructs are called *multi-dimensional constructs* because they have multiple underlying dimensions, all of which are relevant to our understanding and use of the construct and all of which must be measured separately using dedicated variables. Taking the example of intelligence again, the IQ (intelligence quotient) score is the standardised outcome of a complex test that contains measurements of intelligence and abilities, like abstract thought, communication, creativity, learning, memory, problem-solving, reasoning, and visual processing.

Variables are measurable representations of constructs, and these representations create precise operationalisations of concepts that present mental abstractions of the properties of phenomena in the real world. By using variables, we can also speculate about links between empirical phenomena that feature in operationalised hypotheses. A *hypothesis* is the empirical formulation of a proposition of a testable relationship between two or more variables. Hypotheses are formulated so they are directly empirically testable as true or false and such that they allow for precise reasoning about the underlying proposition they represent. For example, the hypothesis that the "highest degree earned is related to annual gross salary" is a <u>weak hypothesis</u> because it fails to specify *directionality* (does the earning of a degree cause an increase or a decrease in annual gross salary?) or *causality* (does annual gross salary cause a specific degree or vice versa?). A <u>strong hypothesis</u>, by contrast, is "the higher the degree earned, the more annual gross salary is earned." As this example shows, hypotheses specify directionality as well as causality by delineating which variable leads to which effect on which other variable. Saying that "Europeans earn high annual gross salaries," for example, is not a hypothesis because it does not specify a directional/causal relationship between two variables, so we cannot collect meaningful data to evaluate the hypothesis, which violates the principle of falsification.

2.5 Further Reading

I found Chalmers' (1999) introductory book on the philosophy of science worthwhile for its elucidation of the common principles of good scientific inquiry. Popper's (1959) seminal book, *The Logic of Scientific Discovery*, provides a more detailed follow-up to my explanations of falsification. For a more critical view of the principles of scientific inquiry and their limitations, you can consult Feyerabend's (2010) *Against Method*. If you are interested in how interpretive scholars challenge typical principles of scientific inquiry, such as those I introduced, I can recommend several papers written by or co-authored by Myers (Klein & Myers, 1999; Myers, 1997) and the articles by Walsham (1995b, 2006).

A good introduction to essential concepts in information systems research is Bhattacherjee's (2012) book on social science research. Similar term definitions can also be found in other introductory textbooks, such as those by Creswell (2009) and Reynolds (1971). Burton-Jones and Lee (2017) wrote a paper that does a good job defining the differences between constructs and measurements well.

References

Bhattacherjee, A. (2012). *Social Science Research: Principles, Methods and Practices* (2nd ed.). Global Text Project.
Burton-Jones, A., & Lee, A. S. (2017). Thinking About Measures and Measurement in Positivist Research: A Proposal for Refocusing on Fundamentals. *Information Systems Research, 28*(3), 451–467.
Chalmers, A. F. (1999). *What Is This Thing Called Science?* (3rd ed.). Hackett.
Creswell, J. W. (2009). *Research Design: Qualitative, Quantitative, and Mixed Methods Approaches* (3rd ed.). Sage Publications.
Feyerabend, P. (2010). *Against Method* (4th ed.). Verso Books.
Giddens, A. (1993). *New Rules of Sociological Method*. Polity Press.
Hirschheim, R. (2019). Against Theory: With Apologies to Feyerabend. *Journal of the Association for Information Systems, 20*(9), 1340–1357.
Klein, H. K., & Myers, M. D. (1999). A Set of Principles for Conducting and Evaluating Interpretive Field Studies in Information Systems. *MIS Quarterly, 23*(1), 67–94.

Myers, M. D. (1997). Interpretive Research in Information Systems. In J. Mingers & F. Stowell (Eds.), *Information Systems: An Emerging Discipline?* (pp. 239–268). McGraw- Hill.

Nature Videos. (2016). *Is There a Reproducibility Crisis in Science?* Scientific American. Retrieved January 18, 2020 from https://www.scientificamerican.com/video/is-there-a-reproducibility-crisis-in-science/

Popper, K. R. (1959). *The Logic of Scientific Discovery*. Basic Books (Logik der Forschung, Vienna, 1935)

Reynolds, P. D. (1971). *A Primer in Theory Construction*. Allyn and Bacon.

Venkatesh, V., Thong, J. Y. L., & Xu, X. (2016). Unified Theory of Acceptance and Use of Technology: A Synthesis and the Road Ahead. *Journal of the Association for Information Systems, 17*(5), 328–376.

Walsham, G. (1995a). The Emergence of Interpretivism in IS Research. *Information Systems Research, 6*(4), 376–394.

Walsham, G. (1995b). Interpretive Case Studies in IS Research: Nature and Method. *European Journal of Information Systems, 4*, 74–81.

Walsham, G. (2006). Doing Interpretive Research. *European Journal of Information Systems, 15* (3), 320–330.

Yong, E. (2012). Replication Studies: Bad Copy. *Nature, 485*(7398), 298–300.

Part II
Conducting Research

Chapter 3
Planning Your Research

3.1 Research Questions

A doctoral program takes a long time. The Australian PhD program takes three years or more, with the average being more than four years. German PhD programs often take between three and five years, and sometimes longer. Doctoral programs in other countries can take even longer—up to seven years in some North American programs. While the length of the program varies, they all start similarly with two challenges of doctoral study:

(1) You will have to read the available literature to learn about methods and theories. This part is nicely structured as there is a set of useful books and papers, and there are typically good classes, workshops, and tutorials to attend. While this challenge should not be underestimated, the process of addressing it is usually well structured and typically has considerable guidance available. This structured challenge comes with the expectation that you will master the relevant methods and theories and be able to apply them appropriately. This challenge is relatively *domain-agnostic* in that it is at least to some extent independent of your field of study or phenomena of interest. You simply build the capacity to use a research method or set of methods well and to understand a particular set of theories, so this first challenge pertains mostly to <u>how</u> you perform research.

(2) You will have to formulate and develop your own research questions and propose a plan to address them. This challenge is much more difficult than the first challenge largely because it is not as structured but is undefined and highly contextual. Formulating and understanding research questions is a *domain-specific* challenge that pertains closely and directly to <u>what</u> you want to research.

The difference between these two challenges is important. One of the great scholars in information systems (IS) put it much better than I can (Weber, 2003, pp. iii–iv):

© Springer Nature Switzerland AG 2021
J. Recker, *Scientific Research in Information Systems*, Progress in IS,
https://doi.org/10.1007/978-3-030-85436-2_3

I believe that the choice of research problem—choosing the phenomena we wish to explain or predict—is the most important decision we make as a researcher. We can learn research method. Albeit with greater difficulty, we can also learn theory-building skills. With some tutoring and experience, we can also learn to carve out large numbers of problems that we might research. Unfortunately, teasing out deep, substantive research problems is another matter. It remains a dark art.

The point is that a good doctoral study starts and ends with the right research questions. Finding and specifying them—not even answering them—is not easy. I have grouped some of the problems that are related to the formulation of research questions into five categories:

1. **The "monologuing" problem**: students with this problem cannot tell what research question they are tackling unless they engage in a five-minute monologue. If it takes an extended monologue just to explain the question they seek to answer, they typically do not understand the research question well enough to articulate it concisely. A good research question is simply a short question. Needing to elaborate for five minutes on this question or to explain its components indicates that they have not grasped the essence of the problem or discovered how to scope it in a way that it can be distinguished easily from related phenomena or problems.
2. **The "so what" problem**: in these cases, students can state a research question but not why it would matter to anyone. The relevance of a problem is particularly important in applied fields of research like information systems, where we seek to solve a specific problem or provide innovative solutions to issues that affect an individual, group, or society, such as how new technology shapes the work practices of employees. You may have a so-what problem if you have trouble justifying its practical merit, that is, why it is worth asking the question.
3. **The "solving-the-world" problem**: students who have this problem can state a research question that has value, but it cannot be answered given the students' resource constraints. For example, in most PhD programs, your resources are basically limited to you. Your timeline may also be constrained either because the program's regulations stipulate completion after so many years or because funding runs out. Students often have two to three years to complete their research, and a topic that is too broad ("The cure for cancer lies in the Amazon jungle") has no chance of completion given the available time and resources.
4. **The "insolvability" problem**: your research question simply cannot be answered meaningfully because of a logical problem in the question, because the information needed to answer the question cannot be logically or legally obtained, or because the answer is so hard to obtain that feasibility of the research in the constraints is not possible. A good example that I often give is that of longitudinal studies, in which research is meant to examine the evolution of phenomena into the future. Such research, by definition, must be carried out over many years. For instance, studying the impact of early childhood abuse on the development of social morale in adolescence would require examining individuals in a sample over many years, and most PhD programs must be completed in much less time.

5. **The "multitude" problem**: students who have this common problem ask (too) many questions instead of one. I always tell my students that a good study sets out to answer one question with one answer—maybe two if they are ambitious. Nothing is gained by setting out to answer six questions as most of them will fall into five inappropriate categories:

- *Obvious questions*: "Are there challenges in using information technology?" Of course there are. Obvious questions have answers to which everyone would agree.
- *Irrelevant questions*: "What is the influence of weather on the salaries of technology professionals?" There is no reason to believe that there is any influence whatsoever.
- *Absurd questions*: "Is the earth flat after all?" Absurd questions have answers to which everyone would agree, although I read that almost two percent of people still believe the earth is flat (Branch & Foster, 2018).
- *Definitional questions*: "Is technology conflict characterised by disagreement?" The answer is simply a matter of creating a concept that says it does. A definition is a form of description, not research.
- *Affirmation questions*: "Can a decision-support tool be developed to facilitate decision-making for senior retail executives?" Yes.

Use these categories as a "black list" (an exclusion list) to ensure that your proposed research questions do not fit any of these problems, and if they do, go back and revise them. Alternatively, use the questions above as a checklist of *what not to do* when creating your research questions in the first place.

A research question should be a key statement that identifies the phenomenon to be studied. **The research question(s) is/are the fundamental cornerstone around which your whole doctoral research revolves and evolves.** For you, your supervisory team, and other stakeholders (external examiners and reviewers, for example), the research question provides the frame that brackets your whole investigation and its representation in the final thesis. We set out in our study to answer a particular question, and when we find an answer, we turn back to the question to determine whether we have sufficiently and comprehensively answered the question. A number of guiding questions can help you find a good research question:

- Do you know in which field of research your research questions reside?
- Do you have a firm understanding of the body of knowledge (the domain's literature) in that field?
- What are important open research questions or unsolved problems in the field that scientists agree on?
- What areas need further exploration?
- Could your study fill an important gap in knowledge? Could it help clarify a problem we are having with the knowledge already available?
- How much research has already been conducted on this topic?
- Has your proposed study been done before? If so, is there room for improvement or expansion?

- Is the timing right for the question to be answered? Is it a sustainable and important topic, or is it currently a fad but risks becoming obsolete?
- Who would care about obtaining an answer to the question? What is the potential impact of the research you are proposing? What is the benefit of answering your research question? Who will it help, and how will it help them?
- Will your proposed study have a significant impact on the field?
- Is your proposed research question based only on the fact that you think it is "interesting" but nothing else?

Using these criteria and guidelines can help you formulate a good research question, but three key components should also be considered: motivation, specification, and justification

Motivation of the Research Question

A good research question does not fall out of thin air. It is the logical, necessary, and inevitable conclusion to a set of arguments that find (1) an *important problem domain* with (2) an *important phenomenon* that deserves attention from the research community and that relates to (3) an *important problem with the available knowledge* about this type of phenomenon. A motivation is not necessarily extensive, as long as it addresses these three points. A simple example is the following chain of arguments. The argument that reveals the important problem domain is as follows:

Organisations invest heavily in new information technology to seek benefits from these investments.

In this statement, we learn about a problem domain: investments into IT and benefit realisation from IT. This is an important problem domain for businesses because it involves money. As a tip, motivating research problems by citing data that confirm the quantifiable value associated with the problem (dollars spent, money lost, for example) might be valuable. Within this domain, we then learn about one important phenomenon:

Many of these benefits never materialise because employees do not use the technologies.

Here we drill down to a particularly important phenomenon of interest, individuals' rejection of IT (i.e., their unwillingness to use IT), which narrows the problem domain down and will be useful in focussing the research later on. Finally, we learn about an important problem in the available knowledge that relates to this phenomenon:

The literature to date has studied only why individuals accept new technologies but not why they reject them.

Here we make a statement about the current body of knowledge. The problem with the body of knowledge we have (i.e., the literature available to date) is that it has a gap—that is, we do not know enough yet to address the specific phenomenon in the problem domain. For example, as the Covid-19 pandemic spread across the globe in 2020, at the beginning we had very little knowledge about the virus, its infection rates, and its possible cures or vaccinations. The problem then was a gap of knowledge.

A "gap" in knowledge is a typical problem with the available knowledge, but it is not necessarily the best or only problem (Alvesson & Sandberg, 2011). For example, we could develop a set of arguments to strengthen the proposition that our theories on technology acceptance (e.g., Venkatesh et al., 2003) fail to predict the opposite, rejection of technology, conclusively. Other typical problems with the knowledge could be that they have yielded inconsistent results: study A suggests one thing and study B suggests an opposite thing, so which is correct? That is a problem. Another problem might be that the knowledge to date rests on assumptions that are no longer current or realistic, such as when studies assume that findings for a sample of men must also apply to women.

Having introduced an important problem domain with a specific phenomenon and a substantial problem with the knowledge to date allows us to formulate a research question as the logical conclusion to these arguments:

Why do people reject new information technology?

This question is one that Centefelli and Schwarz (2011) set out to answer in their paper, "Identifying and Testing the Inhibitors of Technology Usage Intentions." They do a good job in motivating why research on technology rejection is important, why the question of individual unwillingness to use technology is an important specific phenomenon, and why an answer to their research question helps alleviate a problem with the available literature.

Specification of the Research Question

With appropriate motivation, a good research question can be precisely defined. Research questions are typically one of two types based on the issues they address:

1. "What," "who," and "where" questions tend to focus on issues we seek to *explore* or *describe* because little knowledge exists about them.
2. "How" and "why" questions are *explanatory* as they seek to answer questions about the causal mechanisms that are at work in a particular phenomenon.

Exploratory and descriptive questions (type 1) are different kinds of research questions from explanatory questions (type 2). Type 1 questions seek to learn what the situation of a phenomenon looks like. We ask these questions about phenomena that are new to the world. For example, at the onset of the Covid-19 pandemic, the world realised that there was a new virus. The first step was then to find out everything about it: what it looks like, what it does, what its genetic structure is, where it occurs, who can be infected by it, and so forth. We are not explaining (or curing) anything at this stage; we are exploring the virus in order to describe it fully.

Type 2 questions then seek to explain the cause and effect mechanisms behind why and how something works. For example, we wanted to find out how the Covid-19 virus infects people so we could devise treatments and vaccinations that hinder the mechanism by which the virus infects people.

Often, type 2 questions temporally succeed type 1 questions as it is difficult to explain a phenomenon without first systematically exploring and describing it. For example, one of the most significant scientific breakthroughs of all time was the description of the double-helix structure of a deoxyribonucleic acid (DNA) molecule. Watson and Crick described it in 1953, and this description gave rise to modern molecular biology, which explains how genes control the chemical processes in cells. The double helix also paved the way for new and powerful scientific techniques, such as recombinant DNA research, genetic engineering, rapid gene sequencing, and monoclonal antibodies. A description is fundamental to being able to build explanations.

As you may have gleaned from the differences between description and explanation in the two types of questions, research questions also unveil clues about how the research question can be answered. The research processes for exploration and description differ from those for explanation. In other words, certain types of questions favour certain research methods.

Developing the research question as your problem statement is probably one of the most important steps in your doctoral study, so you should be both patient and flexible in doing so. Give yourself time to revise questions as your knowledge and experience grow over time, and resist being rigid and fixed on one type of problem if you realise that your doctoral study takes you down a path where what you do is not quite what you originally set out to do.

If you struggle with this important task, you may find that guidelines for structuring research questions hierarchically can be beneficial. For example, a common approach to hierarchical structuring begins with a *managerial* question before moving on to *research* and *investigative* questions (Cooper & Emory, 1991):

1. The *managerial question* states the driving question of the study: who the interested audience is and why the question is important to them.
2. The *research question* captures the general purpose of the study. It is derived from the managerial question and translates it into a research problem.
3. The *investigative question* then identifies what must be answered to address the research question.

Justification of the Research Question

As a final step, a good research question comes together with a convincing argumentation for why the particular problem is significant and deserves our attention. Thus, for each question that indicates a problem with knowledge in a particular area (our problem statement), we should be able to offer an argument regarding why that particular focus, aspect, or question deserves our focus. Think of the research question formulation as a top-down process in which you narrow down a particular domain or field of investigation to bring it to one specific question in the domain. In the motivation process, you argue why the domain should be examined, and you identify a phenomenon in the domain that warrants attention. In the specification of the research question, you define one particular aspect of some phenomenon that you propose to examine from a particular angle. In this final step, you offer arguments regarding why the particular focus demonstrated in the research question(s) is warranted.

After specifying your research questions, it can be useful to reflect on them. The following criteria can be applied to evaluate the quality of your research questions and assess critically your set of research questions:

- *Feasiblity*: Are adequate subjects, technical expertise, time, and money available, and is the scope manageable?
- *Interestingness*: Are you confident that you can maintain an interest in the topic and maintain your motivation to study it for several years?
- *Novelty*: Will an answer to the research question confirm or refute previous findings or provide new findings?
- *Ethicality*: Will pursuing and answering the question violate ethical principles for the conduct of research or put the safety of the investigators or subjects at risk?
- *Relevance:* Will both the question and its answer(s) inform scientific knowledge, industry practice, and/or future research directions?

3.2 Research Design

Once your research question is well specified, the next challenge is to craft a plan of action to answer the question: a *research design*. A well-specified question will suggest the most appropriate course of study for answering the question.

A research design is a blueprint for the collection, measurement, and analysis of the data used to answer the stated research question. It should be economical and reflect complex research planning decisions that require compromises and trade-offs among the demands of resources, time, quality, and data access. But before discussing different types of research designs, let us explore the core methods of intellectual reasoning that form the basis of all types of research designs: *induction, deduction,* and *abduction.*

Intellectual Reasoning: Induction, Deduction, and Abduction

There is no series of events that commonly and consistently unfolds in a scientific process and would, therefore, be common to all research designs. However, all research designs help researchers engage in systematic forms of intellectual reasoning to generate knowledge from data or test knowledge against data. The aim of science is to advance human knowledge through such approaches as extension and intension (Kaplan, 1998/1964). Extension in this context refers to exploring new areas by applying existing knowledge in one area to other areas. Intension refers to seeking more complete knowledge in a single area. In other words, we can go outside to build new knowledge, or we can go deeper into the knowledge we have already accumulated.

This distinction is important because these two modes of advancing knowledge rest on different forms of intellectual reasoning: knowledge growth by extension relies on inductive reasoning, which is used to explore new knowledge, whereas knowledge growth by intension relies on deductive reasoning, which is used to refine and test existing knowledge.

Induction is a form of logical reasoning that involves inferring a general conclusion from a set of specific facts or observations. By developing patterns and commonalities, inductive reasoning allows tentative hypotheses and propositions to be formulated that declare general conclusions or theories. In other words, induction is used to infer theoretical concepts and patterns from observed data or known facts to generate new knowledge by proceeding from particulars to generals. A simple example of induction is as follows:

- Every life form we know of depends on liquid water to exist.
- Therefore, all life, including that we do not know of, depends on liquid water to exist.

Inductive arguments can be weak or strong. The induction "I always hang pictures on nails. Therefore: All pictures hang from nails" is an example of a weak induction because the observation is too limited to lead to such a broad generalisation.

The problem with induction is that inductive arguments cannot be proven or justified, only supported or not supported. Still, inductions are an accepted and often useful pathway for constructing explanations or hypotheses because conclusions are offered based on educated predictions. Case study research is a good example of research involving inductive reasoning because this kind of research collects observations that form the basis of educated speculations, which could form the basis of a more general theory. Inductive reasoning typically goes as follows: "I studied phenomenon X in Y number of cases and I have always found the particular relationship or phenomena Z to be at work. Hence, the evidence collected in my observation leads me to formulate the tentative proposition that Z is related to X in this or that way."

Deduction is a form of logical reasoning that involves deriving arguments as logical consequences of a set of more general premises. It involves deducing a conclusion from a general premise (i.e., a known theory) to a specific instance (i.e., an observation).

Deduction is commonly used to predict the results of hypotheses or propositions, an approach to science called the hypothetico-deductive model (Mertens & Recker, 2020). That is, to predict what observations one might make if an inquiry is conducted, a hypothesis is treated as a premise, and from it some not obvious conclusions are logically derived, tested, and revised if necessary. In other words, through deductive reasoning, we attempt to show that a conclusion necessarily follows from a set of premises or hypotheses.

Deduction can be seen as an attempt to test concepts and patterns known from theory using new empirical data. You may already recognise that the principle of falsification is core to deductive reasoning as by deriving hypotheses from general knowledge and testing them in new settings, we can demonstrate a theory to be wrong or right in those settings, but we can never prove it. A simple example of deduction is as follows:

- All men are mortal.
- Socrates is a man.
- Therefore, Socrates is mortal.

Similar to induction, deduction has potential drawbacks, the most obvious of which are related to deductive soundness and validity. Consider this deduction:

- Only quarterbacks eat steak.
- John eats steak.
- Therefore, John is a quarterback.

We can see here that the deductive reasoning as it is applied is logically sound (the conclusion that John is a quarterback), but we don't know whether the final statement is valid because the premise "Only quarterbacks eat steak" is not true. In other words, we can deductively reason in good faith but still end up with incorrect conclusions when the premise may not be valid (other people like eating steak, too).

At this point, you may recognise that induction and deduction play a role in many scientific processes, from setting up a plan to collecting data to the intellectual challenges of developing a new theory. However, neither is sufficient or complete. Mechanically executing induction or deduction cannot guarantee that knowledge will be advanced or new theory generated.

Abduction, a third form of intellectual reasoning, is the process of making sense of an observation by drawing inferences about the best possible explanation. The key point here is that abduction is not a process of inference or deduction but a trial-and-error search for a satisfactory explanation for an observed consequence after the fact. Some people refer to abduction as a form of educated or informed guessing (Peirce, 1958).

One key difference between abduction and induction or deduction is that abduction involves a creative process rather than a logical process. It is an operation geared

Table 3.1 Induction, deduction, and abduction

Form of reasoning	Example
Induction	Observation: These beans are from this bag. Reasoning: These beans are white. Conclusion: All the beans from this bag are white.
Deduction	Premise: All the beans in this bag are white. Observation: These beans are from this bag. Conclusion: These beans are white.
Abduction	Rule: All the beans from this bag are white. Observation: These beans are white and near the bag. Conclusion: These beans are probably from this bag.

towards the discovery of entirely new ideas (e.g., a new theory) rather than a mode of justification (through deduction) or formal inference (through induction). One could see abduction as a form of intellectual reasoning that is more concerned with discovery or design than rationalisation or validation.

Table 3.1 compares the three forms of intellectual reasoning using an example adapted from Fischer and Gregor's (2020) discussion of the topic.

Exploration, Rationalisation, and Validation

No research process relies on induction, deduction, or abduction in isolation. Consciously or not, we usually use multiple, if not all, of these strategies to explore and reason about phenomena, facts, and assumptions when we generate new knowledge. All of these modes of reasoning have some advantages and some disadvantages. Induction is useful for developing theories from observations and other singular facts and evidence, but it is insufficient for demonstrating the validity of any emergent theory. Deduction in itself can be used to test theories using some or many individual cases, but it must rely on a robust set of premises to begin with. Abduction may lead to entire new ideas or breakthroughs, but it rests on careful observation of facts and an understanding of existing rules and assumptions as a point of departure.

In any of the three forms of reasoning, **observation** plays a key role. Observation concerns the systematic discovery of things or phenomena encountered in common experience. It supports attempts to understand these observable things by discovering a systematic or structural order in them. Much of scientific work relies on observation. Many scientific advances began with scientists exploring and documenting previously unknown or understudied phenomena and scoping their magnitude, extent, or boundaries.

As part of a scientific study, observations must be made in adherence with the principles of scientific inquiry, so observations must be precise, reliable, and independent. An observation is conducted to gain an initial understanding of a phenomenon in its context and to generate ideas about the phenomenon or its relationships to

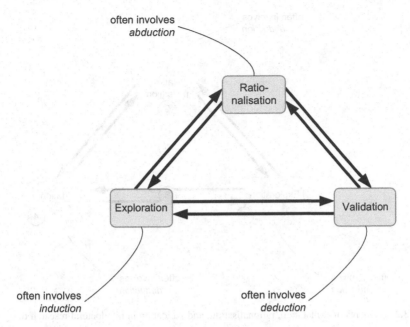

often involves
abduction

often involves
induction

often involves
deduction

Fig. 3.1 Exploration, rationalisation, and validation in research design

other phenomena that may lead to the formulation of speculative propositions or theories of explanation.

Sound research designs often employ <u>combinations</u> of strategies that rely on induction, deduction, and/or abduction to achieve a meaningful mix of **exploration**, which generates an initial understanding and description of a phenomenon; **rationalisation**, which we use to begin to make sense of the puzzle or problem; and **validation**, which subjects our emergent or developed theory to rigorous examination and testing.

Exploration, rationalisation, and validation do not necessarily follow each other in a defined linear or temporal manner. Good research typically moves back and forth among them, as shown in Fig. 3.1.

The exploration of a phenomenon can provide a basis for rationalising about it. For instance, using observations, we can rationalise about a solution to a problem, begin to explain a behaviour, or begin abduction to generate likely explanations or solutions. The rationalisation process can result in the need for further exploration (as shown in Fig. 3.1 by the arrow moving from rationalisation back to exploration). We may find that explaining a particular behaviour requires that we collect additional observations about other behaviours that we did not identify as relevant to our initial exploration. The interplay between rationalisation and exploration can also provide a set of initial evidence against which we can test the outcomes of our rationalisation process or evaluate a set of tentative propositions between constructs that capture a phenomenon. The rationalisation should be valid in light of any observations that we collected.

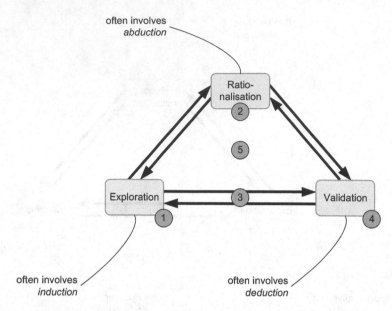

often involves
abduction

Ratio-
nalisation
2

5

Exploration
1

3

Validation
4

often involves
induction

often involves
deduction

Fig. 3.2 Elements of exploration, rationalisation, and validation in my doctoral research design

Once a rationalisation, in which tentative general propositions are created through inductive reasoning from observations or through abduction, has been made, we can proceed to validation, where we develop testable hypotheses or propositions for a particular context or scenario from our more general theory. These hypotheses can be subjected to further empirical tests using new or existing cases. The results or evidence collected may suggest that we revise our rationalisation (moving from validation back to rationalisation), which could involve abduction. For example, our validation may find an observable mechanism that speaks against the logic of our propositions, requiring us to make an educated guess about why it happened or how these observations can otherwise be explained.

Validation often also employs findings from exploration as a basis by defining the sample frame, the target population, or other contextual parameters that initial observations suggested were important. Likewise, the results might prompt a further exploration of the phenomenon, so we move from validation to exploration. For instance, observations might be collected that can be used to refine results, like those that are, at least on the surface, contradictory to the developed theory.

To illustrate this view of research designs, consider Fig. 3.2 and Table 3.2, which list elements of my own doctoral research program and how they relate to exploration, rationalisation, and validation. Study 1 reported on observations gathered through a survey, a type of exploration of the phenomenon, the adoption of the Business Process Model and Notation (BPMN) standard. Study 2 involved rationalising the phenomenon analytically through a deductive comparison of the standard against alternatives. Study 3 contained elements of deductive validation (empirical testing of propositions) and inductive exploration (identification of new,

Table 3.2 Studies in my doctoral research design

Number	Prominent research design principle	References
1	Exploration	Recker (2010)
2	Rationalisation	Recker et al. (2009)
3	Validation and exploration	Recker et al. (2010)
4	Validation	Recker et al. (2011)
5	All	Recker (2011)

Table 3.3 Research design decisions (adapted from Cooper & Emory, 1991)

Spectrum	One end of continuum		Other end of continuum
Aim	Exploratory	vs.	Explanatory
Method	Qualitative	vs.	Quantitative
Boundary	Case	vs.	Statistical
Setting	Field	vs.	Laboratory
Timing	Cross-sectional	vs.	Longitudinal
Outcome	Descriptive	vs.	Causal
Ambition	Analysing	vs.	Designing

unexpected findings) on the basis of qualitative research (interviews). Study 4 was a typical deductive form of the empirical validation of two propositions that were based on quantitative survey data. The entire research program was later published in a book covering all four studies. Abduction did not feature prominently in my PhD research. I worked deductively for large parts of the research and inductively to some extent. I did not create a breakthrough idea or an entirely new discovery.

Choosing a Research Design

A good research design typically includes work that combines induction, deduction, and abduction. You can use these three themes to reflect on whether your research design involves an appropriate way to rationalise, validate, or explore.

Fig. 3.1 also shows that a research design is the outcome of a process with many choices, none of which are trivial. Their implications regarding the potential of your research and its likely outcomes are significant. Table 3.3 summarises some of the important design decision parameters beyond the focus on the mode of intellectual reasoning alone. By no means are these decisions binary (either-or) in nature; rather, they are key points along a continuum of choices.

The rows in Table 3.3 describe the spectra by which we can examine our research design choices:

- The "aim" spectrum between exploration and explanation: Is the overall aim of the research more about exploration or explanation or somewhere on the continuum between them? For example, perhaps the aim of a research project is not only exploratory observation but also explanatory in determining an intervention. Intervention can, for example, help an organisation with its struggle to introduce new digital technologies and avoid issues like rejection and decreased performance.

- The "method" spectrum between qualitative and quantitative modes of scientific inquiry: Which sets of procedures and techniques will allow obtaining the best possible answer given the research aim? Will the methods involved rely more on qualitative, quantitative, or some other data?
- The "boundary" spectrum between case related and statistical: your research might be limited to a particular case (such as the case of an organisation or an individual) or by statistical properties (such as the required sample size for a survey or experiment). Variations along the spectrum might include research on several cases at one point in time or one case over time.
- The "setting" spectrum between field and laboratory: Where will the location of your research mainly be? Will it be in the field—in the real world, within an organisation or community? Or will it involve participants, such as students, that are recruited to undertake experiments or other data collection efforts in controlled, simulated environments (i.e., a laboratory)?
- The "timing" spectrum between cross-sectional and longitudinal: the focus of the "timing" might be one case over time (longitudinal) versus several cases at one point in time (cross-sectional) or somewhere in between.
- The "outcomes" spectrum between descriptive and causal: your research might focus on descriptions of a previously undiscovered phenomenon or on the discovery of certain causal mechanisms that explain why a phenomenon manifests the way it does. The focus might also be on both outcomes.
- The "ambition" spectrum between understanding and designing: the goal of your research might be to analyse the root causes or inner mechanics of a problem or situation, or to design a solution or a novel artefact, or some combination of both.

At this stage, the researcher should go back to the research questions to determine how to make a selection alongside these different dimensions of choice. The key benchmark against which your research design must be aligned is the problem statement as specified in the research question(s), so the research design must match logically the research question, not the other way around. The research question determines to a large extent the choices one makes in selecting a research design. It dictates, for example, whether a more qualitative, explorative inquiry is warranted or a more quantitative, statistical one.

This point is important because one key downfall of doctoral students that I have come to encounter is the "I do research method X syndrome." When I ask students about their research, they often say things like "I'm doing case study research," "I'm doing design science," or "I'm doing an experiment." In all these cases, the students are focussing on one aspect of their research design—the choice of method—which they have often chosen independently of the projected research outcome or the research question they seek to answer.

Finally, one of the key choices in research design relates to the **research methodology**. We will discuss this challenge in more detail in Sect. 3.3, but let me just say here that, while the research methodology is critical, the research design must account for several other considerations as well. The most important ones have to do with data, risks, theory, feasibility, and instrumentation:

- **Data**: What type of data is required? What type of data is or might be available? Where and how can I collect observations or other forms of evidence? How will I sample the data I gather?
- **Risks**: What are the dangers associated with executing the research design? For example, how likely is it that a case organisation will not be available for study? What strategies are available to minimise these risks?
- **Theory**: How much literature concerning the phenomena I am interested in is available? What are the problems with the knowledge base, and what form do they take? What findings have been produced that might have an effect on my work and influence the choices in my research design?
- **Feasibility**: Can my research design be executed within the constraints associated with a doctoral study, such as time limitations, resource limitations, funding, experience, and geographic boundaries?
- **Instrumentation**: How will my concepts of interest manifest in reality? How can my constructs be measured? Will my operationalisations be appropriate given the choice of research methodology and the set of available data?

In selecting a research design, you may be able to evaluate your progress by determining whether you have appropriate answers to the questions above and have maintained alignment with the type of research problem that is specified in your research question. The alignment does not have to be unidirectional (from the question to the design); in fact, most research questions are tweaked and altered over time to reflect an updated research design, although research questions should retain their prominence over the research design. Since research sets out to answer an important question, it is not appropriate to find an answer through your research design and then devise a question that fits the answer.

In making decisions about their research designs, students and their supervisors need to work together to select a research design that they feel comfortable with and with which they have experience. This is not to say that new research designs should not be pursued, but many problems I have seen originated largely from the fact that neither the student nor the supervisory team had any experience with the research design they chose. Executing such studies then becomes unnecessarily difficult because of limited resources for meaningful feedback based on experience.

3.3   Research Methodology

One critical element in the development of a research design is the selection of a research methodology. Many scholars even argue that the research methodology is the most important design choice in the research process.

Research methodology is a term that describes the **strategy of inquiry** used to answer a research question. Creswell (2009) states that strategies of inquiry are "types of qualitative, quantitative and mixed methods designs that provide specific direction for procedures in a research design." I would add design science and computational methods to Creswell's list of strategies of inquiry, both of which are recent advances in research methodology:

- **Quantitative strategies** are procedures that feature research methods like experiments and surveys. Quantitative strategies are characterised by an emphasis on quantitative data (a focus on "numbers").
- **Qualitative strategies** are procedures that feature research methods like case study, ethnography, and phenomenology. Qualitative strategies are characterised by an emphasis on qualitative data (a focus on "words").
- **Mixed methods** are procedures that feature a combination of qualitative and quantitative strategies in either sequential or concurrent fashion (a focus on both "words" and "numbers").
- **Design science methods** are procedures that feature methods for building and evaluating novel artefacts like new models, methods, and systems as the outcome of a research process. Design science methods are characterised by an emphasis on the construction of the artefact and demonstration of its utility in solving an organisational problem (a focus on "artefacts").
- **Computational methods** are procedures for data visualisation and pattern identification that rely on software to analyse digital trace data automatically for the purposes of classification, description, or theory generation. Computational methods are characterised by an emphasis on the digital records of activities and events captured and stored through digital information and communication technologies (a focus on "digital traces").

Setting aside the mixed-method strategy for a moment (because it combines characteristics of two or more strategies of inquiry), we can differentiate qualitative, quantitative, design science, or computational strategies using the methodological requirements imposed by the research questions or elements of the research design. These requirements are summarised in Table 3.4.

Controllability refers to the extent to which events that occur during a study are under the researcher's control. In a qualitative inquiry, where the researcher often enters an organisation to observe behaviours, processes, or events, control over what happens is low compared to quantitative inquiries like surveys and experiments, where control is exerted through the operationalisation of a measurement instrument that defines what will be measured and how. In design science research, control over

Table 3.4 Differences in research strategies

Requirement	Qualitative	Quantitative	Design science	Computational
Controllability	Low	Medium to high	High	Low to medium
Deducibility	Low	Medium to high	Low	High
Repeatability	Low	Medium to high	High	High
Generalisability	Low	Medium to high	Low	Low to medium
Explorability	High	Low to medium	Low to medium	High
Complexity	High	Low to medium	Medium to high	Medium to high

progress and effects is typically in the hands of the person who is designing the artefact, the researcher.

Deducibility refers to the extent to which the strategy allows for deductive reasoning. Through the emphasis is on quantitative data, quantitative strategies allow for strong deductive reasoning through statistical or other quantifiable conclusions, whereas deducibility is typically limited when doing qualitative inquiries such as single-case research or ethnography. Deducibility is often low in design science research because of the challenge involved in embedding hypothesis testing into the design of an artefact.

Repeatability refers to the extent to which the findings are reliable in the sense that the research procedures can be repeated with similar results. This requirement is easier to meet in quantitative inquiries, where instruments of measurement tend to be precisely defined. Repeatability is high in design science research because the artefact is typically designed to be stable. Repeatability is also often high in research that uses computational methods because the digital trace data can be used to run and rerun our algorithms for analysis and discovery any number of times.

Generalisability refers to the extent to which the findings and observations can be generalised beyond the data that are examined. Quantitative inquires, especially surveys, tend to provide greater generalisability beyond the sample than qualitative inquiries do because the latter are more deeply immersed in the context of the inquiry. Design science and computational methods are typically low in generalisability: design science creates situated artefacts for the most part that are meant to work for a particular problem in a particular setting. Likewise, the data basis for computational methods comes from a particular set of digital records (and only those records that are digitally available), so they typically do not allow broader conclusions beyond the boundaries of the data itself.

Explorability refers to the extent to which a research strategy encourages or enables the discovery of previously unknown or unconsidered observations or findings. Explorability is typically built into qualitative inquiries through an emphasis on broad and open measurements, while quantitative inquires, with their precise and formalised measurements, are more limited in terms of exploring beyond the focus of the study. Explorability can be an attribute of some artefact designs, but it is not a key requirement for creating novel artefact designs. Explorability is often high in computational methods because the key area of application is the use of automated

Fig. 3.3 Qualitative and quantitative methodologies

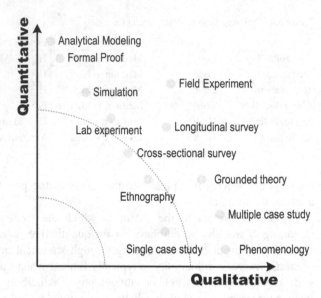

algorithms to discover patterns, themes, and associations in data that are typically too large for manual analysis and interpretation.

Complexity refers to the extent to which a research design leads to comprehensive, exhaustive, and multifaceted contributions to knowledge. Quantitative inquiries are characterised by selected, precisely defined measurements of phenomena, whereas qualitative inquiry's broader and more open data-collection procedures allow for more findings and contributions. Complexity in design science research depends heavily on the type of artefact, but it is often a key characteristic of the design since all simple artefacts have already been discovered and designed. Complexity in computation methods is also medium to high because of the nature or format of the digital trace data that are the subject of inquiry or the complexities of the automated methods and algorithms—or both.

Mixed-method designs are not mentioned in Table 3.4 because, as their name suggests, their key characteristic is that they combine, usually in a favourable way, different methods with the view to meeting several or all of the requirements.

Most often, mixed-method designs involve a combination of some qualitative and some quantitative methods. In such a situation, depending on the choice of research methods to be combined, the overall methodology may lean towards either purely qualitative or purely quantitative inquiries. A valuable mixed-method design is one that combines strong qualitative characteristics, like explorability and complexity, with strong quantitative characteristics, like generalisability and deducibility. This way, requirements that one method may not fully meet can be compensated by the other. Figure 3.3 groups several research methods in each of the two major strategies of inquiry and illustrates the extent to which different methods can meet desired characteristics of quantitative or qualitative strategies.

There are different reasons for choosing a mixed-method research design (Venkatesh et al., 2013). For example, the rationale for choosing a mixed-method strategy of inquiry can be to *compensate* for the limitations of one method (e.g., a survey) with the advantages of another method (e.g., a case study). Other reasons are to ensure a more *complete* observation of a phenomenon or to test the propositions that emerge inductively from one method, such as a case study, deductively through another method, such as a survey (Gable, 1994) or experiment (Chatman & Flynn, 2005). This type of mixed-method design is called *developmental* because it involves testing the results of one method by means of another method.

Selecting an appropriate strategy of inquiry to determine the research methodology is critical to the success of any research project and must be driven by the research question and by the current state of knowledge in the area of study. For example, an emerging problem domain or topic area is often initially explored through predominantly qualitative strategies because these strategies score highly on the characteristics of explorability and complexity and in turn allow researchers to develop a first comprehensive picture of that area and to identify and describe important concepts or phenomena within it. Conversely, as research in an area matures over time, the share of studies that use quantitative methodologies typically increases, building on more precisely defined concepts and exploring in a more controlled manner the studied behaviours, processes, events, or other phenomena, with a view to deducing generalisable findings. This is because demands for controllability and repeatability, for example, increase as more and more research in an area is being done.

Selecting a design science methodology indicates an entirely different strategy as the aim of design science research is not exploration, description, or explanation but instead intervention and problem-solving by constructing novel artefacts as solutions to problems. Even so, design science can be combined with or complemented by qualitative or quantitative research.

Computational methods, a new methodological approach to research, rely on automated collection and analysis of digital trace data. This strategy is new because such methods rely on the wide availability of large samples of digital records. Records of events and actions were once restricted to a computer system in a particular organisation (e.g., a transaction system in a bank), but so many business and social activities now involve digital technology that vast quantities of digital records about actions and events that occur in our lives are becoming available to researchers. Advances in the automated analysis of such data have led to algorithms that identify sequences, match patterns, mine associations, classify data into clusters or categories, and extract semantics from text, audio, and video. This field of inquiry is subject to substantial ongoing research and development itself, and it will be exciting to follow these developments and their implications for scientific activities, like discovery, theory generation, and hypothesis testing.

Personally, I like doctoral research programs that feature a combination of research methods. For example, when a subject area is not well understood, qualitative methods may be used to collect observations in an effort to build theory and testable hypotheses, after which such theory may be tested by means of deductive reasoning using quantitative methods like surveys and experiments. It should be noted, however, that such mixed-method approaches increase the learning burden for doctoral students—they need to learn not one but several methods and also understand ways to combine them appropriately. I should also point out that many excellent theses have been completed on the basis of one strategy alone.

3.4   The Role of Literature in the Research Process

A colleague of mine always tells his students: "you should read before you write." There is a lot of truth in this advice. One of the key tasks in your effort to contribute to knowledge during your PhD journey will be to acquire knowledge. You need to know the current state of the knowledge in your area of study (codified in the literature) so you can demonstrate how you can contribute to it by adding new knowledge to the literature. Earlier in this book, we have discussed that you need to acquire at least three types of knowledge before you can even start your research:

(1) Knowledge about the domain and topic of interest that relate to your chosen phenomena
(2) Knowledge about relevant theories and available evidence that help you frame questions and phenomena, and
(3) Knowledge about relevant research methods that you can apply to develop new knowledge, build innovative artefacts, or articulate new questions

   Knowledge in the scholarly field is available predominantly in the form of articles and books because writings have historically been the most persistent and replicable medium in which to store and distribute knowledge. We build a cumulative tradition of knowledge by adding our own research to this repository of knowledge in the form of published books, book chapters, journal articles, and papers in conference proceedings, among other vehicles.

   Doing research demands that you spend a significant amount of time and effort to acquire and critically appraise this cumulative knowledge base, constantly, repeatedly, continuously. You will not be able to add substantially to the body of knowledge without knowing where that body of knowledge currently stands, and because research is being done and published every day, the body of knowledge is not static; it moves and grows every day. A researcher has to be a good and avid reader.

   I mention this role of the literature in the midst of discussing the research design process because it is already at this stage that a firm understanding of the body of knowledge is essential to many of the decisions regarding the *planning* stages of research:

• The literature informs the extent, type, and nature of potential research problems because the research problem only exists if a problem is identifiable in the literature, and we can find that problem only if we have cumulative knowledge about it.

- The literature informs where gaps of knowledge are about a particular phenomenon or question and where other problems with the extant knowledge are (e.g., inconsistency, false assumptions, inconclusiveness). Critically appraising literature helps in identifying an important academic research question, that is, one that deserves scholarly attention because its answer will contribute to the body of knowledge.
- The literature informs the extent to which current theories can explain the particularities of a phenomenon or problem and where they fail to do so adequately.
- The literature contains strategies and methodologies that have been used to research the same phenomena or problem and similar phenomena or problems.
- The literature contains theories that can be used to frame an investigation.
- The literature contains the current body of knowledge about research methodologies that are available.

A firm understanding of the literature is critical to the design and conduct of a doctoral study. Often, to beginning students, the list of readings appears large—maybe overwhelming. And even when you start with what looks like a long reading list (say, 50 papers), rest assured that the volume over time will easily be doubled, quadrupled, or more than that. Believe me: any "reading list" you may come across will be nowhere as long as the list of readings you will have consumed by the end of your journey. Therefore, start reading straight away, that is, from the start of your journey. Many doctoral students overlook parts of the literature because they underestimate how important the literature is to their ability to formulate sound research questions and research methodologies. As a rule of thumb, you can never read too much, but it is easy not to read enough.

In consuming the literature, it helps to follow a process of read-think-interpret. Reading a paper or book does not always mean consuming every sentence from start to finish as not all of the literature or even all sections of a piece of reading material will be relevant to your area of interest. Therefore, after you *read*, *think* about the piece's relevance and *interpret* it based on your assessment of its relevance to you, that is, evaluate whether there are useful ideas, theories, concepts, methods, or findings in a reading that you should investigate in more depth. In following this process of read-think-interpret, the following questions can guide you:

- What is the reading's core contribution with respect to the contemporary practice in your field of inquiry?
- How does it relate to other articles and practices?
- Does it espouse a theoretical or methodological perspective that would be useful in studying the phenomena that are of interest to you? And why is this, or is this not the case?
- How may it influence your own thinking of the field?
- How do you think the reading influenced the body of knowledge in the field at the time it was published?

Following these guiding questions should benefit you in your quest to master the body of knowledge as it pertains to your research. In my own reading, I take several passes of read-think-interpret: I scan new papers when I come across them to develop an impression—Is this reading relevant to me? Do I find the idea, theory, evidence, data, method, or phenomena useful or interesting? My goal at this stage is to build passing knowledge about the paper, so when at some stage it becomes relevant to my research, I will remember it and engage in a second, more thorough reading that is more detailed and deliberate. In this second pass, I read a paper to determine exactly what was done and how: I read the title and the abstract, scan the introduction, move to findings and discussion, and in some cases go back to methods or implications. I read background sections only when I really need to.

Beyond my suggestions, there is ample guidance available for doing literature reviews using more or less structured processes. I suggest some "readings about reading." The information systems discipline also has excellent web resources that are dedicated to the literature about theories and methodologies.

For example, in terms of **theories**, Larsen and Eargle (2015) created a wiki with summarised information on theories that are widely used in information systems research. At http://is.theorizeit.org/, you can explore theories by name and type of application, along with details about the theory, some examples of papers that use the theory, and links to related information.

IS scholars have also crafted online resources as a starting point to learn about and apply research **methodologies**. The most prominent of these resources are the following:

- The *AIS World Section on Quantitative, Positivist Research Methods in Information Systems* (http://www.janrecker.com/quantitative-research-in-information-systems/): maintains an introductory material to address the needs of quantitative researchers in information systems, whether seasoned veterans or those just beginning to learn to use these methods
- The *AIS World Section on Qualitative Research in Information Systems* (http://www.qual.auckland.ac.nz/): provides useful information on the conduct, evaluation, and publication of qualitative research in information systems
- The *AIS World Section on Design Research in Information Systems* (http://desrist.org/design-research-in-information-systems/): provides useful information on understanding, conducting, evaluating, and publishing design science research

I am not aware of any online resource for computational methods that is comparable to these resources, but such a resource would be welcome, and I am expecting that someone will develop such a resource soon.

The literature about **problem domains** varies depending on the domain's type, nature, and maturity. Many domains have their own outlets of coverage through practitioner communities, blogs, forums, journals, and so forth (e.g., *CIO* magazine). It is useful to explore the range of literature that connects various communities of technology practices. This literature is often valuable in, for instance, justifying the relevance and significance of a study. Good examples of such literature include market research reports by institutions like Gartner, Forrester, WinterResearch, and other technology-related research agencies.

A final suggestion is to be prepared to expand the scope of your reading. Many good papers on methods, domains, theories, and other aspects of the research process are published in outlets that you may not necessarily associate with the information systems field but that belong to some of its reference disciplines (e.g., management, computer science, organisational science, psychology). These fields have top journals whose papers are often useful. Expanding your literature search outside of your immediate domain can help you discover theories that are used in other research fields, see how methods are applied in other research, and learn how other scholars in other fields frame, examine, and solve real-world problems. Considering these adjunct fields of literature, a journey can be a source of inspiration and can even be a tipping point in your journey.

3.5 Further Reading

Finding a research question is an unstructured, domain-specific problem, so it can be difficult to find guidance in the literature. One article that can inspire your thinking is Weber's (2003) editorial, "The Problem of the Problem." Editors and senior scholars in other disciplines and journals have published similar pieces, such as in the *Academy of Management Journal* (Grant & Pollock, 2011). A particularly useful strategy in finding research questions is *problematisation* (Alvesson & Sandberg, 2011), a structured approach to finding problems like gaps, inconsistencies, and inconclusiveness in the literature, which then serves as the starting point for adding to the body of knowledge.

As for creating a pathway for answering a research question, many books are dedicated to research designs. One good example is Creswell (2009), which discusses research design choices from the perspective of favoured research methods. Leedy and Ormrod (2001) also include criteria for judging the quality of research designs.

The paper by Lee (1991) is an excellent resource on how to build research designs that combine what the author calls subjective, interpretive, and objective understanding. While these terms are different from mine (exploration, rationalisation, and validation) and the paper's focus is much on the interplay between research paradigms (interpretivism versus positivism) in use at these levels, much of the argumentation and conclusions are similar.

Concerning the selection of a research methodology, ample readings are available that summarise research strategies, such as the 19 strategies Wolcott (2001) discusses and Creswell (2009), mentioned above. We discuss the literature on design science in Chap. 5, but if you are interested in the growing stream of research on computational strategies, Berente et al. (2019), Lazer et al. (2009), and Pentland et al. (2020) are good starting points.

Information about literature reviews and search strategies are widely available, varying in their aims, approaches, systematicity, and structure. Wonderful overviews of the types of literature reviews and their aims and approaches are Paré et al. (2015) and Templier and Paré (2015). Several other good resources include the following:

- Webster and Watson's (2002) guide to writing a literature review
- The relevant section in Leedy and Ormrod's (2001) book on research planning and design
- The essays on conducting research reviews in Cooper (1982) and Strange & Strange (1972)
- For inspiration and as good examples for how literature reviews can be conducted and lead to new knowledge, all articles in the theory and review sections of the information systems discipline's top academic journal, *MIS Quarterly*.

References

Alvesson, M., & Sandberg, J. (2011). Generating Research Questions Through Problematization. *Academy of Management Review, 36*(2), 247–271.

Berente, N., Seidel, S., & Safadi, H. (2019). Data-Driven Computationally-Intensive Theory Development. *Information Systems Research, 30*(1), 50–64.

Branch, G., & Foster, C. A. (2018). Yes, Flat-Earthers Really Do Exist. *Scientific American*. Retrieved January 19, 2020 from https://blogs.scientificamerican.com/observations/yes-flat-earthers-really-do-exist/

Centefelli, R. T., & Schwarz, A. (2011). Identifying and Testing the Inhibitors of Technology Usage Intentions. *Information Systems Research, 22*(4), 808–823.

Chatman, J. A., & Flynn, F. J. (2005). Full-Cycle Micro-Organizational Behavior Research. *Organization Science, 16*(4), 434–447.

Cooper, D. R., & Emory, C. W. (1991). *Business Research Methods* (4th ed.). Richard D Irwin.

Cooper, H. M. (1982). Scientific Guidelines for Conducting Integrative Research Reviews. *Review of Educational Research, 52*(2), 291–302.

Creswell, J. W. (2009). *Research Design: Qualitative, Quantitative, and Mixed Methods Approaches* (3rd ed.). Sage Publications.

Fischer, C., & Gregor, S. (2020). Forms of Reasoning in the Design Science Research Process. In H. Jain, A. P. Sinha, & P. Vitharana (Eds.), *Service-Oriented Perspectives in Design Science Research: DESRIST 2011* (Vol. 6629, pp. 17–31). Springer.

Gable, G. G. (1994). Integrating Case Study and Survey Research Methods: An Example in Information Systems. *European Journal of Information Systems, 3*(2), 112–126.

Grant, A. M., & Pollock, T. G. (2011). Publishing in AMJ—Part 3: Setting the Hook. *Academy of Management Journal, 54*(5), 873–879.

Kaplan, A. (1998/1964). *The Conduct of Inquiry: Methodology for Behavioral Science*. Transaction Publishers.

Larsen, K. R. T., & Eargle, D. (2015). *Theories Used in IS Research Wiki*. University of Colorado. Retrieved May 28, 2021 from https://is.theorizeit.org/

Lazer, D., Pentland, A. P., Adamic, L. A., Aral, S., Barabási, A.-L., Brewer, D., Christakis, N., Contractor, N., Fowler, J., Gutmann, M., Jebara, T., King, G., Macy, M., Roy, D., & Van Alstyne, M. (2009). Computational Social Science. *Science, 323*(5915), 721–723.

Lee, A. S. (1991). Integrating Positivist and Interpretive Approaches to Organizational Research. *Organization Science, 2*(4), 342–365.

Leedy, P. D., & Ormrod, J. E. (2001). *Practical Research: Planning and Design* (7th ed.). Prentice Hall.

Mertens, W., & Recker, J. (2020). New Guidelines for Null Hypothesis Significance Testing in Hypothetico-Deductive IS Research. *Journal of the Association for Information Systems, 21*(4), 1072–1102. https://doi.org/10.17705/1jais.00629

Paré, G., Trudel, M.-C., Jaana, M., & Kitsiou, S. (2015). Synthesizing Information Systems Knowledge: A Typology of Literature Reviews. *Information & Management, 52*(2), 183–199.

Peirce, C. S. (1958). On the Logic of Drawing History from Ancient Documents Especially from Testimonies. In A. W. Burks (Ed.), *Collected Papers of Charles Sanders Peirce, Volumes VII and VIII: Science and Philosophy and Reviews, Correspondence and Bibliography* (pp. 162–255). Harvard University Press.

Pentland, B. T., Liu, P., Kremser, W., & Hærem, T. (2020). The Dynamics of Drift in Digitized Processes. *MIS Quarterly, 44*(1), 19–47.

Recker, J., Indulska, M., Rosemann, M., & Green, P. (2010). The Ontological Deficiencies of Process Modeling in Practice. *European Journal of Information Systems, 19*(5), 501–525.

Recker, J., Rosemann, M., Green, P., & Indulska, M. (2011). Do Ontological Deficiencies in Modeling Grammars Matter? *MIS Quarterly, 35*(1), 57–79.

Recker, J., Rosemann, M., Indulska, M., & Green, P. (2009). Business Process Modeling: A Comparative Analysis. *Journal of the Association for Information Systems, 10*(4), 333–363.

Strange, J. R., & Strange, S. M. (1972). How to Read a Scientific Research Report. In J. R. Strange & S. M. Strange (Eds.), *Reading for Meaning in College and After* (pp. 54–66). Brooks/Cole Publishing.

Templier, M., & Paré, G. (2015). A Framework for Guiding and Evaluating Literature Reviews. *Communications of the Association for Information Systems, 37*(6), 112–137.

Venkatesh, V., Brown, S. A., & Bala, H. (2013). Bridging the Qualitative-Quantitative Divide: Guidelines for Conducting Mixed Methods Research in Information Systems. *MIS Quarterly, 37*(1), 21–54.

Venkatesh, V., Morris, M. G., Davis, G. B., & Davis, F. D. (2003). User Acceptance of Information Technology: Toward a Unified View. *MIS Quarterly, 27*(3), 425–478.

Weber, R. (2003). Editor's Comments: The Problem of the Problem. *MIS Quarterly, 27*(1), iii–ix.

Webster, J., & Watson, R. T. (2002). Analyzing the Past to Prepare for the Future: Writing a Literature Review. *MIS Quarterly, 26*(2), xiii–xxiii.

Wolcott, H. F. (2001). *Writing up Qualitative Research* (2nd ed.). Sage.

Chapter 4
Theorising

4.1 What Is Theory?

Chapter 3 took us through the steps of designing a research inquiry, the *planning* stage of the research. Chapters 4 and 5 address two key challenges in *executing* the research, by discussing **theory** and **method**. Let us start by looking at theory.

Earlier in this book, we stated that scientific knowledge is the collection of theories built, derived, and tested using methods for scientific inquiry, and theories are our current explanations for how our world looks and how phenomena in it behave and function.

So why are theories important? Theories are at the core of any research process. As scholars, it is our job to develop theories, evaluate them, reject them when necessary, and revise, extend, or modify them. Theories represent the main element in the accumulation of our body of knowledge. Therefore, we can only do science if we work *with* the existing theories or find a way to discard them or replace them with new ones.

In addition to being the core *outcome* of scientific research, theories are important to the *planning* process in research: to scholars, a theory can provide guidance in terms of where to direct the attention of study. An existing theory serves as a framework for where current, past, and future empirical work can be incorporated. From a larger perspective, theories can be the material that integrates sets of individual studies into a larger research program (Burton-Jones, 2009).

Theories also have plenty to offer to the *execution* process in research as they provide a framework for synthesising, analysing, and integrating empirical findings and observations; aid us analysing empirical data and observations by identifying patterns and themes in the data; and help us explain our findings or observations so we can make sense of the data we collect. Theories are also the basis for the derivation of hypotheses that can be examined in subsequent scientific, empirical work. As such, theory is a key component that adds rigor to the research process

© Springer Nature Switzerland AG 2021
J. Recker, *Scientific Research in Information Systems*, Progress in IS,
https://doi.org/10.1007/978-3-030-85436-2_4

(Steinfield & Fulk, 1990) and can be of help when we have observations and
evidence that seem contradictory, anomalous, or inconsistent.

Definition of Theory

Simply put, theories are proposed explanations of empirical natural or social phenomena, constructed in a way that is consistent with the principles of scientific
inquiry. For example, a theory in medicine involves understanding the causes and
nature of health and sickness, which is what we call *explanatory theory*.
Foreshadowing our discussion of different types of theories below, let me add that
medicine also contains *design theories*, which are about making people healthy.
Note here that explanatory and design theories are related but can also be independent: One can research health and sickness (explanatory theory) without curing a
patient (design theory), and one can cure a patient without knowing how the cure
worked.

Still, most would argue that theories contain an explanatory component, that is, a
logic about the mechanisms that connect phenomena and a story about *how and why*
actions, events, structure, and thoughts occur. In that sense, theory emphasises the
nature of causal relationships, identifying what comes first and the timing of events.
Therefore, a more formal definition is that theory is a system of constructs and
relationships between constructs that, taken together, present a logical, systematic,
and coherent explanation of a phenomenon (Bacharach, 1989).

It may be helpful to explain what theory *is not* to explain what theory *is*:

- Theory is not *data*: sets of evidence, observations, or arguments do not make up a
  theory. Think of raw materials and the design of a building: we need bricks,
  mortar, or perhaps wood to build a house, but these materials themselves are not
  the house, just as data, evidence, or observations are not theories.
- Theory is not *idiographic*: an explanation of a single situation or phenomenon, in
  whatever detail, is not a theory as it cannot be generalised to other situations,
  events, or phenomena. By extension, therefore, theory is *nomothetic*; that is, it
  pertains to classes of events, behaviours, situations, or phenomena as it is broader
  than one instance or one example. Some even say that the more general a theory
  is, the better.
- Theory is not *description* or *prediction* only: a mere description or classification
  of a phenomenon does not constitute a theory because such descriptions (taxonomies, typologies, classifications, and so forth) operate at the empirical, observational level. A theory delves into underlying processes to explain the systematic
  reasons for a particular occurrence or non-occurrence. It comes with suggested
  explanatory mechanisms that tell not only *that* a phenomenon occurs but also *how*
  and *why* it occurs in the way we observed it. Similarly, prediction alone, without
  explanation, is typically not considered a theory. With advances in machine
  learning, algorithms can generate fairly accurate predictions of future behaviours

based on past behaviours, but they do not explain the mechanisms that yielded these behaviours in the past or will yield them in the future.

- Theory is not *design*: the construction of an artefact, however novel and useful it is, is in itself not a theory. Just as we may be able to predict future events without understanding why the events will occur, we may be able to construct artefacts that operate well without understanding how and why. However, it is possible that a design artefact embodies knowledge, and so is a manifestation of theory if it informs us about why this artefact is constructed in a particular way and why it provides the utility or novelty that it provides; in such a case, a design may involve or yield a theory.
- Theory is not *self-perpetuating*: theory is not an activity that is an end in itself such that it is important to you only because you think it is important, not because it will help you achieve something. Instead, theory has implications that inform our current and future understanding of a phenomenon.
- Theory is not *universal*: some scholars in the natural sciences (e.g., physics) have long searched for one universal theory of everything—the current candidate is super symmetric string theory—but a universal theory does not exist in the social sciences, nor is one necessarily needed. While striving for comprehensiveness, theories have their share of limitations in the form of assumptions and boundary conditions, which specify the limits to which the theory is held. For example, some theories pertain only to large and complex organisations rather than to all types of organisations.

Equipped with this basic understanding of what a theory is and is not, we can turn to examining the elements that make up a theory and to the structural components that are common to all types of theories.

4.2 Building Blocks of Theory

Constructs, Relationships, Mechanisms, and Boundary Conditions

Independent of what a theory is, the phenomena to which it pertains, and the goals it strives to reach, several structural components occur commonly across all theories. Whetten (1989) called these the building blocks of theory:

1. *What* (constructs)
2. *How* (relationships)
3. *Why* (justifications), and
4. *Who, where,* and *when* (boundary conditions)

The most fundamental components of theory are the constructs of which it is composed. In Chap. 2, we defined constructs as operationalised concepts, which meant that we attempt to take the abstract meaning of a concept (such as education) and operationalise it to something in the real world that can be measured. Typically, constructs relate to properties of things, both tangible and intangible, in the real world, so our theory can explain or predict what happens to the thing if one of its properties changes. For example, we may theorise about how users' perceptions of an e-commerce website change depending on how data are represented on that website (e.g., as texts, as graphics, as animation).

Which constructs compose a theory is a fundamental question. The choice of constructs determines both the locus (the domain addressed) and the focus (the level of abstraction) of the theory. The number of constructs determines the theory's comprehensiveness (how much does the theory account for?) and parsimony (what is the simplest account possible?), but the fundamental question goes deeper than that. For example, above I said that constructs relate to the properties of things, both tangible and intangible, in the real world, but this view assumes that the world is made up of things, a substantialist view of the world. A relationalist view would be that the world is in a continuously unfolding process and that the dynamics of this process are its fundamental building blocks (Emirbayer, 1997). Therefore, our constructs are often about things with properties, but they could also be about changes to relationships in a dynamic process. Either way, theory needs constructs that describe its essential elements.

Thinking about theoretical constructs in this way allows us to define at least two key ways we can contribute to advancing theory:

- We can articulate *new constructs* as the basis for a new theory regarding previously unknown phenomena or as a new way to look at existing phenomena. Alternatively, we can articulate new constructs to form part of an existing theory. For example, scholars have introduced the constructs of habit and inertia to explain why some people continue to use an old information system rather than accept a new one (Polites & Karahanna, 2012). The concept of habit is by no means a new one, yet its operationalisation as a construct in the nomological net of technology acceptance was a novel addition to theory at that time.
- We can *delete constructs* from a theory to increase the parsimony of the account offered by the theory. A good example is an early work around the technology acceptance model, which showed that the effects of the construct "attitude" are fully mediated by the other constructs in the theory, so they could be omitted (Davis et al., 1989).

Typically, constructs can be specified further in terms of their importance to the theory. We distinguish between *focal* constructs and *ancillary* constructs, where focus constructs are those that are the key components in our theory and determine its locus and focus. Other constructs might describe other phenomena or properties of interest and be associated with the focal constructs in some way, perhaps because they moderate or mediate some constructs' effects on another construct. It is also possible not to have a focal construct.

Having identified a set of constructs that describe *what* the theory is about, the next question is *how* the constructs are related to one another. In this step, we describe the <u>relationships</u> between constructs. A typical example of a relationship is how changes in the state of one property (e.g., a person's level of happiness) change the state of another of that thing's properties (e.g., a person's ability to sleep peacefully) or another thing (e.g., the level of happiness in a person with whom they engage often). Through relationships, we are essentially describing *laws of interactions*, that is, patterns for how the values of one construct change in accordance with changes in the values of another construct.

These laws of interactions are typically attempts to define a sense of causality in a conceptualisation of some phenomenon, in that we describe certain patterns of behaviour for the properties that are captured in our theory. The nature of the relationship depends on the purpose of the theory and may be any of several types, such as associative, compositional, unidirectional, bidirectional, conditional, or causal. In a sense, specifying the form of the relationship between constructs provides a key step towards explaining the mechanisms that explain how and why the constructs behave the way they do or the way we expect them to.

Thinking about relationships between theoretical constructs allows us to identify three other ways in which we can contribute to theoretical advancement:

- We can articulate *new laws of interaction* in the relationships among existing or new constructs.
- We can *delete laws of interactions* among the constructs of a theory.
- We can *redefine the existing laws of interaction* among constructs in a different way.

In general, the laws of interaction can be specified with varying levels of precision. For instance, some theories merely state that the values of their constructs are associated with one another by showing that high values of one construct are associated with high or low values of another construct or that the existence of one value of a construct signals the existence of a certain value of another construct. In some cases, the functional relationships between constructs can be specified more precisely, such as when a certain value range of one construct mediates, mitigates, or moderates the value range of another construct or the relationships between two or more other constructs.

The next step is then to ask *why*—why are the chosen constructs relevant and complete, and why are the laws of interactions as specified? This part of theory relates to the justificatory or explanatory mechanisms: the reason that a theory is a credible account of the phenomenon to which it pertains. Justificatory mechanisms are the key vehicles for the credence of the particular account that the theory offers, and they describe the logic of the key assumptions that underlie the theory. They also provide the basis for gauging whether the proposed conceptualisation is reasonable.

This focus on mechanisms is probably the most essential but perhaps also the most difficult part of theoretical development. There are several ways to identify these mechanisms.

Historically, justificatory mechanisms for theories in information systems were often deductively drawn from existing fundamental, general theories of human behaviour, organisational behaviour, or social behaviour. For example, the technology acceptance model (Davis, 1989) builds on premises from the theory of reasoned action (Ajzen & Fishbein, 1973), which describes human volitional behaviour in terms of the individual's attitude towards that behaviour and the beliefs about the consequences of performing it. We can see how such a theory of human behaviour can provide a logical assumption about how people might behave when confronted with new information technology. It is a good example of deductive reasoning. You may also get a sense that the theoretical advancement is, well, limited: by deducing a theory about an information systems phenomenon from broader, more abstract theories about the same but more general phenomena (how humans behave in principle), the research essentially demonstrates the validity of the broader theory in the information systems context: it corroborates existing knowledge but does not yield entirely novel knowledge. On the other hand, this way of constructing theories and mechanisms is perhaps easier to do (because the building blocks of our explanation are provided) and less risky (because we can typically rely on evidence that already supports the theory).

A different approach to developing justificatory mechanisms is through decisively inductive research. One prominent example of such an approach is grounded theory (Glaser & Strauss, 1967). We discuss grounded theory in more detail in Chap. 5. Here it suffices to say that the idea is to identify and understand through systematic empirical research justificatory or explanatory mechanisms that manifest in the setting(s) we examine and to propose or develop claims to causality that can be generalised beyond the setting we study.

Finally, a third—and probably the least understood—approach is abduction. Accounts of the history of science include many stories about when scientists "had a hunch," "took a guess," "had an epiphany," or other kinds of ways in which they found out how a particular phenomenon worked. I think this is an entirely valid way of constructing theory: if we figure out what the mechanisms are and find evidence to support or corroborate that view, who cares where the ideas, explanations, and logic came from? In the history of science, the question concerning how a hypothesis arose in the first place or what the explanatory mechanism that underlies some phenomena is has not been of interest because it is not itself part of a scientific process (Popper, 1959): the understanding or idea could be the result of a creative process, a psychological process, or luck. In this interpretation, science should then be concerned with systematically testing and justifying the idea, not developing the mechanisms in the first place. Still, in information systems and many other disciplines, scientists have a strong interest and emphasis on the justificatory mechanisms that explain how and why constructs and relationships are proposed in the way they are.

Thinking about justificatory mechanisms allows us to identify two additional ways in which we can contribute to theoretical advancement:

- We can *articulate new justificatory mechanisms* for the constructs or relationships of a new or an existing theory. A good example in the vein of studies on the basis of the technology acceptance model is expectation-confirmation theory (Bhattacherjee, 2001), which demonstrates a logic based on the cognitive-dissonance theory, which explains why people might perceive technology to be useful and then be inclined to use it.

• We can *delete a justificatory mechanism* that underlies a theory by showing that the assumptions contained in it are violated, unrealistic, or otherwise deficient.

Let me reiterate the importance of justificatory mechanisms: they describe the intellectual logic of a good theory on which the trust is built that others (other academics, reviewers, readers, practitioners, policy makers, and so forth) will believe in our theory. Gradually, in the research process, the logic built on the key assumptions can be supported or corroborated by research data that show that the constructs and relationships behave as expected. Still, a theory will always be challenged to explain *why* its assertions should hold, and, indeed, an answer to this "why" question is often what separates a primarily empirical contribution of a study, in which scholars discovered qualitatively/quantitatively that certain relationships between certain constructs exist, from a strong theoretical contribution, where scholars can offer an explanation for why such is the case.

A final component of theory is the set of boundary conditions. Boundary conditions describe the circumstances under which the theory is expected to hold—that is, the scope and limitations of a theory. The scope of a theory is specified by the degree of generality of the statements of relationships signified by modal qualifiers, such as "some," "many," "all," or "never," and other boundary statements showing the limits of generalisations. These limits can be uncovered by specifying conditions of "who," "when," and "where," all of which place limitations on the propositions articulated through the chosen set of constructs and the laws of interaction between them. These contextual, spatial, and/or temporal factors set the limits of generalisability; they thus define the scope of the theory.

The boundary conditions of a theory can be specified, for example, when the constructs are selected for the theory (e.g., *experienced* computer users, as opposed to *all* computer users). They can also be specified by considering only certain value ranges of one or more constructs (e.g., computer use during *business hours*, as opposed to computer use *at night*).

Boundary conditions allow us to identify two additional ways in which we can contribute to theoretical advancement:

• We can *articulate new conditions* that specify where a theory will or will not hold.
• We can examine our theory thoroughly in *situations that violate some conditions* of the original theory to explore whether the theory will hold.

Boundary conditions are often not explicitly considered or explored at first in theory-building efforts. Typically, we see how work concerning that theory over time adds to our understanding of the boundary conditions. Again, perusing the work around the technology acceptance model as an example, over time scholars have explored the boundary conditions under which the premise of the original theory holds, such as in situations of mandated versus voluntary technology use (Brown et al., 2002); in usage scenarios, such as for work or enjoyment purposes (van der Heijden, 2004); or in different cultural contexts (McCoy et al., 2005).

Constructs Can Play Multiple Roles in Theories

Equipped with an understanding of constructs, relationships, justificatory mechanisms, and boundary conditions, we can further dissect a theory by focussing on the role of the constructs in the theory. Depending on their intended position in the theory, we can classify constructs as *independent, dependent, mediating,* or *moderating* variables. This classification of constructs is called a nomological net of constructs, a representation of the constructs of a theory, together with their observable manifestations and the interrelationships among and between them. An example is shown in Fig. 4.1.

One construct in our theory might be affected by another construct if a change in the property values in one construct, the independent variable, will invoke a change in the property values of another construct. If so, we denote this construct as the dependent variable in our nomological net (Fig. 4.1a). For example, our theory could stipulate that age (the independent variable) leads to memory loss (the dependent variable). Both constructs have a clear position. For example, it would be illogical to assume that memory loss is the independent variable (memory loss does *not* lead to ageing).

It could also be that a relationship between an independent and a dependent variable is intervened upon by a third construct. We call such a construct a mediating variable. In the example given in Fig. 4.1b, for instance, we see that the effect of age on confusion is mediated by memory loss. In other words, an increase in age can increase the chance of memory loss, which then contributes to confusion. Mediating variables typically add to the explanatory power of a theory because we can specify the exact causality between constructs better. For example, we realise that age per se does not necessarily lead to confusion, but it might lead to memory loss, which can, in turn, lead to confusion. We can also interpret that confusion is a likely consequence of memory loss, which allows us to extend the conceptualisation of our initial nomological net (in Fig. 4.1a).

Finally, other factors might be present that moderate the strength of the relationship between two or more constructs. We call such constructs moderating variables. For example, we might envision how the positive effect of age on memory loss (a negative consequence, of course, but the relationship between age increase and memory loss increase is positive because both are increases) might be strengthened when an individual experiences stress. In turn, stress moderates the relationship because memory loss *also* depends on the stress levels experienced; for instance, between two equally old people, the one who has the higher stress level will have a higher chance of memory loss.

Nomological nets—the description of constructs as well as their manifestations, consequences, and interactions—are important tools with which researchers can argue a theory's soundness and reasonableness. A good theory is one that can be embedded and mentally visualised in a net of constructs that specify antecedents (independent variables that cause some changes in the values of the constructs),

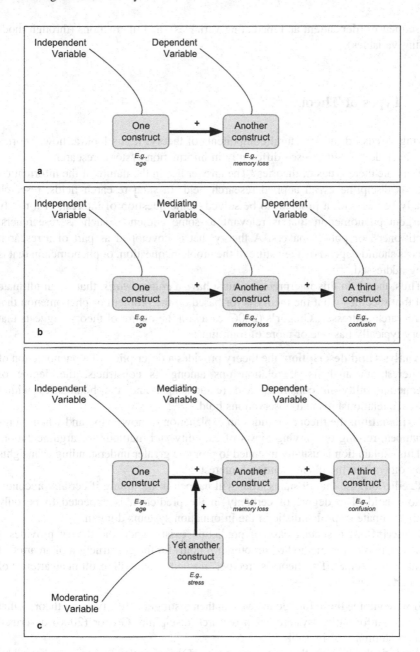

Fig. 4.1 Roles of constructs in a nomological net

consequences (dependent and mediating variables), and interactions (through moderating variables).

4.3 Types of Theory

Having discussed the structural components of theory, let us look at how theories have been developed or used differently in information systems research.

Why are there types of theories? The answer lies in the nature of the information systems discipline as an applied research field. In such research fields, research usually begins with a problem to be solved, some question of interest, or a newly emergent phenomenon that is relevant to some audience, such as researchers, practitioners, or policy makers. A theory that is developed as part of a research process should depend on the nature of the problem, question, or phenomenon that is being addressed.

Thus, theory in this interpretation must have a *causa finalis*, that is, an ultimate goal that specifies what the theory is for based on the problem or phenomenon that the research addresses. Gregor's (2006) essay on the nature of theory suggests that theory typically has one or more of four aims:

- **Analysis and description**: the theory provides a description of a phenomenon of interest, an analysis of relationships among its constructs, the degree of generalisability in constructs and relationships, and the boundaries within which relationships and observations hold.
- **Explanation**: the theory provides an explanation of how, why, and when things happen, relying on varying views of causality and methods for argumentation. This explanation is usually intended to promote greater understanding or insights by others into the phenomenon of interest.
- **Prediction**: the theory states what will happen in the future if certain preconditions hold. The degree of certainty in the prediction is expected to be only approximate or probabilistic in the information systems domain.
- **Prescription**: a special case of prediction exists when the theory provides a description of the method or structure (or both) for the construction of an artefact (akin to a recipe). The theory's "recipe," if acted upon, will result in an artefact of a certain type.

If we combine these four goals, we can then distinguish five types of theories that pertain to information systems as a research discipline. Gregor (2006) described them as summarised in Table 4.1.

Analysis theories are the most basic types of theories; they describe "what is" by classifying specific dimensions or characteristics of phenomena, like individuals, groups, situations, or events. Such theories are needed in particular when little or nothing is known about the phenomenon in question. We know these theories as taxonomies, typologies, classifications, schemas, frameworks, or even ontologies. A well-known example of an analysis theory is the DNA double helix, a model that

Table 4.1 Types of theories (Gregor, 2006)

Theory type	Description
Analysis	*Says what something is* The theory does not extend beyond analysis and description. No causal relationships among phenomena are specified, and no predictions are made.
Explanation	*Says how, why, when, and where something is* The theory provides explanations but does not predict with any precision.
Prediction	*Says what is and what will be* The theory provides predictions but does not have well-developed justificatory mechanisms or other causal explanations.
Explanation and prediction	*Says how, why, when, where, and what something will be* The theory provides predictions and has both testable propositions and causal explanations.
Design and action	*Says how to do something* The theory gives explicit prescriptions (e.g., methods, grammars, principles of form and function) for constructing an artefact

describes the structure of the genetic instructions used in the development and functioning of all known living organisms. The theory makes no statements about *why* living organisms function a particular way or *how* their development takes place. Other examples include the classifications of species and animals drawn up by Darwin after his voyage on The Beagle.

Explanation theories focus on how and why some phenomenon occurs. Such theories also function as models for understanding because they often present a view or conceptualisation of some real-world phenomena or domains. The emphasis lies on explaining some phenomenon but not necessarily predicting future phenomena or variations of phenomena. A prime example is given in Yin (2009): the Cuban Missile Crisis. Allison and Zelikow (1999) develop a new explanation, in the form of an organisational process and governmental politics model, for the confrontation between the Soviet Union and Cuba with the United States in October 1962. They also demonstrate that the then-prevalent explanatory model (mutually assured destruction as a barrier to nuclear war) was unfounded. As this example shows, explanation theories can be used to expound a particular event and the processes that unfolded at that event; but such theories do not necessarily predict a second event. For example, the explanation of the Cuban missile crisis cannot readily be used to explain other crises, such as the Israel-Palestine conflict.

Prediction theories describe what will be without focussing on why that might be the case. Such theories use a range of independent variables to predict an outcome without including the justificatory mechanisms that would explain the causal connections between dependent and independent variables, perhaps because the "internal workings" of the phenomena have not yet been found or because an understanding of the causality is irrelevant to the theory's purpose. As an example, consider Moore's Law, which predicts that the number of transistors that can be placed inexpensively on an integrated circuit doubles approximately every two years. This law also holds for most other electronic devices and attributes, such as processing speed, memory capacity, sensors, and even the number and size of pixels in digital cameras. The law has been deduced empirically by plotting the graph of the log of the number of components per integrated function against the years from 1959 to 1965 and even farther, but no causal model or nomological net is offered that explains why the number of transistors doubles rather than triples or quadruples.

At this place, I should point out that, personally, I disagree with Gregor's (2006) inclusion of prediction as a type of theory. I argued already above that I find predictions not to be theories. In my interpretation, predictions alone do not yield a sense of understanding or explanation. This is my own view of what a theory is (an explanation) and what it should do (help me understand). Others, including Gregor, view the matter differently. You might agree with me or with Gregor or with neither of us.

Explanation and prediction theories predict and explain the underlying causal conditions that lead to a predicted outcome. This type of theory focuses on understanding underlying causal mechanisms and predicting a phenomenon. Explanation and prediction theories are the most common type of theories in the information systems research field. The often-cited technology acceptance model is a good example of a model that attempts to predict whether individuals will accept new technologies and offers an explanatory account of why that should be the case. (Acceptance depends on positive beliefs about usefulness and ease of use.)

Explanation and/or prediction theories often take the form of variance or process theories (Burton-Jones et al., 2015; de Guinea & Webster, 2014). Process theories look at the unfolding of events and actions over time and explain the unfolding of such a process and/or a prediction about future events in or outcomes of that process. Variance theories look at the degree to which one variable can predict changes in another variable and why that would be the case. Good examples include the theory of evolution, which explains and predicts the process of change in all forms of life over generations. The causal mechanisms identified by the theory are mutations, genetic drift, and natural selection. An example of a variance theory in information systems is the theory of representation (Wand & Weber, 1990, 1995; Weber, 1997), which models the desirable properties of information systems at a deep level and predicts consequences when these properties are not present.

Finally, design and action theories are theories that specify how to do something. These theories give normative, prescriptive rules, such as principles of form and function, methods, and techniques, along with justificatory theoretical knowledge about how to construct an artefact (e.g., a type of information system). Good examples are widespread in many applied research disciplines. For instance, the design theory in architecture consists of all the knowledge that an architect uses in his or her work, from how to select the best site and the most suitable construction materials to advice on how to design practical buildings to designing for ease of maintenance and repair. In software engineering, Gamma et al. (1995) described a set of design patterns that specify recurring solutions to common problems in software design. In education, progressive learning theory builds on the view that humans are social animals who are highly interactive with other members of their species to the point of having a recognizable and distinct society. Based on this view, the theory asserts that humans should learn best in real-life activities with other people. From this assertion, the progressive learning theory offers prescriptive advice for the construction of teaching materials: teaching materials should provide not only reading and drill but also real-world experiences and activities that centre on the students' real lives. In information systems research, the focus on design-type research has led to the formulation of many instances of design theories. Examples that I know include theories for designing tailorable technologies (Germonprez et al., 2007), systems that support emergent knowledge processes (Markus et al., 2002), systems that support convergent and divergent thinking (Müller-Wienbergen et al., 2011), or social recommender systems (Arazy et al., 2010).

Having reviewed different types of theories, we should address their logical and temporal interrelationships. For example, analysis theories are useful for the development of all other theories because they offer systematic accounts of the constructs and attributes that are relevant to describing phenomena. Explanation or prediction theories can provide the basis for the development of a theory for explanation and prediction, and both analysis and explanation theories can inform a design theory. A design theory and theory for explanation and prediction can also be closely related as a design can be informed by an explanation of how a phenomenon works. In the same way, designed artefacts can be examined in terms of the changes in events, processes, and behaviours they induce.

To conclude, remember that a doctoral thesis may (but does not have to) include one or many types of theories. Doctoral research often focusses on developing a theory for explanation, along with an attempt to collect evidence systematically in support of that theory. Other theses might offer an analysis theory about a previously unknown phenomenon or as a first contribution in an emerging domain. Of course, contributions have and will be made in the form of design theories and artefacts as instantiations of that theory. It is also possible to do research that is entirely atheoretical. For example, research could be carried out that systematically collects and reports data on new phenomena without attempting to conceptualise the data in some theoretical format or to identify or develop any explanatory or predictive mechanisms. Such work is being done and has its merits, but you will find that the information systems field, like many other fields, has a strong institutional interest and emphasis on theory.

4.4 Theorising as a Process

We have discussed what a theory is, what some of its common structural components are, and how we can distinguish different types of theories. That should equip us with a good understanding of theory as the outcome (or artefact) of the research process. What we still need to discuss is the process that leads to the generation of theory, the theorising process.

Theorising refers to the application or development of theoretical arguments to make sense of some real-world phenomenon. One of the first characteristics of that

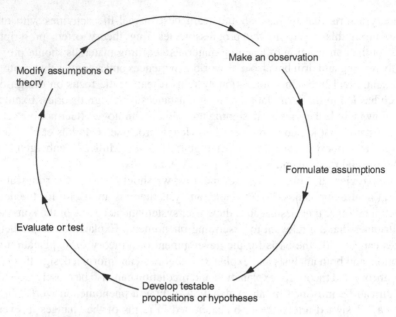

Make an observation

Modify assumptions or
theory

Formulate assumptions

Evaluate or test

Develop testable
propositions or hypotheses

Fig. 4.2 The theorising process

process is that theorising is cyclic (Fig. 4.2), meaning that we typically carry out the steps in theorising over and over again; we usually develop, test, refine, or discard theoretical ideas iteratively. Cyclic also means that we can enter the cycle at any stage and we can stop at any point or we can repeat the cycle of formulation, testing, and modification forever.

As shown in Fig. 4.2, theorising usually involves making observations and formulating assumptions at some point. It does not specify what form or structure the observations or the assimilated knowledge should have as they may or may not be derived through scientific inquiry. In fact, they may depend on rigorous data analysis, happenstance, creative thinking, inspiration, or simply good luck.

Theorising can involve induction, deduction, or abduction. Using inductive reasoning means that in theorising, we would move from a set of facts to a general conclusion. For example, we may gather some observations and inductively develop assumptions or propositions from this data, an entirely plausible and accepted way of theorising. Although induction is impossible to prove, it is an accepted pathway towards theory construction because (interim or final) arguments are informed by data from which they were induced.

We might also proceed deductively in our theorising, deriving arguments as logical consequences from a set of more general premises. For example, we could start with a theory from the literature and deduce a new proposition about a phenomenon or context from the assumptions of a broader theory that is already available. That, too, is an entirely plausible and accepted way of theorising, and it is also a strategy that is often followed in information systems research (Grover & Lyytinen, 2015).

Theorising may also be done through abductive reasoning, a logical inference that leads to an explanatory hypothesis or proposition through "informed guessing." Abductive reasoning occurs when an inquirer considers a set of seemingly unrelated facts and thinks that they are somehow connected. Consider the example of the observation "the lawn is wet." There might be an unlimited set of potential reasons for the lawn's being wet, although it would be unsurprising that the lawn is wet if it had rained the night before. Therefore, by abductive reasoning, the most reasonable theory for why the lawn is wet is that it rained the previous night.

Abductive reasoning reduces the search space for reasons through informed guessing, such that the "leap of abduction" is characterised by simplification and economy. Despite the danger that abductive reasoning offers no means to prove that a proposed reason is indeed a causal factor, it is a useful tool for reducing the solution space to the most likely or economical reason for an observed phenomenon.

Whatever the intellectual reasoning employed, theorising typically proceeds by arriving at a plausible set of propositions or hypotheses between concepts or constructs that are situated in a nomological net and tightly coupled through justificatory mechanisms.

Research often proceeds at this stage through some sort of an evaluation or test of the theory against data, often called the validation stage of the research process. In information systems research, this stage typically, but not necessarily, means subjecting the theoretical propositions to empirical examination, where data are systematically collected and analysed to contrast the observations (the data) against the theory in development. Research methods are the tools scientists use for that purpose. However, you will also find many theories that are proposed but not (yet) evaluated. In management science, for example, an entire journal, *The Academy of Management Review*, is a forum for proposing new theoretical ideas without the need to evaluate or falsify them.

In the cyclic model of theorising, shown in Fig. 4.2, the process of theorising continues with modifying the theory in development based on the outcomes of testing and evaluation. Modification could mean anything, from discarding constructs or relationships to updating the justificatory mechanisms to expanding the set of boundary conditions to refuting the entire theory. It is not the typical outcome of theory testing to support a theory in its entirety, at least not in the first iteration of the cycle. It is much more likely that theoretical ideas will be initially entirely refuted until, over time and over many iterations of the cycle, the ideas, logic, and expectations behind them match reality more and more closely and their evaluation against data shows more and more support until, at some stage, we believe we can step out of the cycle.

An Example

Consider an example of theorising that explains this cyclic, iterative process and introduces a number of attributes that allow us to gauge the quality of our theorising, such as its generality, circularity, fertility, and falsifiability. My example is based on Borgatti's (1996) adaptation of Lave and March's (1993) textbook on theories in the social sciences. Think through each step of the following illustration before proceeding with the suggested theorising outcomes.

We start with an observation. For example, imagine you are in college and attending a class, and the guy next to you, a member of the football team, says an unbelievably dumb thing. You ask yourself, "Why?"

Theorising about reasons might lead to a leap of abduction. For example, one of the first ideas for an explanation that I would come up with is as follows:

• Football players are dumb.

This statement can be considered a theory, an assertion of belief. It is not a good one, but it is a start. What would make it better?

One problem with this initial draft of a theory is that it is not **general** but narrow. It refers only to football players. Theories that are too narrow are not particularly useful, even if they are correct. (What good does it do anyone to theorise that you choose the blue nail polish because the bottle was closest to your hand?) Instead, generalisation (towards universality) is a key attribute of a good theory.

This is not to say that all theorising must strive for wide generalisation or even universality. The generality of a theory is usually classified as one of three types depending on its breadth of focus: *Substantive theory* is developed for a specific area of inquiry, while *abstract* (also called *general or meta*) *theory* is developed for a broad conceptual area. Between these extremes, *mid-range theory* is moderately abstract and has a limited scope. Many theories in information systems, like the technology acceptance model, are mid-range theories. Examples of general or meta theories include complex systems theory, system dynamics theories, and others. The statement "football players are dumb" is an example of a substantive theory.

Let us explore how a more general theory would look. To develop a mid-range theory, we might state the following:

• Athletes are dumb.

The range of this statement is broader than the previous one as it refers to all sorts of athletes, not just football players, but it is still limited in scope since it is restricted to athletes only, not every human being. Thus, it is a mid-range theory.

You probably still do not like this theory much, and rightfully so. Our proposition has no sense of *process* and no sense of *explanation*. It says athletes are things that have the property of being dumb, and that is why they say dumb things. It does not account for why they say dumb things.

Another problem with our statement is that it contains **circularity**. What do we mean when we say that a person is dumb? It means that he or she consistently behaves stupidly. The problem with being dumb as a property is that it cannot be observed or measured directly. It is a latent construct, intangible in nature, like so many other constructs in the social sciences. The only way we can know whether people are dumb is by examining what they say and do. Since what we are trying to explain is the dumb thing someone said, in effect our statement is that athletes say dumb things because they say dumb things. Circularity is a problem because it prevents theories from being *falsifiable*.

We can avoid circularity and the problem of falsifiability by building into our theory so-called **explanatory and justificatory mechanisms** as an account of the processes that explain how things unfold to cause a particular phenomenon to occur or to behave in a particular way. Every good theory provides such a sense of explanation and contains mechanisms that describe the process by which A makes B happen, like the way a car's gears transfer the rotation in the engine to the rotation of the tires. In this sense, theorising involves imagining an observation as the outcome of a (hidden) process that has produced the outcome. This process is called a **mechanism**.

What is an explanatory mechanism that we can build into our athlete theory? Try to develop your own suggestion before reading my suggestion:

- To be a good athlete requires practice time, while being smart in class requires study time. Available time is limited, so practicing a sport means less time for studying, which means being less smart in class.

The focus of this version of our theory now is a **mechanism**, not an enduring **property** of a class of people (in our case, athletes). You can also probably see how much more thinking had to go into identifying this mechanism that we ascribe to the behaviour we witnessed. Identifying the explanatory mechanism of a theory is probably the hardest part of theory building.

Although we moved away from examining how one property begets another property, using mechanisms in a theory means that we can apply the same reasoning to other people and other situations. I can expand the range of our mid-range theory to be broader (and hence more generalizable and more useful) because I now have fewer boundary conditions:

- There is limited time in a day, so when a person engages in a time-consuming activity, such as athletics, it takes away from other time-consuming activities, such as studying.

An implication of this version of the theory is that it can be generalised more easily (because we refer to a time-consuming activity rather than just athletics), which means we can apply the logic to more situations. This scenario is a good one for empirical researchers because more ability to generalise suggests that there are more settings from which we can collect data to test our theory. For example, we can observe whether good musicians, who also practice many hours a day, also say dumb things in class, and if such is not the case, our theory is wrong. Otherwise, we may extend our observations to include other classes of people who engage in time-consuming activities and use that data to continue testing the theory. A good theory is general enough to generate implications for other groups of people and other contexts, all of which serve as potential testing grounds for the theory. If such is the case, we call the theory **fertile** as it creates many opportunities to expose our theory to data that can be used to falsify our theory.

We have now conceived a potential explanation for the phenomenon we are studying by imagining the observation as the outcome of a (hidden) processual mechanisms. We stated our theory in a way that is reasonably general, has a sense of process, is falsifiable, and is fertile. It carries implications for a range of scenarios that we could formalise as hypotheses and test against data. Therefore, we have many of the building blocks of theorising covered. Of course, our limited time theory is but one possible explanation for the observation we started with. Good theorising involves moving forward and not only supporting our theory through data but also **ruling out alternative theories**. For example, through the same theorising process, we could have ended up with other theories:

- The "excellence theory": everyone has a need to excel in one area. Achieving excellence in any one area is enough to satisfy this need. Football players satisfy their need for accomplishment through football, so they are not motivated to be smart in class.
- The "jealousy theory": we are jealous of others' success. When we are jealous, we subconsciously lower our evaluation of that person's performance in other areas, so we *think* football players ask dumb questions.

These alternative theories also provide an explanation for our initial observation. Much like the limited time theory, they are also general and fertile because they generate implications for other groups of people, such as musicians and beauty queens.

A theory that is general, fertile, and non-circular has a decisive advantage for making our theorising even stronger by ruling out alternative theories through testing or evaluation. Simply put, if we have competing general and fertile theoretical arguments, we can throw them into a real-world scenario where they each yield different predictions about what will happen. Then we can observe reality to see which prediction was correct and which alternative theoretical predictions can be ruled out.

If a theory is specific enough, a situation can be plugged into the theory to determine the outcome. The idea is to collect a set of situations that, when applied to different theories, would result in different predictions.

Consider, for example, how football players should behave (or appear to behave) in class when it is not the football season. Will they still be asking dumb questions? According to the limited time theory, football players should not ask dumb questions out of season because there is plenty of time to study. However, according to the excellence theory, members of the football team should continue to ask dumb questions out of season because they are still football players and are still getting recognition, so they still don't feel the need to excel academically. The jealousy theory would also yield the expectation of continued dumb questions because we are still jealous, and jealousy may not be dependent on the football season.

Table 4.2 Expectations generated by each theory

Question	Limited time theory	Excellence theory	Jealousy theory
Do football players ask dumb questions out of season?	No	Yes	Yes
Do athletes who do not look like athletes ask dumb questions?	Yes	Yes	No

Studying football players' behaviour out of season could thus help to distinguish between the limited time theory and the other two, no matter how the data turn out. If football players appear to be smart out of season, then the excellence and jealousy theories are likely wrong, and we can rule them out. If football players appear to be dumb out of season, then our original limited time theory might be wrong. In that case, however, we still do not know whether excellence or jealousy is the better explanatory account for our observation.

What we can do is to conceive another scenario by which we can distinguish all our competing theoretical accounts. For example, consider athletes who do not look like athletes because they are not unusually large (like football players), tall (like basketballers), or heavy (like sumo wrestlers). Would those athletes appear to ask dumb questions? The limited time theory will again say "yes" because practice time required for these sports is unaffected by physical appearance. The excellence theory will also say "yes" because, even if people can't recognise them on the street, they are still fulfilling their need to do one thing really well, so they will still not feel the need to excel in class. However, the jealousy theory would say "no" (for most people anyway) because if the athlete is not recognizable as such (by virtue of being large, tall, or heavy), we would not realise that we are in the presence of an athlete.

What we have done here is to conjure situations for which we have different expectations as to the propositions of our theory, and these situations were sufficient to reach a verdict about the theories (Table 4.2).

You should see now how this set of expectations would allow us to collect data that, on analysis, should allow us to rule out two theories in favour of one remaining theory. In other words, we have created testable hypotheses that allow us to determine the validity of our theories.

Of course, this example is simplistic, but it still demonstrates important principles of theorising. You should have also noted that in each theorising instance, we made a set of **assumptions** on which our theory is based, such as that there is a time (out of season) when football players are not consumed by the sport, which might not always be true. The jealousy theory also builds on an assumption that we ascribe negative characteristics to people who look like they have high social status. Assumptions are always critical components of any theorising.

4.5 Guidelines and Techniques for Theorising

We end this chapter by reviewing some general guidelines about the act of theorising. One guideline is not to underestimate the significance of theorising in scholarly work. Many of the editors of prominent journals stress that reviewers of scholarly work expect your method to be sound and rigorous and your research plan and execution to be effective and appropriate. As a result, a paper will not be accepted simply because you executed the survey or case study method well. Carrying out procedures well is a necessary but not sufficient criterion for successful research. Papers are inspected primarily for novelty and theoretical contribution. As Straub (2009), former editor-in-chief of *MIS Quarterly*, explained:

> Theory is King and it is in the evaluation of the theoretical contribution that most reviewers become convinced, or not.

You might already glean from this statement that theory is viewed in a particular way in the information systems field. Rivard (2021) called it a romantic view:

> The romantic view of a theory portrays it as a complete, detailed, flawless, deep, and exhaustive explanation of a phenomenon, an object that Weick (1995) refers to as "Theory That Sweeps Away All Others" (p. 386).

You might recognise here that this romantic view is not particularly helpful for engaging in theory development. It is full of intimidating expectations about the explanatory or predictive power of a theoretical account, and one would have to be all but omniscient to meet these expectations. As a result, I do not think this view is actionable in any sense: it does not tell me what I should be doing when developing a theory; it just formulates outrageous expectations about the outcome.

To help demystify this romantic view of theory, several scholars have worked to formulate procedures and templates to assist with theorising. Rivard (2021) suggested a spiral model that involves the activities read-reflect-write in iterations that move from erudition to motivation, definition, imagination, explanation, and presentation. Hassan et al. (2019) suggested a procedure for theorising that involves moving between generative practices, like analogising or metaphorising, and foundational practices, like problematising or discourse forming, to construct theorising components like frameworks, concepts, and boundaries.

Such procedural models add clarity and systemacity to the opaque and messy activity of theory development. However, I do not believe there is such a thing as one procedure for theorising that we can all follow nor that following one such procedure will guarantee good theory as an outcome. To me, theorising is not a mechanical process in the sense that following certain guidelines or steps closely will guarantee that you develop a theory. Instead, theorising involves having a good idea as an outcome of systematic or structured ideation or design processes, but they can also occur spontaneously. Weick (1989) called theorising an act of disciplined imagination—generating ideas, followed by systematic processes for selection and evolution—which is an example of adding some systemacity to "having a good idea."

Let me reiterate that I still see value in models like those of Rivard (2021) and Hassan et al. (2019). They draw attention to several elements that can be helpful with theorising and provide suggestions for practices like metaphorising and mythologising, which we can use to generate ideas. They also emphasise that a good idea is still not enough as there is considerable craftsmanship and hard work involved in developing a theory: it must be defined well, it must be explained well, and it must be presented well. Aspects of high-quality theory, like generalizability, fertility, and circularity, are not obvious or automatic; they must be carefully explicated.

Aside from such procedural suggestions, I have found a number of techniques and tools helpful during theory development as ways for constructing mental schemas and cognitive aids. Three the tools I find particularly helpful are counter-factual thinking, thought experiments, and constructing mystery.

1. *Counterfactual thinking* (Cornelissen & Durand, 2014; Roese, 2000) refers to imagining "what might have been" in a given situation by reflecting on the outcomes and events that might have occurred if the people in the situation had acted differently than they did or if circumstances had been different. We can use counterfactual thinking to generate hypotheses and competing predictions as mental representations of alternatives to an experienced or observed past.
2. *Thought experiments* (Folger & Turillo, 1999) are mental exercises in which we zero in on problematic assumptions and construct imaginary worlds to draw out the implications of new assumptions. We give one such example in von Briel et al. (2018), where we theorise about how one emergent venture could have carried out its product development process in different ways.
3. *Constructing mystery* (Alvesson & Kärreman, 2007) relies on the idea of discovering or else creating a mystery by (re-)framing empirical materials in different ways such that a mystery manifests, and then subsequently constructing a theory by solving the mystery. This approach rests on the assumption that facts and evidence are themselves constructed so they can be reconstructed: empirical material is not discovered but interpreted, so it is possible to identify or formulate a mystery that requires solving. In their paper, they use the example case of an advertising agency where a mystery involved how male and female work colleagues carried out their work.

In concluding this chapter, I want to share four tips I have received over the years from other colleagues and senior scholars.

First, theories should be <u>well argued</u>. Theorising relies heavily on building trust in your account of a phenomenon. That we go out and test our theory against empirical data does not change the fact that the theory itself should be built on solid arguments and logical conclusions. Therefore, theorising should be inspired by data or theoretical/logical arguments.

Second, theorising should be <u>insightful</u>. By engaging in theorising, we should come to develop a new perspective on a new or existing phenomenon. Theorising becomes striking when we know instantly that we have not read something like this before, at least not from this perspective. It should give us a new idea about how to look at the world or how to solve a problem.

Third, theorising should <u>challenge existing beliefs</u> and offer a set of new beliefs. Our theoretical account should be characterised by novelty—a new lens through which to see the world differently. The case of the Cuban Missile Crisis shows how the organisational process and governmental politics model of the theory challenged the widely held belief that a nuclear war would not occur because the threat of mutual destruction acted as a barrier.

Fourth, theorising should have (surprising) <u>implications</u> <u>that make sense and are intuitively logical</u>. A good theory is often characterised by a sense of "obvious-ness"—the feeling that the consequences of the tenets of the theory are what is truly happening in the world, which is what a theory aspires to do!

In aspiring to meet these four key attributes of good theorising, these several suggestions might be useful:

1. *Do not hide unique findings; focus on them.* When you set out to collect and examine data and you find something that is inconsistent with prior research, chances are that this finding can lead to a new account of that phenomenon—and to a new theory in turn. We often seek to ensure that our findings are in line with current theories, so propositions and hypotheses that are not supported by data are a bad thing. However, the opposite might be the case: if your data shows findings that you cannot explain through the existing body of knowledge, then surely there is something to theorise about.

2. *Use easy yet convincing examples* in your theorising. Theorising is like storytell-ing (Dyer & Wilkins, 1991; Eisenhardt, 1991), so theory development can be argued using simple examples that can be described in a narrative. The idea here is to use examples that any reader can follow. The case of the dumb football player is an example.

3. *Be familiar with reference theories.* Reference theories are theoretical accounts from research disciplines related to the domain of inquiry. For example, if you study the organisational adoption of social media technology, a reference disci-pline could be organisational psychology, the study of work with and within global organisations. Reference theories are often formal theories that can provide a framework with which to identify the types of constructs that are probably relevant to the phenomenon you are studying. Being able to relate to such theories allows you to build your theory and also to contrast your account to others in an effort to rule out competing theories.

4. *Iterate between theory and data.* Build, read, apply, evaluate, reiterate, build, read, apply, evaluate.... This suggestion assumes that there is some sort of close connection between rationalisation and exploration (and perhaps even validation, as per Fig. 3.1), which might not always be the case or always be required, but let us assume it is true for a moment. Theorising is often a close cyclic and iterative interaction between an idea that is forming in your head and the data you are collecting about a phenomenon. A new development in the theory might cause you to re-analyse your data or collect more data, and you may revise or extend

parts of your theory based on your findings. In this process, reference to other theories is often woven in.

In closing, a few guiding questions may help you determine whether you are finished with theorising because you have developed a good theory:

- Is your account insightful, challenging, and perhaps surprising, and does it seem to make sense?
- Does it connect disconnected or disconnect connected phenomena in a new way?
- Is your account (your arguments) testable (falsifiable)?
- Do you have convincing evidence and arguments to support your account?
- Is your account as parsimonious as it can be?
- What can you say about the boundary conditions of the theory?
- How general is your theory?

4.6 Further Reading

Theorising is of interest to many scholars, so a large variety of literature about theory and theorising is available. It would be futile to try to list all of it, so I suggest a few historical and recent classics to get you started:

- Gregor's (2006) essay on the nature of theory in information systems research
- The debates on the role and position of theory in information systems research (Avison & Malaurent, 2014; Gregor, 2014; Silverman, 2014)
- A good historical debate about theory building outside of information systems (Dyer & Wilkins, 1991; Eisenhardt, 1989, 1991)
- Attempts to define theory and its constituting elements from Wacker (1998), Weber (2003a, 2003b, 2012), Bacharach (1989), Weick (1989, 1995, 1999), and Whetten (1989).

Textbooks about theorising are also available. A simple introduction is Reynolds' (1971) primer on theory construction. Other good reads are Dubin's (1978) *Theory Building* and the articles on some of the processes that have been developed based on Dubin's account (e.g., Holton & Lowe, 2007). Several papers have also provided accounts and guidelines on how to theorise (e.g., Borgatti, 1996; Byron & Thatcher, 2016; Compeau & Olivera, 2014; Cornelissen & Durand, 2014; Hassan et al., 2019).

There is also a growing literature on techniques and tools that facilitate creative thinking and theoretical development. I mentioned counterfactual thinking and thought experiments as examples. Others include thickening thin abstractions (Folger & Turillo, 1999), contrastive explanations (Tsang & Ellsaesser, 2011), problematising assumptions (Alvesson & Sandberg, 2011), concept bricolage (Boxenbaum & Rouleau, 2011), a combination of scientific logics (Kilduff et al., 2011), event narration (Pentland, 1999), storytelling (Shepherd & Russady, 2017), and the borrowing and blending of reference theory (Truex et al., 2006). All these techniques have one thing in common—they provide guidelines on how to identify or promote a new theory.

This chapter does not deal comprehensively or exhaustively with every type of theory that scholars distinguish. It introduces the general building blocks of theory, such as construct, associations, and boundary conditions, because concepts and relationships are needed regardless of the type of theory we are developing. However, this nomenclature is associated most often with the explanatory and predictive theory and with a particular theoretical perspective that is called the *variance theory* (e.g., Bacharach, 1989; Dubin, 1978). Variance theories focus on properties of conceptual entities that have varying values and try to identify the variables that explain that variance. Other common perspectives of theory include the *process perspective* (e.g., Langley, 1999; Pentland, 1999) and the *systems perspective* (e.g., Churchman, 1972; von Bertalanffy, 1968). A process perspective emphasises changes in concepts over time and the sequence of events that is involved in these changes (Pentland et al., 2017). A systems perspective emphasises collections of interacting elements that form a holistic whole. It focusses on wholes, parts, and emergent properties that arise from interactions among them (Demetis & Lee, 2016). There is not enough room in this book to pay due attention to these and other perspectives of theory (design theory perspectives, for example). A good overview of these perspectives is in Burton-Jones et al. (2015). Other good readings about this topic include de Guinea and Webster (2017) and Thompson (2011).

Finally, many experiential accounts of senior researchers exist in which they reflect on their attempts to develop a theory (e.g., Byron & Thatcher, 2016; Grover & Lyytinen, 2015; Henfridsson, 2014), and editors often give advice from years of dealing with article submissions that attempt at theory development (Lee, 2001; Rivard, 2014; Straub, 2009). A particularly good book is the edited volume *Great Minds in Management*, which collects accounts of ideas and theories by influential scholars (Smith & Hitt, 2007).

References

Ajzen, I., & Fishbein, M. (1973). Attitudinal and Normative Variables as Predictors of Specific Behavior. *Journal of Personality and Social Psychology, 27*(1), 41–57.

Allison, G. T., & Zelikow, P. (1999). *Essence of Decision: Explaining the Cuban Missile Crisis* (2nd ed.). Longman.

Alvesson, M., & Kärreman, D. (2007). Constructing Mystery: Empirical Matters in Theory Development. *Academy of Management Review, 32*(4), 1265–1281.

Alvesson, M., & Sandberg, J. (2011). Generating Research Questions Through Problematization. *Academy of Management Review, 36*(2), 247–271.

Arazy, O., Kumar, N., & Shapira, B. (2010). A Theory-Driven Design Framework for Social Recommender Systems. *Journal of the Association for Information Systems, 11*(9), 455–490.

Avison, D., & Malaurent, J. (2014). Is Theory King? Questioning the Theory Fetish in Information Systems. *Journal of Information Technology, 29*(4), 327–336.

Bacharach, S. B. (1989). Organizational Theories: Some Criteria for Evaluation. *Academy of Management Review, 14*(4), 496–515.

Bhattacherjee, A. (2001). Understanding Information Systems Continuance: An Expectation-Confirmation Model. *MIS Quarterly, 25*(3), 351–370.

Borgatti, S. B. (1996). *How To Theorize*. Retrieved December 14, 2011 from http://www.analytictech.com/mb313/howto.htm

Boxenbaum, E., & Rouleau, L. (2011). New Knowledge Products As Bricolage: Metaphors and Scripts in Organizational Theory. *Academy of Management Review, 36*(2), 272–296. https://doi.org/10.5465/amr.2009.0213

Brown, S. A., Massey, A. P., Montoya-Weiss, M. M., & Burkman, J. R. (2002). Do I Really Have To? User Acceptance of Mandated Technology. *European Journal of Information Systems, 11*(4), 283–295.

Burton-Jones, A. (2009). Minimizing Method Bias Through Programmatic Research. *MIS Quarterly, 33*(3), 445–471.

Burton-Jones, A., McLean, E. R., & Monod, E. (2015). Theoretical Perspectives in IS Research: From Variance and Process to Conceptual Latitude and Conceptual Fit. *European Journal of Information Systems, 24*(6), 664–679.

Byron, K., & Thatcher, S. M. B. (2016). Editors' Comments: "What I Know Now That I Wish I Knew Then"—Teaching Theory and Theory Building. *Academy of Management Review, 41*(1), 1–8.

Churchman, C. W. (1972). *The Design of Inquiring Systems: Basic Concepts of Systems and Organization*. Basic Books.

Compeau, D. R., & Olivera, F. (2014). From 'Theory Light' to Theorizing: A Reaction to Avison and Malaurent. *Journal of Information Technology, 29*(4), 346–349.

Cornelissen, J. P., & Durand, R. (2014). Moving Forward: Developing Theoretical Contributions in Management Studies. *Journal of Management Studies, 51*(6), 995–1022.

Davis, F. D. (1989). Perceived Usefulness, Perceived Ease of Use, and User Acceptance of Information Technology. *MIS Quarterly, 13*(3), 319–340.

Davis, F. D., Bagozzi, R. P., & Warshaw, P. R. (1989). User Acceptance Of Computer Technology: A Comparison Of Two Theoretical Models. *Management Science, 35*(8), 982–1003.

de Guinea, A. O., & Webster, J. (2014). Overcoming Variance and Process Distinctions in Information Systems Research. In *35th International Conference on Information Systems, Auckland, New Zealand*.

de Guinea, A. O., & Webster, J. (2017). Combining Variance and Process in Information Systems Research: Hybrid Approaches. *Information and Organization, 27*(3), 144–162.

Demetis, D. S., & Lee, A. S. (2016). Crafting Theory to Satisfy the Requirements of Systems Science. *Information and Organization, 26*(4), 116–126. https://doi.org/10.1016/j.infoandorg.2016.09.002

Dubin, R. (1978). *Theory Building*. The Free Press.

Dyer, W. G., & Wilkins, A. L. (1991). Better Stories, Not Better Constructs, To Generate Theory: A Rejoinder to Eisenhardt. *Academy of Management Review, 16*(3), 613–619.

Eisenhardt, K. M. (1989). Building Theories from Case Study Research. *Academy of Management Review, 14*(4), 532–550.

Eisenhardt, K. M. (1991). Better Stories and Better Constructs: The Case for Rigor and Comparative Logic. *Academy of Management Review, 16*(3), 620–627.

Emirbayer, M. (1997). Manifesto for a Relational Sociology. *American Journal of Sociology, 103*(2), 281–317.

Folger, R., & Turillo, C. J. (1999). Theorizing as the Thickness of Thin Abstraction. *Academy of Management Review, 24*(4), 742–758.

Gamma, E., Helm, R., Johnson, R., & Vlissides, J. (1995). *Design Patterns: Elements of Reusable Object Oriented Software*. Addison-Wesley.

Germonprez, M., Hovorka, D. S., & Collopy, F. (2007). A Theory of Tailorable Technology Design. *Journal of the Association for Information Systems, 8*(6), 351–367.

Glaser, B. G., & Strauss, A. L. (1967). *The Discovery of Grounded Theory: Strategies for Qualitative Research*. Aldine Publishing Company.

Gregor, S. (2006). The Nature of Theory in Information Systems. *MIS Quarterly, 30*(3), 611–642.

Gregor, S. (2014). Theory—Still King but Needing a Revolution! *Journal of Information Technology, 29*(4), 337–340.

Grover, V., & Lyytinen, K. (2015). New State of Play in Information Systems Research: The Push to the Edges. *MIS Quarterly, 39*(2), 271–296.

Hassan, N. R., Mathiassen, L., & Lowry, P. B. (2019). The Process of Information Systems Theorizing as a Discursive Practice. *Journal of Information Technology, 34*(3), 198–220. https://doi.org/10.1177/0268396219832004

Henfridsson, O. (2014). The Power of An Intellectual Account: Developing Stories of the Digital Age. *Journal of Information Technology, 29*(4), 356–357. https://doi.org/10.1057/jit.2014.18

Holton, E. F., & Lowe, J. S. (2007). Toward a General Research Process for Using Dubin's Theory Building Model. *Human Resource Development Review, 6*(3), 297–320.

Kilduff, M., Mehra, A., & Dunn, M. B. (2011). From Blue Sky Research to Problem Solving: A Philosophy of Science Theory of New Knowledge Production. *Academy of Management Review, 36*(2), 297–317.

Langley, A. (1999). Strategies for Theorizing from Process Data. *Academy of Management Review, 24*(4), 691–711.

Lave, C. A., & March, J. G. (1993). *An Introduction to Models in the Social Sciences*. University Press of America.

Lee, A. S. (2001). Editor's Comments: Research in Information Systems: What We Haven't Learned. *MIS Quarterly, 25*(4), v–xv.

Markus, M. L., Majchrzak, A., & Gasser, L. (2002). A Design Theory for Systems that Support Emergent Knowledge Processes. *MIS Quarterly, 26*(3), 179–212.

McCoy, S., Everard, A., & Jones, B. M. (2005). An Examination of the Technology Acceptance Model in Uruguay and the US: A Focus on Culture. *Journal of Global Information Technology Management, 8*(2), 27–45.

Müller-Wienbergen, F., Müller, O., Seidel, S., & Becker, J. (2011). Leaving the Beaten Tracks in Creative Work—A Design Theory for Systems that Support Convergent and Divergent Thinking. *Journal of the Association for Information Systems, 12*(11), 714–740.

Pentland, B. T. (1999). Building Process Theory with Narrative: From Description to Explanation. *Academy of Management Review, 24*(4), 711–725.

Pentland, B. T., Recker, J., & Kim, I. (2017). Capturing Reality in Flight? Empirical Tools for Strong Process Theory. In *38th International Conference on Information Systems, Seoul, Republic of Korea*. http://aisel.aisnet.org/cgi/viewcontent.cgi?article=1208&context=icis2017

Polites, G. L., & Karahanna, E. (2012). Shackled to the Status Quo: The Inhibiting Effects of Incumbent System Habit, Switching Costs, and Inertia on New System Acceptance. *MIS Quarterly, 36*(1), 21–42.

Popper, K. R. (1959). *The Logic of Scientific Discovery*. Basic Books (Logik der Forschung, Vienna, 1935)

Reynolds, P. D. (1971). *A Primer in Theory Construction*. Allyn and Bacon.

Rivard, S. (2014). Editor's Comments: The Ions of Theory Construction. *MIS Quarterly, 32*(2), iii–xiii.

Rivard, S. (2021). Theory Building is Neither an Art Nor a Science. It is a Craft. *Journal of Information Technology*, forthcoming. https://doi.org/10.1177/0268396220911938

Roese, N. J. (2000). Counterfactual Thinking. *Psychological Bulletin, 121*(1), 133–148. https://doi.org/10.1037/0033-2909.121.1.133

Shepherd, D. A., & Russady, R. (2017). Theory Building: A Review and Integration. *Journal of Management, 43*(1), 59–86.

Silverman, D. (2014). Taking Theory Too Far? A Commentary on Avison and Malaurent. *Journal of Information Technology, 29*(4), 353–355.

Smith, K. G., & Hitt, M. A. (Eds.). (2007). *Great Minds in Management: The Process of Theory Development*. Oxford University Press.

Steinfield, C. W., & Fulk, J. (1990). The Theory Imperative. In J. Fulk & C. W. Steinfield (Eds.), *Organizations and Communication Technology* (pp. 13–25). Sage.

Straub, D. W. (2009). Editor's Comments: Why Top Journals Accept Your Paper. *MIS Quarterly, 33*(3), iii–x.

Thompson, M. P. A. (2011). Ontological Shift or Ontological Drift? Reality Claims, Epistemological Frameworks, and Theory Generation in Organization Studies. *Academy of Management Review, 36*(4), 754–773. https://doi.org/10.5465/amr.2010.0070

Truex, D. P., Holmström, J., & Keil, M. (2006). Theorizing in Information Systems Research: A Reflexive Analysis of the Adaptation of Theory in Information Systems Research. *Journal of the Association for Information Systems, 7*(12), 797–821.

Tsang, E. W. K., & Ellsaesser, F. (2011). How Contrastive Explanation Facilitates Theory Building. *Academy of Management Review, 36*(2), 404–419. https://doi.org/10.5465/amr.2009.0153

van der Heijden, H. (2004). User Acceptance of Hedonic Information Systems. *MIS Quarterly, 28* (4), 695–704.

von Bertalanffy, L. (1968). *General System Theory: Foundations, Development, Applications.* George Braziller.

von Briel, F., Recker, J., & Davidsson, P. (2018). Not All Digital Venture Ideas are Created Equal: Implications for Venture Creation Processes. *Journal of Strategic Information Systems, 27*(4), 278–295.

Wacker, J. G. (1998). A Definition of Theory: Research Guidelines for Different Theory-building Research Methods in Operations Management. *Journal of Operations Management, 16*(4), 361–385.

Wand, Y., & Weber, R. (1990). An Ontological Model of an Information System. *IEEE Transactions on Software Engineering, 16*(11), 1282–1292.

Wand, Y., & Weber, R. (1995). On the Deep Structure of Information Systems. *Information Systems Journal, 5*(3), 203–223.

Weber, R. (1997). *Ontological Foundations of Information Systems.* Coopers & Lybrand and the Accounting Association of Australia and New Zealand.

Weber, R. (2003a). Editor's Comments: The Problem of the Problem. *MIS Quarterly, 27*(1), iii–ix.

Weber, R. (2003b). Editor's Comments: Theoretically Speaking. *MIS Quarterly, 27*(3), iii–xii.

Weber, R. (2012). Evaluating and Developing Theories in the Information Systems Discipline. *Journal of the Association for Information Systems, 13*(1), 1–30.

Weick, K. E. (1989). Theory Construction as Disciplined Imagination. *Academy of Management Review, 14*(4), 516–531.

Weick, K. E. (1995). What Theory is Not, Theorizing Is. *Administrative Science Quarterly, 40*(3), 385–390.

Weick, K. E. (1999). Theory Construction as Disciplined Reflexivity: Tradeoffs in the 90s. *Academy of Management Review, 24*(4), 797–806.

Whetten, D. A. (1989). What Constitutes a Theoretical Contribution? *Academy of Management Review, 14*(4), 490–495.

Yin, R. K. (2009). *Case Study Research: Design and Methods* (Vol. 5, 4th ed.). Sage Publications.

Chapter 5
Research Methods

As a science, information systems (IS) research is diverse and pluralistic, as the field accepts many forms of inquiry, theory, and outcomes. As it is a cross-sectional field to begin with, situated between the engineering disciplines that develop technology and the social sciences that examine human behavior, it has always been receptive to a range of methods, ideas, and approaches.

One consequence of this diversity and pluralism in methods is that the way information systems research is conducted, as well as the goals, theories, and assumptions it uses, can vary widely. This variance is probably most evident in the choices related to the selection of an appropriate research methodology, as we discussed in Sect. 3.3. This pluralism and diversity is one of the great advantages of being an information systems scholar, as not all scientific disciplines accept all sorts of methodologies and paradigms.

Even so, diversity and pluralism do not mean that all methods are equally pursued. Fig. 5.1 shows which research methods were used in articles published in eight journals that are considered the field's top journals (*MIS Quarterly, Information Systems Research, Journal of Management Information Systems, Journal of the Association for Information Systems, European Journal of Information Systems, Information Systems Journal, Journal of Strategic Information Systems*, and *Journal of Information Technology*) over the period from 2007 to 2018, based on data reported by Mazaheri et al. (2020). Quantitative methods are used in just over half of the papers in this sample of journals, and qualitative methods are used in about a third of the papers. Design science methods featured in 2–4% of journal articles, and computational methods ranged from about 1% in 2015 to 7% in 2018. The most widely used method was the survey method, followed by mathematical modelling (including formulaic, econometric, optimization, social network analysis, and simulation modelling), case study research, qualitative field research (including ethnography and action research), and experiments (both lab and field). Other such reviews of method use in IS research include (Chan et al., 2006; Chen & Hirschheim, 2004; Galliers & Whitley, 2007; Liu & Myers, 2011), all of whom report similar findings.

© Springer Nature Switzerland AG 2021
J. Recker, *Scientific Research in Information Systems*, Progress in IS,
https://doi.org/10.1007/978-3-030-85436-2_5

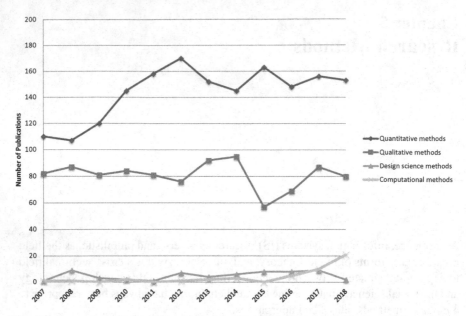

Fig. 5.1 Research methods used in publications in eight top IS journals between 2007 and 2018. (Data from Mazaheri et al. (2020))

This chapter first addresses different quantitative, qualitative, design, and computational methods in some detail, and then briefly discusses their use together in what is called mixed methods. The focus is on key guiding principles that characterize each of these methods. The list of methods discussed is not comprehensive, as the methods used in some strands of research (e.g., structuralist, feminist, or postmodernist research) do not fit easily into the standard methods discussed here. In addition, there are methods for research of a conceptual nature–non-empirical research that emphasizes ideas and concepts for, for example, theory development, literature reviews, and content analysis that are not discussed at length here.

5.1   Quantitative Methods

Quantitative methods describe a set of techniques for answering research questions with an emphasis on quantitative data, that is, types of data whose values are measured in numbers.

In quantitative methods, numbers are used to represent values and levels of theoretical constructs, and interpretation of the numbers is viewed as scientific evidence of how a phenomenon works. Numeric data is often so dominant in quantitative methods that people assume that advanced statistical tools, techniques, and packages are an essential element of quantitative methods, although quantitative methods do not have to involve advanced statistical analyses. Sources of data are of

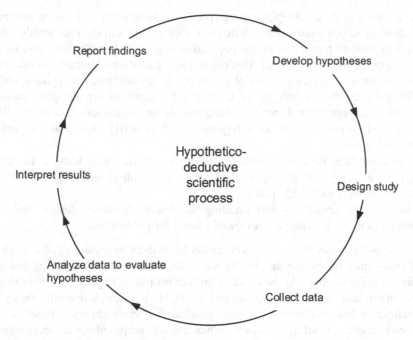

Fig. 5.2 The hypothetico-deductive research cycle

less concern than the fact that empirically derived numbers lie at the core of the scientific evidence assembled. A researcher may, for example, use archival data, gather it through structured interviews, administer questionnaires, or collect digital trace data from electronic systems. In either case, the researcher is motivated by the numerical outputs and how to derive meaning from them.

Traditionally, quantitative methods have been associated with with a particular approach to scientific inquiry, called the hypothetico-deductive model of science. Using quantitative methods does not automatically equate to following this particular model as, for example, using quantitative methods in inductive ways is certainly possible, appropriate, and acceptable. However, many studies that have used quantitative methods in information systems have followed the hypothetico-deductive process (Fig. 5.2), which has six sequential steps:

1. Researchers posit one or more hypotheses (e.g., "people with small hands type faster than people with large hands") expressed in contrast to a null hypothesis of no effect (e.g., people with small hands do not type faster).
2. They design an empirical study to obtain data (e.g., measures of typing speed and hand size).
3. They collect the data from a sample (e.g., a group of students).
4. They test their hypotheses, by analyzing the gathered data and calculating one or another test statistic (e.g., a t-test comparing typing speed of those with large hands to those with small hands). The researchers calculate a probability (the p-value), under the assumptions of a specified statistical model, that a particular

test statistic (e.g., the average typing speed) would be equal to or more extreme than its observed value. Through this test, they examine in the data whether the null hypothesis holds true in the population (e.g., people with small and large hands type at the same speed). This prediction is called a null hypothesis because it typically assumes the absence of an effect (i.e., no difference in typing speed). The p-value—the probability of finding a difference in typing speed in our sample, assuming that there is no difference in the population—is then usually compared to certain thresholds (typically 0.05 or 0.01) known as the alpha protection level.

5. The researchers interpret the results based on the statistical tests. If the null hypothesis is rejected, they typically construe this result as denoting "acceptance of" or "support for" the hypothesis.

6. Finally, they submit a report detailing the theory, the study design, and the outcomes to a scientific peer-reviewed journal for publication.

The hypothetico-deductive research model lends itself to research that is guided by a philosophy of science that involves a realist and objectivist ontology and an empiricist epistemology. At the heart of this philosophy is Popper's (1959) differentiation between "scientific" theories and "myth." In his view, a scientific theory is one whose predictions can be empirically falsified. Einstein's Theory of Relativity is a prime example, according to Popper. When Einstein proposed it, the theory might have ended up in the junk pile of history had its empirical test not been supportive, despite the enormous amount of work put into it and despite its mathematical appeal. The reason Einstein's theory was accepted was because it was put to the test. Eddington's eclipse observation in 1919 confirmed its predictions, predictions that were in contrast to what should have been seen according to Newtonian physics. In this view, Eddington's eclipse observation was a test-or-break event for Einstein's theory. The theory would have been discredited had the stars not appeared to move during the eclipse because of the Sun's gravity.

According to Popper, a contrasting example is Freud's theory of psychoanalysis, which he claims can never be disproven because the theory is sufficiently imprecise to allow for convenient "explanations" and the addition of ad hoc hypotheses to explain observations that contradict the theory. The ability to explain any observation as an apparent verification of psychoanalysis is no proof of the theory because it can never be proven wrong to those who believe in it. Because it cannot be falsified, Popper argues, Freud's theory of psychoanalysis is not a scientific theory.

These worldviews have shaped the idea that proposed theories can be falsified by comparing the theory to empirical data. More precisely, realist ontology presupposes a reality that exists objectively, independent of human consciousness and perception, and that rests on natural laws. Objectivist ontology describes reality and truth as existing objectively, as discoverable, and as measurable. Therefore, researchers can attempt to uncover this reality and its hidden truths. An empiricist epistemology supposes that knowledge comes through experience, mediated by the senses. Hence, observation and experience of empirical facts form the basis of knowledge. Together, these views suggest that observations can be used to support or falsify theories. In fact, in this view, it would be enough, according to Popper's way of thinking, to have one observation that contradicts the prediction of a theory to falsify it and render it incorrect.

Researchers that follow the hypothetico-deductive model to science set out to study events in the real world, theorize and hypothesize about them and their relationships, test these hypotheses, rule out incorrect hypotheses, and ultimately identify and document general laws. This approach, which is common to scientists across many fields, has several advantages:

- It provides a strong foundation for building a cumulative knowledge tradition.
- It supplies means for both novel theory generation and incremental theoretical advancements through intension and extension (Kaplan, 1998/1964).
- It allows study results to be compared and reproduced across a range of settings and samples.
- Relatively standard scripts can assist in creating and assessing scientific knowledge in academic papers that are easy for readers to consume and evaluate.

Quantitative Methods Depend on Measurement

Because of its focus on quantities that are collected to measure the state of some variable in real-world domains and because measurement provides the fundamental connection between empirical observation and theoretical and mathematical expression of quantitative relationships, quantitative methods depend heavily on exact measurement. Exact measurement is particularly vital because many constructs of interest to information systems researchers are latent, that is, abstract and not tangible or readily measurable. Appropriate measurement is the most important thing that a quantitative researcher must do to ensure that the results of a study can be trusted.

Fig. 5.3 describes the process of quantitative research. In the hypothetico-deductive tradition, quantitative research typically starts with developing a theory that the researcher hopes offers an insightful and novel conceptualization of an important real-world phenomena. In attempting to falsify the theory or to collect

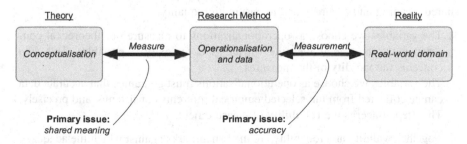

Fig. 5.3 The process of quantitative research. (Adapted from Burton-Jones and Lee (2017))

evidence in support of that theory, operationalizations in the form of measures (individual variables or statement variables) are needed, and data must be collected from empirical referents (phenomena in the real world to which the measure supposedly refers).

Fig. 5.3 points to two key challenges in quantitative research. Moving from theory to the research method, the first issue is that of "shared meaning." If researchers fail to ensure shared meaning between their theoretical constructs and their operationalizations through measures they define, their ability to measure empirically the constructs about which they theorized will be limited. Taking steps to obtain accurate measurements—the connection between the real-world domain and the concepts' operationalization through a measure—can reduce the likelihood of problems that affect the data (accuracy of measurement). However, if there is no shared meaning, even complete accuracy of measurements would still not reflect the construct theorized. For example, imagine that your research is about individuals' emotions when they work with information technology and the behavioral consequences of such emotions. An issue of shared meaning could occur if, for instance, you are attempting to measure "compassion," and you do not make clear the difference between "compassion" and, say, "empathy," which is a concept that has a similar meaning?

Likewise, problems manifest if "accuracy of measurement" is not assured. No matter how the degree of sophistication with which researchers explore and analyze their data, they cannot have faith that their conclusions are valid (and, thus, reflect reality) unless they can demonstrate the faithfulness of their data.

Understanding and addressing these challenges are important, independent of whether the research is validation or exploration (Fig. 3.1). Burton-Jones and Lee (2017) explained it this way: In research that is concerned with validation, problems can accumulate from theorizing to operationalizing. If researchers fail to ensure shared meaning between their theoretical constructs and operationalizations, their ability to measure faithfully the constructs they theorized is restricted. In research that is concerned with exploration, problems tend to accumulate from operationalizing to theorizing: no matter how well or systematically researchers explore their data, they cannot guarantee that their conclusions reflect reality unless they first take steps to ensure the accuracy of their data.

Not just any measurement will do in quantitative research if we want to avoid these problems. Measurements must meet two requirements to avoid problems of shared meaning and accuracy and to ensure high quality:

1. The variables we choose as operationalizations to measure our theoretical construct must share their meaning (in all its complexity if possible). This step concerns the **validity** of the measures.
2. The variables we choose as operationalizations must guarantee that accurate data can be collected from the selected empirical referents consistently and precisely. This step concerns the **reliability** of measurement.

Together, validity and reliability are the benchmarks against which the adequacy and accuracy (and, thus, the quality) of our quantitative methodology are evaluated

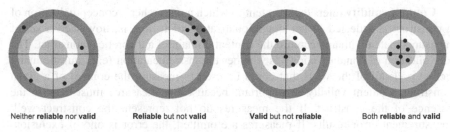

Neither **reliable** nor **valid**   **Reliable** but not **valid**   **Valid** but not **reliable**   Both **reliable** and **valid**

Fig. 5.4 Meeting requirements for validity and reliability

in scientific research. Fig. 5.4 illustrates the importance of validity and reliability through the visual analogy of an archery goal and hitting the bullseye.

The worst situation occurs when our measures are neither reliable nor valid. In such a case, we cannot trust that the measurement variables of our operationalization have shared meaning with the construct we set out to measure, and we cannot trust the accuracy of our data collected with these measures. When measurement is reliable but not valid, it measures something consistently but does not measure validly the meaning of the construct we set out to measure. A good example is that of a mis-calibrated weighing scale that puts an additional ten kilos on your actual weight. The measurements you will receive are consistent, but they do not reflect your actual weight, so they are not valid. A third type of problem occurs when a measurement is valid but not reliable, such as when a measurement approximates the "true" meaning of a construct, but repeated measurements yield inconsistent results.

The notions of reliability and validity are so important that we should take a closer look at them, along with ways to ensure we meet these two key requirements of quantitative research.

Validity

Validity describes whether our operationalizations and collected data share the true meaning of the constructs we set out to measure. Valid measures represent the essence or content on which the construct is focused. For instance, in measuring "compassion," validity requires demonstrating that your measurements focus on compassion and not on empathy or other related constructs.

There are different types of validity that should be identified, some of which relate to the issue of shared meaning (Fig. 5.3) and others to the issue of accuracy. In turn, there are theoretical assessments of validity (for content validity, for example), which assess how well an operationalization fits the conceptual definition of the relevant theoretical construct; and there are empirical assessments of validity (for convergent and discriminant validity as well as concurrent and predictive validity), which assess how well a measurement behaves in relation to theoretical predictions about the similarities and differences between constructs. Both theoretical and empirical assessments of validity are key to ensuring validity of study results.

Content validity refers to the extent to which a researcher's conceptualization of a construct is reflected in her operationalization of it, that is, how well a set of measures match with and capture the content domain of a theoretical construct. The key question of content validity is whether the instrumentation (e.g., questionnaire items) polls all of the ways that could be used to measure the content of a given construct. Content validity is important because the measures must capture the essence of the construct. If the measures do not represent the construct well, measurement error results. If measures are omitted, the error is one of exclusion. Suppose you included "satisfaction with the IS staff" in your measurement of a construct called User Information Satisfaction but you forgot to include "satisfaction with the system" itself? Other researchers might feel that you did not draw well from all of the possible measures of the User Information Satisfaction construct. They could legitimately argue that your content validity was insufficient. Assessments for content validity could include an expert panel that uses a rating scheme, or a qualitative assessment technique such as the Q-sort method (Block, 1961; Thomas & Watson, 2002). There are also statistical tests that can be utilized (Straub et al., 2004)

Construct validity is an issue of operationalization and measurement between constructs. With construct validity, we are interested in whether the instrumentation has truly captured operations that will result in constructs that are not subject to common methods bias and other forms of bias. The instrument items selected for a given construct, when considered together and compared to other constructs, should be a reasonable operationalization of the construct. Maybe some of the questionnaire items, the verbiage in the interview script or the task descriptions in an experiment are ambiguous and are giving the participants the impression that they mean something different from what was intended. These are construct validity issues. The baseline issue here is whether the theoretical constructs are separable from each other or whether they "bleed over" from one to the other.

Problems with construct validity occur in three major ways. Items or phrases in the instrumentation are not related in the way they should be or they are not related in the ways they should not be. If the items do not converge or run together as they should, it is called a **convergent validity** problem. If they do not segregate or differ from each other as they should, then it is called a **discriminant validity** problem. **Nomological validity**, on the other hand, assesses whether measurements and data about different constructs correlate in a way that matches how previous literature predicted the causal (or nomological) relationships of the underlying theoretical constructs. Essentially, we test whether our data supports our suggested classification of constructs as independent, dependent, mediating, or moderating (Fig. 4.1). If there are clear similarities, then the instrument items can be assumed to reasonable in terms by virtue of their nomological validity.

Among the numerous ways to assess construct validity, statistical, correlational logic is typically used to establish empirically that items that are meant to measure the same constructs have similar scores (convergent validity) whilst also being dissimilar to scores of measures that are meant to measure other constructs (discriminant validity). This effort is usually made by comparing item correlations and looking for high correlations between items of one construct and low correlations between those items and items associated with other constructs. Other tests include factor analysis or principal component analysis, which are statistical tests that assess whether items load appropriately on higher-order factors. In this context, loading refers to the correlation coefficient between the measurement item and a latent factor (the variance in factor values explained by variance in variable scores). If items load appropriately (say, above 0.7), we assume that they reflect the theoretical constructs. Tests of nomological validity typically involve so-called omnibus assessments of multiple variables at the same time through, for example, structural equation modelling or moderated mediation models. In such models, we specify the expected relationship between variables and then compare this model to a model constructed by the collected data to see if our expected model fits the data. We also often estimate multiple alternative models (alternative nomological nets) against the data to see which model fits the collected data best. If you are interested in an example of this, have a look at Lange et al. (2016), Recker et al. (2017). Both articles contain tests of alternative models against data to see which nomological net fits the observed reality best.

The process of validating instruments is greatly complicated if some or all of the variables are formatively-measured rather than reflectively-measured. It is beyond the scope of this book to explain the distinctions between these two choices for measurement, but it needs to be noted that validation proceeds along very different lines in such cases. State-of-the-art practices for validating formative measurements are discussed in Centefelli and Bassellier (2009), Kim et al. (2010), Petter et al. (2007), amongst others.

Internal validity assesses whether alternative explanations of the dependent variable(s) exist that have not been ruled out (Shadish et al., 2001). **Internal validity** differs from construct validity in that it focuses on alternative explanations of the strength of links between constructs whereas construct validity focuses on the measurement of individual constructs. Shadish et al. (2001) distinguish three factors of internal validity, these being (1) temporal precedence of IVs before DVs; (2) covariation; and (3) the ability to show the predictability of the current model variables over other, missing variables ("ruling out rival hypotheses").

Challenges to internal validity in quantitative studies are frequently raised using the rubric of "endogeneity concerns." Statistically, the endogeneity problem occurs when model variables are highly correlated with error terms. From a practical standpoint, this almost always happens when important variables are missing from a statistical model. Hence, the challenge is what Shadish et al. (2001) are referring to in their third criterion: How can we show we have reasonable internal validity and that there are not key variables missing from our models?

Historically, internal validity was established through the use of **statistical control variables**. Statistical control variables are added to models to demonstrate that there is little-to-no explained variance associated with the designated statistical controls. Typical examples of statistical control variables in many quantitative IS studies are measurements of the size of firm, type of industry, type of product, previous experience of the respondents with systems, and so forth. Other endogeneity tests of note include the Durbin-Wu-Hausman (DWH) test and various alternative tests (Davidson & MacKinnon, 1993). If the DWH test indicates that there may be endogeneity, then the researchers can use what are called "instrumental variables" to see if there are indeed missing variables in the model.

Manipulation validity is used in experiments to assess whether an experimental group (but not the control group) is faithfully manipulated and we can thus trust that any observed group differences are in fact attributable to the experimental manipulation. This form of validity is discussed in greater detail, including stats for assessing it, in Perdue and Summers (1986), Straub et al. (2004). Suffice it to say at this point that in experiments, it is critical that the subjects are manipulated by the treatments and, conversely, that the control group is not manipulated. One way to do this is to ask subjects. Those who were aware that they were manipulated are testable subjects (rather than noise in the equations). In fact, those who were not aware, depending on the nature of the treatments, may be responding as if they were assigned to the control group.

In closing, we note that the literature also mentions other categories of validity. For example, **statistical conclusion validity** (Garcia-Pérez, 2012) assesses the appropriate use of statistics to infer whether the presumed independent and dependent variables co-vary as predicted. **Predictive validity** (Cronbach & Meehl, 1955) assesses the extent to which a measure successfully predicts a future outcome that is theoretically expected. **Ecological validity** (Shadish et al., 2001) assesses the ability to generalize study findings to real-world settings. High ecological validity means researchers can generalize the findings of their research study to real-life settings.

Reliability

Reliability describes the extent to which a measurement variable or set of variables is consistent in what it is intended to measure. If multiple measurements are taken, reliable measurements will all be consistent in their values. Reliable measurements approach the true "score" of a construct.

Reliability is important to the scientific principles of replicability because reliability suggests that a study's operations can be repeated in the same settings with the same results. For example, an unreliable way of measuring the weight of a chair would be to ask onlookers to guess what its weight is. You are likely to get different answers from different people, and perhaps even different answers from the same person if you ask repeatedly. A more reliable way would be to use a scale, as the scale should consistently give you the same results. Even a mis-calibrated scale would still give consistent (if inaccurate) results. This example shows how reliability ensures consistency but not necessarily accuracy of measurement. Reliability does not guarantee validity.

Reliability problems often stem from reliance on overly subjective observations and data collections. All types of observations made as part of an empirical study carry subjective bias because we can only observe phenomena in the context of our own history, knowledge, presuppositions, and interpretations at that time. This issue is why quantitative researchers often look for opportunities to replace observations made by the researcher or other subjects with other, presumably more "objective" data, such as publicly verified performance metrics rather than subjectively experienced or reported performance. Other sources of reliability problems stem from poorly specified measurements, such as survey questions that are imprecise or ambiguous, or respondents who are either unqualified to answer, unfamiliar with the topic, predisposed to a particular type of answer, or uncomfortable with answering.

Like validity, reliability has several types. **Internal consistency** (Streiner, 2003) is useful with multidimensional constructs because it measures whether several measurement items that propose to measure the same general construct produce similar scores. The most common test is Cronbach's (1951) alpha.

Interrater reliability (Goodwin, 2001) is useful when several subjects, researchers, raters, or judges code the same data. "Objective" data is often approximated through "inter-subjective" measures in which multiple individuals (e.g., multiple study subjects, multiple researchers) all rate the same observation and we look to get consistent, consensual results. For example, scoring a student's thesis submission in terms of originality, rigor, and other criteria typically involves multiple reviewers so that we at least approximate an objective grade through intersubjective rating. In scientific, quantitative research, we have several ways to assess interrater reliability. Cohen's (1960) coefficient Kappa is the most commonly used test, but Pearson's and Spearman correlations and percentage agreement scores are also used (Goodwin, 2001). Straub et al. (2004) introduced several other types of reliability, such as uni-dimensional reliability, composite reliability, split-half reliability, and test-retest reliability, and the tests for examining reliability in all its forms. Their article is a must-read for quantitative researchers in information systems.

In closing, the demonstration of reliable measurements is a fundamental precondition to any quantitative study: The study's results will not be trusted and its conclusions ignored if the measurements are not consistent and reliable. Because even the most careful wording of survey questions or reliance on non-subjective data in data collection does not guarantee that the measurements obtained will be reliable, one precondition of quantitative methods is that instruments of measurement always be tested to ensure they meet accepted standards for reliability.

Processes for Developing and Assessing Measures and Measurements

Establishing the reliability and validity of measures and measurement is a demanding and resource-intensive task. It is by no means optional accepting of shortcuts. The key message bears repeating: Any inferences or conclusions drawn from unreliable or invalid measures are meaningless. Published research contains several studies that contain measurement validation flaws (see, for example Boudreau et al., 2001). Continuous research is being done on measures and measurements to update our knowledge about their challenges, approaches, and solutions.

The largest amount of time and resources is (or should be) devoted to developing and assessing measures and measurement. For example, in my PhD study, I spent about eighteen months developing and assessing measures and measurements for a survey but only five or six months on the data collection and statistical analysis.

Because developing and assessing measures and measurement is time-consuming and challenging, the first rule should always be to identify and re-use (where possible) measures and measurements that have already been developed and assessed. Aside from reducing your own effort and speeding up the research, using such measures ensures the comparability of your results to reported results in the literature such that analyses can be conducted to compare your findings with those of others, side-by-side. Good resources are available that help researchers to identify reported and validated measures and measurements. For example, the Inter-Nomological Network (INN) (https://inn.theorizeit.org/), a tool developed by the Human Behaviour Project at the Leeds School of Business, is designed to help scholars search the available literature for constructs and measurement variables (Larsen & Bong, 2016). Similar initiatives are available also in the broader management literature (https://en.wikibooks.org/wiki/Handbook_of_Management_Scales) or as MetaBUS (e.g., Bosco et al., 2017).

If you find that you need to develop new measures or measurements, the good news is the ample number of guidelines that can help with this task. Historically, scholars in information systems research have often relied on methodologies for measurement instrument development that build on Churchill Jr. (1979) in the marketing field. In the actual instantiation and implementation of his guidelines, many attempts have relied on a varied and disparate set of techniques.

Fig. 5.5 shows a procedural model that researchers can use to create new measurement instruments for conceptually defined theory constructs. It describes in four main stages the tasks to be performed (grey rounded boxes), related inputs and outputs (white rectangles), and the relevant literature or sources of empirical data required to carry out the tasks (dark grey rectangles).

The procedure shown in Fig. 5.5 consolidates and extends several approaches in the literature and incorporates empirical assessments at various stages of the procedure. The model is not concerned with developing theory but applies to the stage of the research where such theory must be tested empirically, as in hypothetico-deductive research. In other words, the procedural model requires a well-defined theoretical domain and well-specified theoretical constructs.

The procedural model blends guidelines from, especially (MacKenzie et al., 2011; Moore & Benbasat, 1991) and (Recker & Rosemann, 2010a, 2010b). The model is not "my" model so much as my interpretation of widely accepted guidelines. I find the model helpful, as it incorporates techniques to demonstrate and assess content validity as well as the reliability and validity of measurements—both (remember, a key issue of accuracy, Burton-Jones & Lee, 2017).

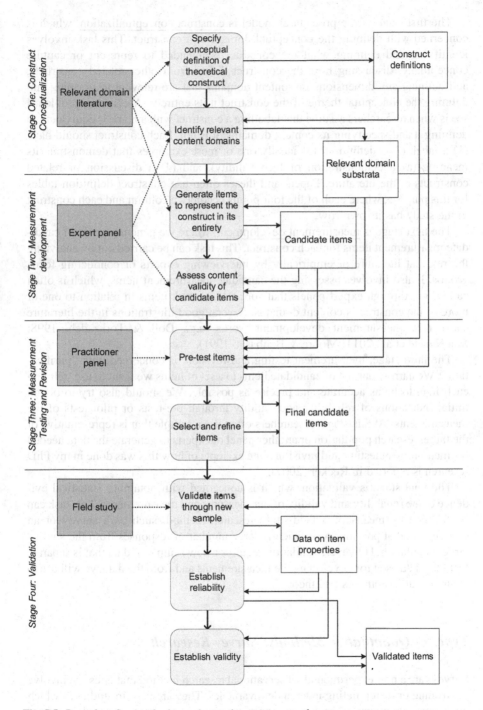

Fig. 5.5 Procedure for developing and assessing measures and measurements

The first stage of the procedural model is <u>construct conceptualization</u>, which is concerned with defining the conceptual domain of a construct. This task involves identifying and defining what the construct is intended to represent or capture conceptually, discussing how the construct differs from other related constructs, and defining any dimensions or content domains that are relevant to grasping and defining the conceptual theme of the construct it its entirety. A common problem I see is when researchers assume that labelling a construct with a name is equivalent to defining it and specifying its content domains: it is not. Each construct should have (1) a label, (2) a definition, (3) ideally one or more examples that demonstrate its meaning (as a demonstration of face validity), and (4) a discussion of related constructs in the literature. Papers and theses often use construct definition tables for this purpose, where each of the four points becomes a column and each construct in the study has its own row.

The next stage is <u>measurement development</u>, where we generate pools of candidate measurement items for each construct. This task can be carried out by analyzing the relevant literature or empirically by interviewing experts or conducting focus groups. It also involves assessing the candidate measurement items, which is often carried out through expert panels that sort, rate, or rank items in relation to one or more of the construct's content domains. Several good illustrations in the literature show how measurement development works (e.g., Doll & Torkzadeh, 1998; MacKenzie et al., 2011; Moore & Benbasat, 1991).

The third stage, <u>measurement testing</u> and revision, is concerned with "purification": We narrow our list of candidate items to a set of items we want to use, refining each item to be as accurate and precise as possible. We should also try to obtain initial indications of reliability and validity through pre-tests or pilot tests of the measurements. At this stage, researchers often use a sample that is representative of the target research population or another panel of experts to generate the data needed for measurement testing and revision. One example of how this was done in my PhD research is reported in Recker (2007).

The final stage is <u>validation</u>, which is concerned with obtaining statistical evidence of the reliability and validity of our measures and measurements. This task can be fulfilled by means of a field-study research method, such as a survey or an experiment, that provides a sufficiently large number of responses from the study's target population. However, validation requires a new sample of data that is separate from the data used for developing the measurements and from the data we will use to evaluate our hypotheses and theory.

Types of Quantitative Methods: Survey Research

Surveys are a non-experimental, observational research method that does not involve controlling or manipulating independent variables. They are used in studies in which we do not intervene in reality but only observe it. A survey is used to gather information about the characteristics, actions, perceptions, attitudes, or opinions of a large group of units of observations (such as individuals, groups, or organizations), referred to as a "population." Surveys involve collecting data about a population from a random sample of that population through questionnaire-type instruments that can be distributed and completed via mail, online, telephone, or, less frequently, through structured interviews. The resulting data is analyzed, typically through descriptive or inferential statistical techniques.

Surveys have historically been the dominant technique for data collection in information systems (Mazaheri et al., 2020). The method is preferable when the central questions of interest about a phenomenon are "what is happening?" and "how and why is it happening?" and when control of the independent and dependent variables is not required or not possible.

Research involving survey instruments in general can be used for at least three purposes, these being exploration, description, or explanation. The purpose of survey research in exploration is to become more familiar with a phenomenon or topic of interest. It focuses on eliciting important constructs and identifying ways to measure them. A good example is in Gable et al. (2008), who use an exploratory survey to identify a wide range of theoretical factors that may influence the impact of an information system on end users. Exploratory surveys may also be used to uncover and present new opportunities and dimensions about a population of interest.

The purpose of survey research in description is to learn about the situations, events, attitudes, opinions, processes, or behaviors that are occurring in a population. Therefore, descriptive surveys ascertain facts; they do not develop or test theory. One example from my own work is a survey of early adopters of a standard called BPMN, through which I collected data to describe systematically who is using the standard, how much, where, and why (Recker, 2010). It needs to be noted that there are relatively few academic outlets for purely descriptive studies, however valuable these studies might be. We tend to find such studies in consultant reports, academic-practitioner journals, and white or technical papers.

The purpose of survey research in explanation is to test theory and hypothetical causal relationships between theoretical constructs. It is the most common form of the survey method used in information systems research. Explanatory surveys ask about the relationships between variables, often based on the theoretically grounded expectations about how and why the variables ought to be related. Typically, the theory behind survey research involves some elements of cause and effect in that hypotheses are made not only about relationships between variables but also about the directionality of these relationships. Surveys then allow researchers to obtain correlations between observations that are assessed to determine whether the correlations fit with the expected cause-and-effect linkages. However surveys do not (and cannot) prove causality. In other words, as an observational method, surveys allow researchers to examine whether observations relate in a way that matches with the theoretical expectations of a cause-effect relationship. But keep in mind that correlation is not causation: Just because two things correlate does not necessarily mean that one causes the other. An example of survey research in my own work is a study in which I evaluated whether perceptions of certain characteristics of a standard that

Table 5.1 Advantages and disadvantages of the survey method

Advantages	Disadvantages
Surveys are easy to administer and simple to score and code.	Surveys provide just a snapshot of behavior at one place and time.
Surveys can determine the values of and relationships between variables and constructs.	Surveys' validity may vary based on the context. In particular, different cultures may produce different results.
Responses can be generalized to other members of the population studied and often to other similar populations.	Surveys do not provide as rich a description of a situation as a case study.
Surveys can be reused easily and can provide an objective way of comparing responses over different groups, times, and places.	The evidence for causality between surveyed constructs that surveys provide is not as strong as a well-designed experiment can provide.
Theoretical propositions can be tested in an inter-subjective or objective fashion.	Surveys are often susceptible to low response rates, which can diminish the generalizability of the results.
Surveys can help confirm and quantify the findings of qualitative research.	

analysts use correlate with their perceptions of that standard's usefulness and ease of use (Recker et al., 2011).

Like any other research method, surveys have several strengths and weaknesses. Table 5.1 summarizes these.

A general procedure for survey research is shown in Fig. 5.6. The procedure distinguishes five stages: theory development, measurement development, instrument development and testing, survey administration, and data analysis.

Phase I, **theory development,** involves identifying and defining the constructs of interest, their roles in a nomological net, and the definition of the expected relationships between them in a form of (usually several) hypotheses. Explanatory survey research requires such a model. Without a theoretical model that specifies our constructs and the relationships between them, we could not develop measurements because what we would be required to measure would be unknown.

Phase II, **measurement development,** is concerned with developing and assessing measures and measurements for all our constructs in the theoretical model.

Phase III, **survey development and testing**, involves embedding our measurements into a complete survey instrument. Aspects of the instrument to consider beyond its statements or questions include the form of the instrument. Mail surveys had long been the predominant means of data collection until web-based surveys began to proliferating in the early 2000s because they are more time and cost efficient. These advantages of web-based surveys usually outweigh their potential disadvantages, such as dangers of fraud, viruses, issues related to calculating response rates, and response bias. A web-based instrument can reduce the complexity and cost of distribution and processing from that required to distribute the survey via mail, arranging prepaid return envelopes for various countries, and so on. Web-based instruments simplify data entry, transfer, cleansing, and codification, as all data is automatically extracted in computer-readable format and automatically

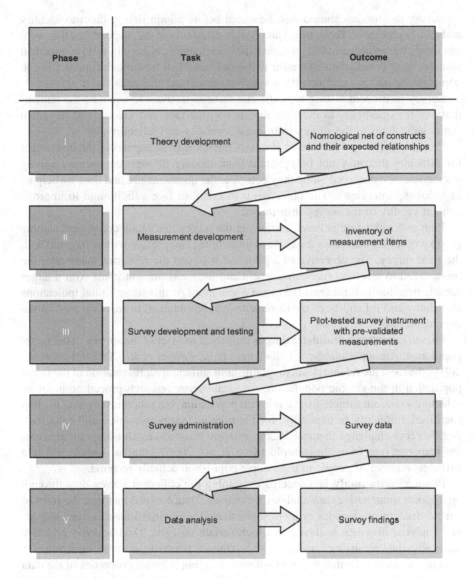

Fig. 5.6 Survey research procedure

stored in a database. A web-based instrument also reduces mistakes by respondents related to item completion by using input validation checks that can be implemented through web scripting languages. In addition, notwithstanding the initial effort required in designing and implementing a web-based survey, the marginal costs are low in comparison to those of traditional techniques, response times are minutes rather than days, mailing and transfer costs are marginal, and data entry is done automatically.

Survey instruments should also be tested before administering them to identify and rectify problems. These tests can provide details about the respondents that were not identified before, establish whether the questionnaire is easy to follow, establish whether there is sufficient space for responses, establish how much time it takes to complete the survey, and identify ways to increase response rates.

Survey instrument testing typically has three objectives: to evaluate the authenticity of the questions, to evaluate the survey interface and layout, and to obtain initial indications of the survey instrument's validity and reliability.

Pre-tests differ from pilot tests. Pre-tests test some or all aspects of the instrument for difficulty that may not be apparent from reading through the survey. Survey respondents are observed while they complete the questionnaire and then participate in follow-up interviews. The objective is to establish face validity and to improve content validity of the survey instrument.

Pilot tests, on the other hand, administer the survey to a small, convenient sample group whose characteristics are close to those of the sample that will be targeted with the final survey. The objective of a pilot test is to test the revisions made after the pre-test and to test the survey instrument and the measurement items with a larger sample that closely represents the target population. At this stage, initial indications of validity and reliability of measurements can be obtained to increase trust in the eventual results.

Phase IV, **survey administration**, is the actual roll-out of the survey to the target population. Among a number of challenges (e.g., Couper et al., 2001; Olsen et al., 2004), the most prevalent relates to establishing sufficient representation of the target population in the sample population. An ideal survey research procedure involves selecting a random sample from a relevant population, but random sampling is often sacrificed, implicitly or explicitly, for the sake of feasibility, costs, and resources. Another core challenge in survey administration relates to establishing an appropriate response rate from the sample (Sivo et al., 2006)—that is, ensuring that a sufficient number of people in the sample population actually respond.

Phase V, **data analysis**, concerns examining the collected survey data through appropriate quantitative data analysis techniques. Data analysis can take the form of simple descriptive statistics or more sophisticated inferential statistics, such as univariate analysis, bivariate analysis, and multivariate analysis. Data analysis typically starts with data cleansing (detecting, correcting, or removing corrupt, inaccurate, or incomplete records from a data set) before describing relevant properties of the data (e.g., demographics or correlations), testing the assumptions required for statistical tests, and performing a variety of data analyses.

Many books address the varieties and intricacies of different quantitative data-analysis techniques, including Bryman and Cramer (2008), Field (2013), Reinhart (2015), Stevens (2001), Tabachnick and Fidell (2001). It suffices to mention that most survey data is analyzed using multivariate analysis methods, broadly defined as statistical methods that simultaneously analyze multiple measurements of each individual or object under investigation. The most popular types of multivariate analysis used in survey research are structural equation modelling (SEM) techniques, such as LISREL (Jöreskog & Sörbom, 2001), and Partial Least Squares

(PLS) (Hair et al., 2013). SEM has been widely used in social science research for causal modelling of complex, multivariate data sets in which the researcher gathers multiple measures of proposed constructs. SEM has become increasingly popular amongst researchers for purposes such as validating measurements and testing the linkages between constructs.

In general terms, SEM is a statistical method for testing and estimating causal relationships using a combination of statistical data and qualitative causal assumptions. It encourages confirmatory rather than exploratory analysis. SEM requires one or more hypotheses between constructs represented as a theoretical model, operationalizes by means of measurement items, and then tests statistically. The causal assumptions embedded in the model often have falsifiable implications that can be tested against survey data. One of the advantages of SEM is that, while it can be used to assess the structural model—the assumed causation amongst a set of multiple dependent and independent constructs—it can also, separately or concurrently, be used to assess the measurement model, the loadings of observed measurements on their expected latent constructs. In other words, SEM allows the researcher to examine the measurements' reliability and validity and the those of the hypotheses contained in the proposed theoretical model.

This introduction to survey methods closes with suggestions for maintaining the rigor and quality of survey research. Good survey research should follow these eight guidelines:

1. Carry out **careful development and assessment of measures and measurements**. The best survey design, administration, or analysis is useless if your measures or measurements are not reliable or valid.
2. **Pre- and pilot-test your survey instrument**. A pre-test is a tryout with the purpose of producing a survey form that is usable and reliable. A pilot test allows you to obtain confidence in your survey results and findings before administering the survey. Both tests help to refine your instrument and ensure it can be executed.
3. **Disclose your sampling strategy**. Include all relevant details of the sampling procedure, such as whether the survey uses simple random sampling, clustering, stratification or other forms of selecting sub-groups of the population. Describing the randomization or selection procedure allows readers to decide for themselves the validity and representativeness of the sample framework and the survey results.
4. **Report a profile of the sample framework**. For a sample to represent the population, the sampling framework should include the characteristics of all members of the target population. Reporting the boundaries of the sample framework is the minimum that a researcher should provide to indicate how it reflects the target population. Describing the characteristics of the respondents also allows readers to determine whether particular characteristics are representative of the sample.
5. **Include your instruments in your reports**. Append your survey questionnaire or other forms of measurement in your paper so readers can evaluate your

measures and measurements. Doing so also enables your research to be replicated.

6. **Report your response rate**. Response rate and non-response error are amongst the most critical issues in survey research. Reporting a large sample would be meaningless without reporting the response rate.
7. **Establish validity and reliability**. Validate your data before carrying out analyses. Confirmatory empirical findings will be strengthened when instrument validation precedes the internal and statistical validity of your conclusions.
8. **Follow the latest guidelines for data analysis**. Guidelines for how to conduct a survey, analyze survey data, and report findings are constantly updated. For example, new tests or thresholds are recommended. Make sure you are following the latest guidelines. Arguments such as "this or that other paper did the same thing" are weak rationales for choosing your approach.

Types of Quantitative Methods: Experimental Research

Observational research methods such as surveys and case studies rely on data sampling, that is, the process of selecting units from a population of interest and observing or measuring variables of interest without attempting to influence them. However, such data is often not suitable for gauging cause-and-effect relationships because of potential confounding factors that may be at play beyond the data that is collected. Said another way, these methods do not guarantee that data about independent variables is collected prior to data on dependent variables, which is one of the conditions of causality (Shadish et al., 2001). Moreover, as noted above, there is the threat of endogeneity, that is, the possibility that there are other explanations of noted effects that are unaccounted for.

Experiments are quantitative methods specifically intended to examine cause-and-effect relationships. They are used to examine such relationships by imposing a treatment on one group of respondents (the treatment group) but not on another group (the control group) while maintaining control over potential confounding factors. A treatment is a manipulation that an experimenter administers to the treatment group so the experimenter can observe a response. The treatment in an experiment is how an independent variable is operationalized or realized into data, typically by dividing the subjects into groups randomly and "treating" each group differently so the differences in these treatments result in differences in responses. Thus, different treatments result in different levels or values of the construct that is the independent variable. When treatments are randomly assigned to groups, causal inference is strong because there are no other explanations, that is, endogeneity threats, that would confound the results.

Why is this so? Take the case of an experiment where scholars are positing that using a self-managed healthcare website will lead to better health outcomes (versus a control group that was not given access to the website). Suppose someone wonders if the differences in experimental results might be explained based on pre-existing health conditions and not whether the experimental group heavily utilized the self-managed healthcare website, which was the espoused treatment by the researchers? Random assignment makes this confound highly unlikely since with real randomization and given a sufficiently large number of subjects there should be roughly the same (statistically equivalent) number of subjects with pre-existing conditions in each group. In short, a hypothesis test of the number or extent of pre-conditions in the experimental control group (or placebo group) versus the experimental treatment group should not find a statistically significant difference. That is, the groups are equivalent, statistically speaking. Therefore, if a difference is found, it effectively rules out any other rival explanation of the findings.

The primary strength of experimental research over other methods is its emphasis on internal validity because of the availability of means to isolate, control and examine a variable (the cause) and the consequence it has on another variable (the effect). This establishes the temporal precedence required for internal validity. Its primary disadvantage is often a lack of ecological validity because the desire to isolate and control variables typically comes at the expense of the setting's realism; real-world domains are often much more complex than the reduced set of variables that are examined in an experiment.

Experimental research is often considered the gold standard in research, as it is one of the most rigorous forms of collecting and analyzing data. However, it is also one of the most difficult research methods because it relies on strong theory to guide the constructs' definition, specification of hypotheses, treatment design, and analysis. Any error in the design of an experiment renders all results invalid. Moreover, experiments without strong theory tend to be ad hoc, possibly illogical, and often meaningless because they reveal mathematical connections between measures without being able to offer a justificatory mechanism for the connection ("you can't tell me why you got these results"). The most pertinent danger in experiments is failure to rule out rival hypotheses (alternative theories that contradict the suggested theory). The second biggest problem is probably the inappropriate design of the treatment and the tasks.

Experiments can take place in the laboratory (**lab experiment**) or in reality (**field experiment**). Lab experiments typically give the researcher the most control over the situation, so they are the classic form of experiment. Think of students sitting at a computer in a lab performing experimental tasks or think of rats in cages that get exposed to all sorts of treatments under observation. Slater (2005) provides some wonderful examples of experiments in psychology. Field experiments are conducted in real world settings, as when researchers manipulate interface elements of the Amazon.com webpage while people use it. Field experiments can be difficult to set up and administer in part because they typically involve collaborating with an organization that hosts a particular technology (say, an ecommerce platform), but they typically achieve much higher levels of ecological and internal validity. Field experiments have become more popular (and more doable) in information systems research over recent years and are probably the real "gold standard" in scientific research.

In both lab and field experiments, the most important basic concepts are the treatment, the treatment manipulation, the controls, randomization, and the type of experimental design.

The **treatment** is the experimental stimulus that is provided to some participants but not to others. A treatment is considered successful if the responses from the treatment group differ as expected from the responses from the control group that did not receive the treatment. In medical research, for example, experimental treatments typically involve administering a drug to one group of patients but not to other groups of patients to measure its efficacy and/or side effects. In information systems research, a treatment could be a particular way that a user interface is designed in an e-commerce setting. For example, Benbasat and Wang (2005) performed an experiment in which one group of online shoppers could complete their purchases on an e-commerce website that had an interactive virtual product-recommendation agent, and the other group of participants did not to determine whether the groups' purchase patterns differed.

Treatment manipulation concerns the control for the cause in cause-effect relationships by identifying the type and number of stimulus levels (provision versus non-provision, low/medium/high levels of stimulus, and so forth). Experimental designs typically involve a phase prior to treatment manipulation called pre-test measures, and usually a phase after treatment manipulation called post-test measures.

Experimental **controls** are mechanisms employed to ensure that the responses observed are due to the treatments and not because of confounding factors. Sources of potential bias and confounding influences that could prevent the effect of the treatment from being observed must be identified and controlled for. For example, in medicine, since many patients are confident that a treatment will have a positive effect, they react to a control treatment that has no physical affect at all, such as a sugar pill, because of the placebo effect. For this reason, it is common to include control, or placebo, groups in medical experiments to evaluate the difference between the placebo effect (no treatment or zero-treatment) and the actual effect of the treatment. Controls are also used in experiments to rule out rival theories, that is, alternative explanations. If we want to demonstrate that differences in a group's responses are due to the treatment that the group received rather than an external factor such as education or experience level, we can control for these potential factors by obtaining measures for the so we can statistically discriminate between the influence of control measures and the effect of our treatment.

Randomization is the process of selecting a sample from a population in such a way that personal characteristics and predispositions do not interfere with the treatment or the response to the treatment. Key biases that can creep into experiments include the effect of the subjects' differences in terms of experience, risk adversity, and knowledge. Therefore, a critical aspect of experimental design is ensuring that either biases are accounted for during data analysis (by administering appropriate controls) or designing the experiment so that biases are evenly distributed across the groups (and cancel each other out). One way to achieve this kind of design is through matched allocation of subjects to different groups to ensure, for example, that equal numbers of risk-taking and risk-averse individuals are in both groups. However, matched allocation can be expensive and is not possible most of the time, as any number of personal characteristics could result in bias, and it is impossible to match subjects for all these characteristics. Therefore, random assignment of participants to experimental groups is usually employed to ensure that experimental groups are similar in their characteristics. Experiments are called true experimental designs if participants are randomly assigned to treatment and control groups. In quasi-experimental designs, random assignment is not followed.

Finally, in both lab and field experiments, the **experimental design** can vary. For example, one key aspect of experiments is the choice between between-subject and within-subject designs: In between-subject designs, different people test each experimental condition. For example, if you had a treatment in the form of three user-interface designs for an e-commerce website, three groups of people would each evaluate one of these designs. By contrast, in a within-subjects design, the same person tests all three experimental conditions, first evaluating one user-interfaces design, then the second one, and then the third.

Fig. 5.7 and Fig. 5.8 use basic experiment design notation to describe some of the most popular types of designs in as either true experimental designs (Fig. 5.7) or quasi-experimental designs (Fig. 5.8).

The simplest form of a true experimental design is a two-group design involving one treatment group and one control group and possible pre- and/or post-tests. Typically, the effects of a treatment in this design can be analyzed using analysis of variance tests between the treatment and the control groups to determine differences in the treatment group's response and whether the differences are statistically significant.

More sophisticated true experimental designs include covariance designs, where measures of dependent variables can be influenced by extraneous variables called covariates. Covariates are not of central interest to the theory but are potential source of bias, so their effect on the dependent variable must be controlled for to identify the true effect of a treatment.

The most common types of experimental studies involve factorial designs, which involve manipulation of two or more independent variables (treatments). Each independent variable then denotes a factor, and each manipulation describes a factor level. For instance, in a 2×2 factorial design, one independent variable could be a drug dose with the levels high and low and the other independent variable could be a medical treatment that is either absent or present. In such a design, we would have $2 \times 2 = 4$ treatment groups (high $\times$ absent, high $\times$ present, low $\times$ absent, and low $\times$ present). Factorial designs have high sample size requirements to ensure sufficient responses from each treatment group ("cell") and allow for meaningful data analysis (stable results with appropriate significance levels).

Quasi-experimental designs (Fig. 5.8) are similar to true experimental designs, except that they lack random assignment of subjects to groups and hence are experiments with non-equivalent groups (Fromkin & Streufert, 1976). In turn, one group (say, the treatment group) may differ from another group in terms of key characteristics. For example, a post-graduate class has more domain knowledge than

True Experimental Designs

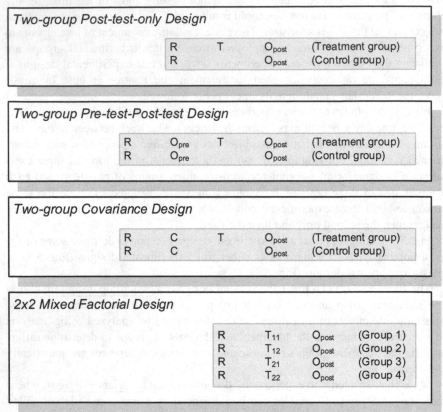

Two-group Post-test-only Design

| | R | T | O_{post} | (Treatment group) |
| | R | | O_{post} | (Control group) |

Two-group Pre-test-Post-test Design

| | R | O_{pre} | T | O_{post} | (Treatment group) |
| | R | O_{pre} | | O_{post} | (Control group) |

Two-group Covariance Design

| | R | C | T | O_{post} | (Treatment group) |
| | R | C | | O_{post} | (Control group) |

2x2 Mixed Factorial Design

	R	T_{11}	O_{post}	(Group 1)
	R	T_{12}	O_{post}	(Group 2)
	R	T_{21}	O_{post}	(Group 3)
	R	T_{22}	O_{post}	(Group 4)

Legend

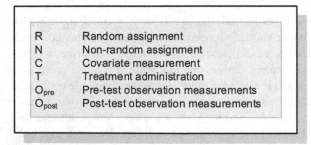

R	Random assignment
N	Non-random assignment
C	Covariate measurement
T	Treatment administration
O_{pre}	Pre-test observation measurements
O_{post}	Post-test observation measurements

Fig. 5.7 Types of true experimental designs

an under-graduate class does. Quasi-experimental designs often suffer from selection bias, which diminishes internal validity. Still, sometimes a research design demands assigning people to an experimental group to, for instance, test the effect

Quasi-Experimental Designs

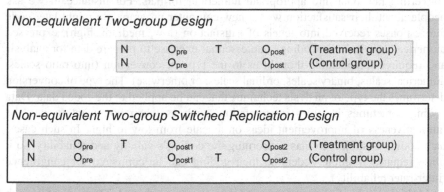

Non-equivalent Two-group Design

| N | O_{pre} | T | O_{post} | (Treatment group) |
| N | O_{pre} | | O_{post} | (Control group) |

Non-equivalent Two-group Switched Replication Design

| N | O_{pre} | T | O_{post1} | | O_{post2} | (Treatment group) |
| N | O_{pre} | | O_{post1} | T | O_{post2} | (Control group) |

Legend

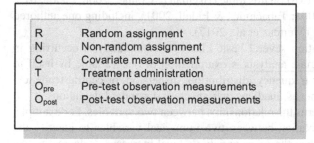

R	Random assignment
N	Non-random assignment
C	Covariate measurement
T	Treatment administration
O_{pre}	Pre-test observation measurements
O_{post}	Post-test observation measurements

Fig. 5.8 Quasi-experimental design types

of an intervention on under-performing students versus well-performing students. The most common forms of quasi-experimental design are non-equivalent groups design–the alternative to a two-group pre-test-post-test design—and non-equivalent switched replication design, in which an experimental treatment is "replicated" by switching the treatment and control groups in two subsequent iterations of the experiment (Trochim et al., 2016).

Data analysis in experimental research concerns examination of quantitative data in a number of ways. Descriptive analysis refers to describing, aggregating, and presenting the constructs of interest or the associations between the constructs to describe, for example, the population from which the data originated and the range of response levels obtained. Inferential analysis refers to the statistical testing of hypotheses–the suspected cause and effect relationships–to ascertain whether the hypotheses receive support from the data within certain degrees of confidence, typically described through significance levels. Most of these analyses are conducted through statistical software packages such as SPSS or SAS, or mathematical programming environments such as R and Mathematica. Knowing these tools is essential for any quantitative researcher.

Data analysis relies on data that is coded appropriately. Data coding refers to converting raw data into appropriate numerical formats. For instance, if we ask people about their satisfaction with a new computer program, we might later code the responses received into levels of satisfaction (low, medium, high), expressed numerically as 1, 2, 3). Coding is an essential exercise to prepare data for analysis and requires considerable thought as to the type of conversion (into ratio scales, numerical scales, binary scales, ordinal scales, or otherwise). The type of conversion determines the type of analysis technique that can be applied to the coded data. Data coding sometimes involves interpretation, such as when you want to rate the innovativeness of improvement ideas on a scale from low to high. In such cases, data coding is subject to bias concerning the coding's validity and reliability, so it often requires multiple coders so their coding can be compared for congruence (inter-rater reliability).

Multiple kinds of analyses of coded data can be conducted. There is not enough space here to cover the varieties or intricacies of different quantitative data analysis strategies. But many books exist on this topic (Bryman & Cramer, 2008; Field, 2013; Reinhart, 2015; Stevens, 2001; Tabachnick & Fidell, 2001), including one authored specifically for IS research (Mertens et al., 2017).

Here it suffices to mention several basic classes of data analysis occurring in experimental work. Univariate analysis is examination of one variable by itself to identify properties such as frequency, distribution, dispersion, or central tendency. Classic statistics involve means, medians, variances, and standard deviations.

Bivariate analysis concerns the relationships between two variables. For example, we may examine the correlation between two numerical variables to identify the changes in one variable when the other variable's level increases or decreases. An example is the correlation between salary increases and job satisfaction, where a positive correlation indicates that job satisfaction increases when pay levels go up (or vice versa). Of course, correlation does not imply causation but only confirms that the changes in variables' levels behave in particular way when another variable's level changes, but it cannot make a statement about which factor causes the change. A common technique relies on the student t-test, which examines whether the mean of a dependent variable differs significantly between two groups, such as whether one group's mean has a statistically significant difference from that of the other group. The analysis is done by computing the probabilistic estimates of population means within a certain confidence interval (typically 95% or higher) for both groups. The computation compares the sample means and standard deviations of the two groups to identify the t-statistic. With the t-statistic, the confidence interval can be found in a t-test table that describes the probabilities (p-values) associated with the t-statistic. (An example can be found at https://www.statisticshowto.com/tables/t-distribution-table/.) Most current statistical packages compute the probability values straightaway, without the researcher's having to consult a t-test table.

Multivariate analysis, broadly speaking, refers to all statistical methods that simultaneously analyze multiple measurements on each individual or object under investigation (Hair et al., 2010); as such, many multivariate techniques are extensions of univariate and bivariate analysis. Examples include general linear models

(GLM) or two-group comparisons to examine hypotheses statistically. Other approaches involve data analysis techniques that can estimate covariates' main and interaction effects.

The choice of the correct inferential analysis technique depends on the experimental design, the number of independent and dependent (and control) variables, the data coding, and the distribution of the data because statistical tests all come with a set of assumptions and preconditions about the data to which they can be applied. Mertens et al. (2017)provide an introduction to these important issues, but the book by Shadish et al. (2001) is standard reading in this area. For example, many experimental and quasi-experimental studies use some form of between-groups analysis of variance such as ANOVA, ANCOVA, repeated measures, or MAN (C)OVA (Lindman, 1974).

This introduction to experiments closes with suggestions for maintaining rigor and quality. Good experimental research should follow these six guidelines.

1. **Carry out experiments only in the presence of strong theory**. Without strong theory and clear hypotheses, you cannot design good treatments or good settings (like the tasks) in which these treatments should manifest as differences.
2. **Design your treatments carefully**. The treatment is the core design element of an experiment because it is how the independent variable (typically the key theoretical construct of interest) finds its way into the study. It is not enough just to split groups; treatments clearly operationalize differences in the meaning of a construct, that is, the different ways a construct can manifest in reality. The design of an appropriate treatment is a key challenge for researchers since the treatment is the key element in the experimental method and deserves careful development during both pre- and pilot-testing. For example, a common error is to use treatments that bundle two or more theoretical properties, rather than just one. I have made this mistake myself: In an experiment comparing two visual-analysis techniques (Recker & Dreiling, 2011), the treatment conditions (technique A versus technique B) actually differ along more than one dimension, as they vary in color, orientation, visual shapes, and text, so while we found differences between the experimental groups, we could not ascertain from where these differences stemmed. Make sure you test your experiment carefully to ensure that your treatment is working.
3. **Perform manipulation checks**. Carefully designing a treatment includes incorporating checks to demonstrate that a particular treatment manipulation was valid and effective. Reviewers often demand manipulation checks (and rightfully so) to demonstrate that a treatment worked.
4. **Rule out alternative hypotheses.** A common problem in many experiment-based studies is that the researchers do not effectively or comprehensively rule out alternative hypotheses. It is not enough to demonstrate that your treatment led to some differences between the experimental groups; you must also establish that this difference stems from the treatment, not some other endogenous or exogenous mechanism that may be at work.

5. **Ensure ecological validity**. Experiments reduce reality into reasonably simple, controlled situations so cause-and-effect relationships between a few conditions (such as groups) can be revealed. We often have to comprise realism in the setting to be able to maintain or ensure control. Reality is complex and messy, and the danger with experiments is that they become internally valid but not plausible in a realistic setting. Aim to demonstrate, or at least discuss, how and to what extent your experiment design resembles reality and your findings generalize (or not) to realistic settings.

6. **Check for the latest guidelines on experiments in the literature.** For example, I have not mentioned other threats to experimental validity, such as fatigue and learning effects. These threats may be relevant to consider as well.

5.2 Qualitative Methods

Qualitative methods are designed to assist researchers in understanding phenomena in context. With its focus on measurement, quantitative research has the tendency to isolate aspects of phenomena by measuring only these. Quantitative methods are nomothetic, meaning that they are used to identify regularities among categories of phenomena, in general (Burrell & Morgan, 1979). This focus typically fails to consider the wider setting in which phenomena occur. In response, qualitative methods have been developed in the social sciences to enable researchers to investigate phenomena in their real-life contexts. They are helpful especially when the boundaries between phenomena and their contexts are not apparent or when you want to study a particular phenomenon in depth. As such, qualitative methods are idiographic, meaning that they are used to identify the meaning of idiosyncratic, contingent, unique, or subjective phenomena.

A good example of a qualitative study is Peshkin's (1986) study of Bethany Baptist Academy, a fundamentalist Christian school, by spending eighteen months interviewing and observing the students, parents, teachers, and members of the community to provide a comprehensive analysis of Christian schooling as an alternative to public education. Peshkin's work is qualitative research as it is an in-depth study using tools such as observations and unstructured interviews, absent assumptions and hypotheses and with the purpose of securing descriptive and non-quantifiable data without attempting to generalize the findings.

As the Bethany Baptist Academy example illustrates, qualitative research often focuses on "why" and "how" things occur. With its emphasis on a phenomenon "within its context," qualitative research often focuses on a small case or sample, unlike many quantitative methods that regularly focus on large, representative samples.

To understand qualitative research, it is helpful to compare qualitative methods to quantitative methods. The simplest distinction between the two is that quantitative methods focus on numbers, and qualitative methods focus on words (as expressed in text, audio but also video or imagery) to capture what people have said, done, believed, or experienced about a phenomenon, topic, or event. Qualitative research emphasizes understanding phenomena through direct observation, communication with participants, or analysis of texts, and may stress contextual subjective accuracy over generality.

Several basic principles are common to qualitative methods:

- **Natural setting**: Qualitative research is usually performed in the field to study a phenomenon in the context in which it occurs (Creswell, 2009). This approach contrasts lab experiments, for example, which use artificial settings ("the lab") to control and manipulate what goes on in this setting.
- **Researchers as a key instrument**: Qualitative researchers collect data and information themselves, rather than through an "objective" instrument, and often by means of interacting face-to-face, observing behavior, studying documents, or interviewing participants.
- **Multiple sources of data**: Qualitative researchers typically gather a variety of data of different sorts, from interviews to documents to observations and so forth.
- **Inductive analysis**: Qualitative methods often (but not always) contrast the hypothetico-deductive model to science that is often (but not always) applied in quantitative methods by focusing on bottom-up analysis of data and building patterns, themes, and concepts into increasingly abstract units from the data.
- **Focus on emergent meaning**: Qualitative methods focus on uncovering the meaning of behaviors, opinions, or views that participants have or develop about a phenomenon.
- **Evolutionary design**: While following a general procedure, qualitative methods typically follow an evolutionary research process in which a research plan, a theory, data collection, and analysis can unfold and change over time as the research progresses. This characteristic contrasts with much of quantitative research, which typically proceeds only in two stages: first design and then execution. Because qualitative methods typically are used in an evolutionary process, the nature of this process needs to be documented transparently to support traceability and replicability.
- **Holistic and contextual**: Qualitative methods are designed to assist researchers in developing a comprehensive, detailed picture of complex phenomena. This approach typically means shedding light on a phenomenon from multiple perspectives, developing a larger picture, and paying attention to various aspects of the phenomenon without isolating or reducing it to one or few dedicated variables.

Prominent qualitative research methods that are discussed in this book include case study research, action research, and grounded theory. Other qualitative methods include ethnography (e.g., the study of a particular culture and its members' understanding of the role of a particular event, such as an illness), phenomenology (a description of the "subjective reality" of an event, as perceived by the study's population), or activist research (research that aims to raise the views of the underprivileged or "underdogs" to prominence in the minds of the elite, who often control the public's view and positions).

Because of its emphasis on non-numerical data (words), qualitative research is not as amenable to quantitative analyses like statistics but relies primarily on analysis techniques such as content analysis or discourse analysis. Another key difference between qualitative and quantitative methods is the purpose of **sampling**. A variety of sampling strategies exist, such as theoretical, random, purposive, or convenience sampling (Miles & Huberman, 1994). In simple terms, however, one can say that quantitative methods often rely on random sampling, where cases are selected randomly from a wider population to ensure representativeness. Qualitative methods, by contrast, often rely on theoretical sampling, where cases are selected because they have certain theoretical properties of interest, so instead of searching for more cases to ensure the ability to generalize statistically, qualitative researchers decide what data to collect next and where to find them so as to develop theory as it emerges, in an attempt to support generalization analytically (Tsang & Williams, 2012).

Qualitative methods have advantages over quantitative methods in exploratory research because qualitative methods may be able to uncover complex, multifaceted, or even hidden phenomena, so they can lead to a more comprehensive, multi-perspective view. They are also often used for theory-building (Fig. 3.1) because of their exploratory, holistic nature and because they can be applied to domains or phenomena that feature little knowledge or theory (and, hence, constructs and measurements).

One disadvantage of qualitative research methods is the difficulty to generalize findings to a larger population. Qualitative methods also often have issues with reliability because the studies' processes are often so contextualized to one case that they cannot readily or faithfully be repeated in other cases.

Traditionally, qualitative methods have been associated with interpretive methods because of their typical focus on developing interpretations of data. However, "qualitative" is **not** a synonym of "interpretive". Qualitative research may be carried out based on a positivist, interpretive, critical, or other worldview, depending on the researcher's philosophical assumptions. For example, case study research can be positivist (Yin, 2009) or interpretive (Walsham, 1995), action research can be positivist (Clark, 1972) or interpretive (Elden & Chisholm, 1993), and grounded theory research can be positivist (Glaser & Strauss, 1967) or interpretive (Gasson, 2004). Without delving too deeply into the distinctions and their implications, positivists generally assume that reality is objectively given and can be discovered by a researcher and described by measurable properties that are independent of the observer (researcher) and his or her instruments. Interpretive researchers start out with the assumption that reality (given or socially constructed) can be accessed only through social constructions such as language, consciousness, and shared meanings. Interpretive researchers generally seek to understand phenomena through the meanings that people assign to them. Table 5.2 contrasts these two perspectives. The assumptions of positivism and interpretivism impact how qualitative researchers conceive and use data, analyze that data, and the research's argumentation and rhetorical style (Sarker et al., 2018).

Table 5.2 Some stylized differences between positivism and interpretivism that are relevant to qualitative research

Positivism	Interpretivism
Experience is objective, testable, and independent of explanation.	Data are not detachable from theory. Data and facts are determined and constructed in light of interpretation.
Generalizations are derived from experience and are independent of the observer.	Generalizations are dependent on the research. Validity hinges on plausibility.
The language of science can be exact and formal.	Languages are equivocal and adaptive.
Meaning is separated from facts.	Meanings are what constitute facts.

Data Collection Techniques

Qualitative researchers use a variety of data, such as texts, videos, images, sounds, and written, spoken, recorded or otherwise communicated accounts of behaviors. This data might be designed (or generated) in that it is prompted by the researcher, as in interviews or focus groups, or it could be organic in that the data naturally occurs, as in observations of everyday conversations or digitally recorded behaviors and communications in online forms, social media, or emails.

Because they seek to use a large variety of data, qualitative methods employ many techniques to gather it. The most prominent form is **interviewing**, "conversations with purpose," so to speak, which can be conducted face-to-face or via telephone/conferencing one-to-one or one-to-many. Some 90% of all social science investigations use interviews in one way or another (Briggs, 1986).

Interviews, as a way to construct knowledge, are typically between the researcher (s) and key informants, subjects whose positions in a research setting give them specialist knowledge about other people, processes, events, or phenomena that are relevant to the research and more extensive, detailed, or privileged than that ordinary people might have. Key informants are particularly valuable sources of information.

Interviews can be descriptive, exploratory, or explanatory. Descriptive interviews are used to provide a rich description of a phenomenon as perceived by the interviewees to reveal subjective understanding. Focus is typically on development and exploitation of multiple individual perspectives regarding the phenomenon with the purpose of arriving at a comprehensive, multi-faceted description or conceptualization. Rationalizing interview data can then generate interpretive understanding.

Exploratory interviews are typically used to define research questions, propose new theoretical concepts, and/or identify the boundary conditions of a phenomenon. Propositions or hypotheses are usually generated based on the observed relationships or on the interpretive understanding generated.

Explanatory interviews are performed to determine whether presumed and/or postulated relationships and causal links between concepts occur and are experienced or perceived as such by subjects in real-life settings.

Interviews have the advantage of being targeted, as the focus is directly on a selected topic, and insightful, as they can provide causal inferences as perceived by interviewees. Interviews also allow some level of control as the interviewee can use follow-up and probing questions to steer the conversation into certain areas of interest. Interviews are furthermore a flexible and responsive method that can accommodate a range of research problems and can be used to explore additional research questions if they arise. They allow the collection of rich and descriptive data, which is ideally suited to examining topics for which multiple levels of meaning need to be explored. Finally, interviews are a familiar method, so most potential participants will accept an invitation to interview readily, and they provide the ability to follow up research participants for clarification or further exploration.

However, interviewing also has weaknesses and challenges. Among these, the challenges of reflexivity, when the interviewee responds with what he or she thinks the interviewer would like to hear, inaccuracy and poor recall, artificiality, as the researcher is typically a stranger to the interviewee, and subjectivity and bias because of poorly constructed questions and the researchers' own views stand out. Other disadvantages include that interviews do not generalize well, and they are time-consuming and slow to conduct and analyze. Other limitations are discussed in Myers and Newman (2007).

Interviewing typically uses more or less formally structured protocols that depend on the purpose of the interview. In some situations, these protocols are provided to the informants in advance (e.g., so they have the opportunity to prepare answers), but in other situations it may be desirable or required to surprise informants with questions.

Similar to surveys, formally structured interviews follow pre-planned sets of questions. Unstructured interviews do not contain any preconceived protocol or sequence; in a sense, they are most comparable to open-ended conversations. Most interviews, however, are semi-structured, where respondents are asked about the topics of the study following a flexible interview structure (a protocol) that allows new questions to be brought up during the interview in response to what the interviewee says. Hence, the interview follows a conversational form that allows for follow-up questions and bidirectional discussions about the topic or other topics that emerge during the interview. Semi-structured interviews usually start with general questions about a topic that are typically formulated ahead of the interview. Then the possible relationships between the questions and potentially related topics and issues become the basis for more specific questions that are typically not pre-formulated. This approach allows both the interviewer and the person being interviewed the flexibility to probe for details or discuss issues if necessary or beneficial. Thus, semi-structured interviews are guided only in the sense that some form of interview protocol provides a framework for the interview. Table 5.3 compares the advantages and disadvantages of the various types of interviews.

A second key technique for data collection is **observation**. Observations allow researchers to obtain first-hand experiences, and they reveal incidents as they occur. Direct observation involves the researcher as a passive and neutral bystander who is not involved in the phenomenon of interest ("looking over the shoulder"), whilst

Table 5.3 Advantages and disadvantages of interviewing formats

Format	Advantages	Disadvantages
Structured	Features consistency and reliability	Cannot follow emergent new lines of inquiry
Semi-structured	Combines strengths and minimizes risk	
Unstructured	Allows free talk by interviewees about what they find important	Requires interviewee to be in a free-flowing, talkative mode. If too talkative, white noise data is generated.

participant observation includes the researcher as an active participant ("influencing the phenomenon"). In some studies, some events or actions are directly observed by the researcher while others are influenced by the researcher. One of the key challenges in observation stems from our typically studying unfamiliar contexts, requiring us to go through a period of enculturation in which we become accustomed to the context. A more modern form of observation is netnography, a form of ethnography that involves the observation of online behaviors or communities (Kozinets, 2002).

A third key technique for data collection is **archival data collection**, where internal and external documents that relate to the unit of observation are gathered and used as a data source. These documents can be structured (e.g., spreadsheets), semi-structured (e.g., emails, reports, policy documents, websites), or unstructured (e.g., music, video, other media). The documentation may be personal, private, or public, which may impact the researcher's ability to access, use, or report on the data. Increasingly, this data is also in the form of digital records, such as social media or blog posts (Levina & Vaast, 2015; Whelan et al., 2016).

These and other data collection techniques, such as focus groups (Morgan, 1997) and social network analysis (Wassermann & Faust, 1994), bring us to another fundamental principle of qualitative research: **triangulation** of data. Data triangulation refers to relating multiple sources of evidence about a phenomenon or topic. Through triangulation of data, researchers can gain a more nuanced picture of the situation and increase their findings' reliability and validity. For example, researchers might triangulate interview data with data published in an organizational report or with observational data. An excellent example of data triangulation is described in Markus' (1994) study of email use by managers, which shows how survey data corroborated findings from interviews and analysis of email messages. As Markus and other authors have shown, triangulation helps researchers increase the robustness of results, as findings can be strengthened through cross-validation when various kinds and sources of data converge and are shown to be congruent or even when explanations account for divergence.

Data Analysis Techniques

In quantitative research, data collection and data analysis are typically separate, sequential stages of the research. This distinction is often not meaningful or productive in qualitative research, where data analysis and data collection can be closely interwoven or even dependent on each other. A researcher who analyzes a set of interviews and develops a theoretical model from the interviews might realize at that stage a need to follow up with the interviewees or other sources of data to explore further an emerging concept in the theory, its associations with other constructs, and so forth. The subsequent analysis of the newly collected data might modify the emerging conceptualization, so data analysis in qualitative research can best be seen as the process of developing meaning from the data.

One of the key attributes of the data analysis stage in qualitative research is the sheer amount of data to be analyzed, typically without a clear understanding of which parts are relevant or not relevant to the final research outcome, or why because qualitative research emphasizes richness, diversity, perspectives, and complexity. In turn, analytical strategies are many and varied since any set of qualitative data can be looked at from any number of perspectives, and various techniques can be applied to the same data to illuminate its various aspects. If you are interested in what this looks like, see Feldman's Feldman (1995) single study of a university housing office, which describes four strategies for interpreting the same set of qualitative data: ethnomethodology, semiotics, dramaturgy, and deconstruction.

Qualitative data analysis, just like quantitative data analysis, can be supported by a variety of tools (e.g., Bandara et al., 2015; Bazeley, 2007), and as usual the choice of tool is not all that critical. Instead, the choice of an analysis technique depends on the purpose of the research. The technique must be included in the planning stage and integrated with other parts of the research. Five common analysis techniques are coding, memoing, critical incident analysis, content analysis, and discourse analysis.

- **Coding**: Coding is probably the most commonly employed, useful set of techniques for analyzing and reducing qualitative data to meaningful information. Coding organizes raw data into conceptual categories, where each code is effectively a category or "bin" into which a piece of data is placed. Coding involves assigning tags or labels as units of meaning to pieces or chunks of data–, whether words, phrases, paragraphs, or entire documents. Coding is often used to organize data around concepts, key ideas, or themes that we identify in the data or to map theoretical expectations to a set of data with the view to corroborating or falsifying the theory. In fact, coding is already analysis, as it requires interpreting the data.

  There are many approaches to coding, but the most common coding techniques—open, axial, and selective—were introduced by Strauss and Corbin (1998). Open coding aims at uncovering and naming concepts in data, which may be grouped in higher-level categories to reduce the number of uncovered concepts. Axial coding involves organizing categories and/or concepts into causal relationships, such as to distinguish conditions from actions, interactions, and consequences. <u>Selective coding</u> might then be used to identify one or a few central categories to which all other categories are then systematically and logically related by selectively sampling the available data to validate and refine categories and relationships. A great general overview of coding is available in Saldana (2016).

- **Memoing**: Memoing, a technique that is typically used during or immediately after data collection, is effectively a subjective commentary or reflection on what was happening at the time or place of the data collection. Memos can be a summary of what was done, what was happening, or how something was achieved. Memos can also be a commentary describing a "hunch" or initial idea about possible interpretations of the data. They can be useful tool in the research process and can guide the identification of concepts and themes. A good introduction to memoing is provided in Miles and Huberman (1994).
- **Critical incident analysis**: Critical incident analysis involves identifying series of "events" or "states" that occur (e.g., in chronological order) and the transitions between them. Such incidents can then be used to develop a storyline or to speculate about temporal or logical relationships between things, events, or actions.
- **Content and relational analysis**: <u>Content analysis</u> is concerned with the semantic analysis of a body of text to uncover the presence of dominant concepts. In general, content analysis approaches fall into two categories: conceptual and relational. In conceptual analysis, text material is examined for the presence, frequency, and centrality of concepts. Such concepts can represent words, phrases, or constructs that are more complex. Relational analysis, on the other hand, tabulates not only the frequency of concepts in the body of text, but also the co-occurrence of concepts, thereby examining how concepts (pre-defined or emergent) in the documents are related to each other. These relationships may be based on, for example, contextual proximity, cognitive mapping, or underlying emotion. Content analysis is performed by trained analysts who tag a corpus of text with pre-defined or emerging codes, thereby introducing a source of bias to the coding process. More recently, however, computational approaches have become available that facilitate more efficient and objective exploration of the content of large bodies of text. Several such approaches have been developed, including hyperspace analogue to language (Burgess & Lund, 1997), latent semantic analysis (Landauer et al., 1998), and data mining tools like Leximancer (Smith & Humphreys, 2006).
- **Discourse analysis**: Discourse analysis looks at the structure and unfolding of an instance of communication, such as a conversation, an argument, or a debate. It is concerned with language in use and can be used to examine the use or evolution of phrases, terms, metaphors, and allegories. Sub-forms of discourse analysis include social semiotics, conversation analysis, and post-structuralist analysis.

These are but a few categories of the techniques that can be used in qualitative data analysis. Each set of techniques has its own focus, advantages, and disadvantages. It is difficult to declare ahead of time whether any one approach is more

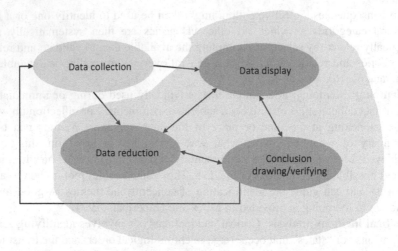

Fig. 5.9 Qualitative data analysis (Miles & Huberman, 1994)

appropriate than another, because the choice will depend on the researchers' philo-sophical stance, the stage of the research process, the research method chosen, the type of data collected, personal interest, and the availability of good advice.

Fig. 5.9 shows a general model for qualitative data analysis consisting of three main stages: data reduction, data display, and conclusion drawing/verifying. As the figure shows, the three stages are inter-dependent and interwoven with data collec-tion, demonstrating the iterative, flexible, and emergent character of qualitative methods.

Data reduction refers to the process whereby a mass of qualitative data–inter-view transcripts, field notes, observations etc.–is reduced and organized by, for example, coding, writing summaries, and discarding irrelevant data to focus on emergent concepts or themes. Access to discarded data is retained, as unexpected findings may require re-examining some data that was previously considered unnecessary.

Data display refers to the process whereby the main findings, themes, patterns, or interpretations from a rich and diverse set of qualitative data is represented in accessible, readable, systematic, and structured formats such as diagrams, tables, charts, networks, and other graphical formats. Data display should be a continual process, rather than one carried out only at the end of the data collection.

Conclusion-drawing and verification refers to the process in which the researcher develops initial conclusions and then verifies and validates them through reference to field notes or additional data collection.

Rigor in Qualitative Research

Many of the mechanisms and analysis used to display **rigor** in quantitative research, such as demonstrating the validity and reliability of measurements through dedicated statistics such as Cronbach's alpha, cross-loadings, and goodness-of-fit measures, do not apply to non-numerical data. Qualitative methods always involve the researcher as the analytical instrument, so they are a more subjective form of research than quantitative research usually is. This is not to say that rigor does not apply to qualitative methods, that rigor in these methods cannot be achieved, or that qualitative methods clash with quantitative methods in terms of rigor, but demonstrating rigor in qualitative research can be difficult because of the various traditions in qualitative research. One example of these traditions is the distinction between positivist and interpretive qualitative research (Table 5.2) but other differences (Sarker et al., 2018) relate to how qualitative researchers conceive and use data (e.g., as facts, as subjective understanding, as socially constructed reality, or as negotiated meaning) and also to how they view the role of theory (e.g., as a set of generalizable, falsifiable propositions or laws or as a conception or mental scheme, lens, or scaffolding through which they look at data). Table 5.4 summarizes several established tests of rigor in qualitative research that apply to these various traditions. These traditions each have aspects of quality and tests that they use to gauge rigor in that tradition. Of course, the traditions are also equivalent in some ways.

The most common research methods under the qualitative paradigm are the case study, action research, and grounded theory. Other methods, such as ethnography, phenomenology, and hermeneutics are few and far less common and, frankly, I am not in the best position to give any advice on them.

Types of Qualitative Methods: Case Study

Case study research is the most popular qualitative method in information systems research and other social sciences, particularly business and management. The top journals provide many examples of excellent cases and the types of studies conducted on these cases.

The case study method involves intensive research on a phenomenon (a case) in its natural setting (one or more case sites) over a period of time. A case study is commonly used to investigate a contemporary phenomenon in its real-life context, especially when the boundaries between phenomenon and context are not clear.

Case study methods are designed for situations in which there are many more variables of interest than data points, so case studies rely on multiple sources of evidence (documentation, observations, interviews, secondary data) so data can be triangulated to enhance its credibility. Well-known examples of case studies include one of the first instances of psychoanalysis, the case of "Anna O," which inspired much of Sigmund Freud's thinking about mental illness (Freeman, 1990), and the

Table 5.4 Rigor in two traditions of qualitative research

Test	Positivist tactic	Interpretivist tactic
Internal validity/credibility. The internal validity or credibility of findings concerns whether the researcher has been able to provide sufficient substantiated evidence for the interpretations offered in qualitative data analysis.	Pattern matching, explanation building, addressing rival explanations.	Transparency and procedural clarity, dialogical reasoning.
Construct validity/Confirmability. Confirmability means that qualitative research findings can be verified or challenged by outsiders such as participants, other researchers, and outside experts. In that sense, confirmability is similar to construct validity.	Multiple sources of evidence, chain of evidence, informant review	Contextualization, multiple interpretations, suspicion
Reliability/dependability. Dependability means that individuals other than the researchers can consider the same observations or data and would reach the same or similar conclusions. Dependability is similar to reliability in that measures provide consistently similar results.	Case study protocols, case study database	Corroboration and reflexivity
Generalizability/Transferability. Generalizability or transferability mean that the findings from a study can be translated and applied in full or in part to other settings, domains, or cases.	Replication logic	Local surprise, abstraction through formal concepts

case of David Reimer, a boy who was raised as a girl and who later learned the truth about his gender reassignment (Colapinto, 2001).

Case studies are used for both confirmatory purposes (theory-testing) and exploratory purposes (theory-building). For example, Dutta et al. (2003) reported on a primarily inductive application of the case study method in which they analyzed data on the pricing process of a large manufacturing firm, compared the data to existing theories, developed a new theory, returned to the data to see how the emergent theory matched the data, and finally returned to the theory for yet another revision. Another well-known example of a theory-testing case study is Markus (1983), which used an in-depth case study to compare three theories of resistance to implementation of a computer system to test the predictions of each theory.

The main strengths of the case study method are that it allows researchers:

- to study information-systems-related phenomena in their natural settings
- to learn about the state of the art and generate theory from practice
- to understand the nature and complexity of processes, events, actions, and behaviors that take place, and
- to gain valuable insights into new, emerging topics

Case study methods also have limitations, with the most significant ones including problems of controlled deduction (a lack of adequate support for evidence), problems of replicability because of the highly contextualized nature of inquiry, and problems related to the lack of control mechanisms to account for rival explanations or potentially confounding factors.

The case study method is sometimes (regrettably) regarded as an "easy" research method because it does not require the student or scholar to learn about quantitative methods, statistics, or complex instrument-development procedures. However, all accomplished case study researchers stress that case studies are highly complex and difficult and time-consuming to do well. As (Hoaglin et al., 1982, p. 134) observed:

> Most people feel they can prepare a case study, and nearly all of us believe we can understand one. Since neither view is well founded, the case study receives a good deal of approbation it does not deserve.

The challenges of case study research lie in its reliance on gaining access to a case site, which is typically an organization, and gaining access to key informants who really have the required insights that help researchers to build explanations and theories. Moreover, case study research often uncovers things that do not bode well in an organization, and access may be restricted to protect confidential or commercial information or because organizations do not like bad news or bad PR. (See how many "failure factor" theories you can find in the literature compared to "success factor models.") Another challenge is the lack of control over the phenomenon being studied, as the importance of the research problem might change over time, sometimes even before the research can be concluded. Challenges also lie in the vast amounts of largely unstructured data that must be analyzed, which is often a particular challenge for inexperienced scholars. Finally, because of the quantity and complexity of data and inferences, it can be challenging to write up a case study,—especially for publication in journals that impose limitations on word or page numbers.

The research process for case studies varies depending on the case, the phenomenon, and other restrictions, but case studies usually follow an interdependent, iterative process that involves planning, designing, preparing data, collecting data, analyzing data, and sharing, as shown in Fig. 5.10. You can clearly see already how case study, as a qualitative method, follows a more intricate logic than the sequential nature of a quantitative method such as surveys (Fig. 5.6).

Planning refers to identifying the research questions and other rationale for doing a case study. The case study method is preferred for research questions that ask "how" and "why," such as how or why a particular technology works or does not work in an organization. Other criteria that might influence whether to use a case study method include the need to have control over events or behaviors, in which case the case study is not likely to be appropriate. On the other hand, if the focus of the study is on a contemporary event, the case study method may be well-suited. Planning requires appreciating the relative strengths and weaknesses of the various research methods and choosing the one that is most likely to lead to a sound study.

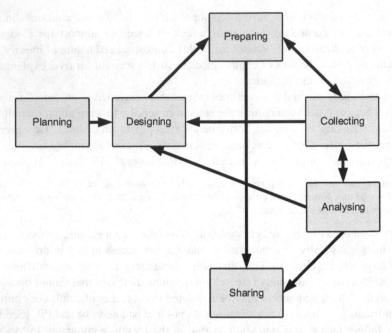

Fig. 5.10 Case research procedure. (Adapted from Yin (2009))

Table 5.5 Classification of case study designs with examples

Dimension	Variants	Examples in IS research
Research objective	Description	Avison and Myers (1995), Hirschheim and Newman (1991).
	Exploration	Bandara et al. (2005), Liu et al. (2014), Orlikowski (1993).
	Explanation	Henfridsson and Bygstad (2013), Markus (1983) Sarker and Lee (2002).
Epistemology	Positivism	Keil (1995), Sarker and Lee (2001).
	Interpretivism	Berente and Yoo (2012), Schlagwein and Bjørn-Andersen (2014).
Case design	Single	Seidel et al. (2013), Silva and Hirschheim (2007).
	Multiple	Ang et al. (2002), Reich and Benbasat (1990).
Unit of analysis	Holistic	Rialp et al. (2005).
	Embedded	Bandara et al. (2005), Bandara and Rosemann (2005).

Designing refers to defining the unit of analysis, the number and types of cases to be studied, and the use of theory or propositions to guide the study. Case study design also involves the development of research procedures, protocols, and other means used to maintain the quality and rigor of the research and to demonstrate reliability and validity of data and findings.

Case studies' have a great variety of designs. Table 5.5 gives four dimensions along which case study designs can be classified: the research objective (what is the aim of the study?), epistemology (what are assumptions caried by the research team about how knowledge can be constructed?), case design (how many cases feature in the case study?), and unit of analysis (is the unit of analysis the case or some unit within the case?).

One of the most important decisions in designing a case study is to identify the appropriate type of case design and the corresponding unit(s) of analysis. With case design, we distinguish whether we study one case or several cases (such as multiple organizations operating in the same industry). With unit of analysis, we distinguish whether the case (most often the organization) is the unit of analysis our research focuses on—then we call it a holistic case, or whether the case we study focuses multiple units of analysis, such as different projects carried out by the organization, or different teams working within the organization. If so, we call the units embedded in the case. Together, we can distinguish four types of designs for case studies (Yin, 2009): single-case (holistic) designs (Type 1), single-case (embedded) designs (Type 2), multiple-case (holistic) designs (Type 3), and multiple-case (embedded) designs (Type 4) (Fig. 5.11).

A single case study (embedded or holistic) is preferable when the researcher wants to identify new and previously unchallenged phenomena or issues. It is most often used to present a unique or extreme case. Single cases are often idiosyncratic, so they do not afford great potential for development of abstract, generalizable theory. However, they are still useful for purposes of exploration or rationalization. In research practice, a clear rationale is often demanded for using a single-case design. The most common arguments for a single case study include:

1. It is a critical case that meets all conditions for testing a theory.
2. It is a unique case that is extreme or rare.
3. It is a representative case that is typical of everyday/commonplace situations.
4. It is a revelatory case that presents a previously inaccessible opportunity.
5. It is a longitudinal case that reflects a change in the subject matter over two more points in time.

A multiple case study (embedded or holistic) is desirable when the researcher wants to build or test a theory. Multiple cases strengthen the results by replicating a pattern and increasing confidence in the robustness of the results. In other words, a multiple-case study is best for enabling an appropriate level of generalization of the findings and eliminating single-case bias. Two types of multiple case studies are embedded and holistic. As noted above, embedded multiple case studies have more than one unit of analysis in a study of one or several cases related to the same object of investigation, while holistic multiple case studies investigate a phenomenon on a more global level. The holistic design is advantageous either when no logical sub-units can be identified or when the theory itself is of a holistic nature, while an embedded design would allow a researcher to define an appropriate set of subunits, thus adding to the sensitivity of the investigation.

In designing case study procedures, attention must be given to demonstrating that the study meets the essential requirements for rigor—dependability, credibility, confirmability, and transferability, for example if you follow an interpretive tradition (Klein & Myers, 1999). Typical components of case study procedures include

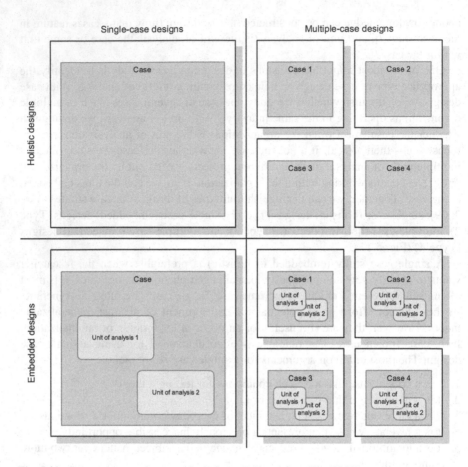

Fig. 5.11 Common types of case study designs. (Adapted from Yin (2009))

defining the case study and interview protocols and setting up a case evidence database in which all records and data can be stored and managed.

Preparing involves taking the necessary steps to conduct high-quality data collection, especially honing the researcher's data-collection skills in interviewing and observation. Case study protocols are further developed, revised, and finalized at this stage, and data-collection procedures are trained and pilot-tested. This stage often involves a pilot test to verify that procedures are applicable and appropriate.

Collecting refers to executing the case study protocol(s) and gathering data, preferably from multiple sources. An important principle in this phase is maintaining a chain of evidence, that is, describing how case study questions link to protocol, citations, other forms of evidentiary sources, elements in the case study database, and inferences and conclusions as described in a case study report. Maintaining a transparent chain of evidence is important to getting a case study published. In my experience, case study papers that do have an unclear chain of evidence struggle in the paper review process.

A case study database is an important tool in this phase for organizing and documenting the data collected. Interviews, a key source of data, should be recorded and transcribed. One of the key pieces of advice that I offer to students involved in data collection at a case site is to gather and maintain complete and precise records of everything that was seen, heard, said, and observed. Data analysis might occur a long time later, and researchers often have to revisit the data they collected data much later. Therefore, maintaining a close record of as much data as possible is a key component to good case study research.

Analyzing consists of examining, categorizing, coding, tabulating, testing, or otherwise combining and studying the evidence collected to draw empirically based inferences and other conclusions. At this stage, qualitative—and perhaps also quantitative—techniques for data analysis are employed. Strategies for data analysis include reflecting on theoretical propositions as to how they fit the data (when the case study is used to test or confirm a theory) and examining rival explanations.

Finally, **sharing** refers to bringing the case study's results and findings to a close by identifying and addressing appropriate audiences with the findings. This stage is important not only for the final write-up (for a thesis or a scientific article) but also for sharing findings and conclusions with case study participants who, one hopes, will find them useful.

Like all research methods, case studies need evaluation to assess the contribution they offer to the research's area of study. Because quantitative criteria such as statistical power, sample size, and goodness-of-fit do not apply, qualitative researchers sometimes use other criteria to gauge a case study's quality (Myers, 2009):

1. It is interesting to the audience of a journal.
2. It displays sufficient evidence.
3. It is complete.
4. It considers alternative perspectives.
5. It is written in an engaging manner.
6. It contributes to knowledge.

Types of Qualitative Methods: Action Research

Action research is an interactive method of inquiry that aims to contribute to both the practical concerns of people in an immediate problem context and the goals of social science by means of joint collaboration within a mutually acceptable, ethical frame-work. In action research, researchers work with practitioners to gain a shared understanding of a complex organizational problem, intervening to improve the situation in real time (during, not at the end of a project), and communicating the knowledge gained through the investigation to the research and practice communities.

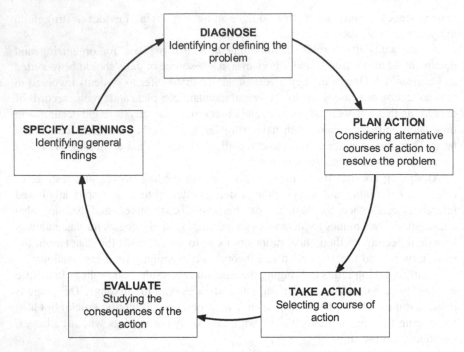

Fig. 5.12 Action research cycle following Susman and Evered (1978)

Action research builds on the idea of introducing changes or other kinds of intervention into a context and studying the effects of those actions. In this mode of inquiry, the researcher acts as the agent of change or intervention (such as in the role of consultant or organizational member) whilst also examining how these actions influence the phenomenon at hand. In effect, action research attempts to solve a current practical problem while simultaneously expanding scientific knowledge, so it involves research that produces immediate practical and academic outcomes and requires various degrees of integration of the researcher and the subject of the research. It can also serve as a means of recording what happened during the process of an event involving change. The distinctive feature of action research–the deliberate introduction of one or more interventions by the researcher–makes it unique from other research methods that typically try <u>not</u> to interfere with the subject of study.

The action research process, as described by Susman and Evered (1978), is cyclical and comprises five stages: diagnosing, action-planning, action-taking, evaluating, and specification of learning (Fig. 5.12).

Diagnosing refers to identifying and defining the problem in context, while **action-planning** involves specifying the organizational actions that will be taken to relieve, mitigate, or rectify these problems. The researcher at this stage employs a theoretical framework that explains why and how the planned actions will bring forth the desired change. **Action-taking** then implements the selected course of action. **Evaluating** involves analyzing the actions and their consequences and considering whether the planned actions achieved their intended effects. The last phase, **specifying learning**, describes what was learnt throughout the process, applies this knowledge in the organization or other problem context, and communicates it to the scientific community. Typically, the second, third, and fourth steps of this cycle are traversed at least twice so that learning from the first iteration can be implemented in the cycle's second iteration.

Several examples for action research studies exist in information systems scholarship that serve as illustrations for how the action research cycle can be carried out. Avison et al. (2018) list 120 such studies published between 1982 and 2016.

While action research also uses interviews, documents, archival analysis, and other data-collection techniques, it relies heavily on participant observation, where the researcher not only observes but also finds a role in the group he or she is observing from which to participate in some manner.

Several key requirements guide the process of action research:

- Establish the research infrastructure, including formalizing the organization's involvement and the researchers' and practitioners' responsibilities in a formal research agreement or contract that also specifics necessary legal and/or ethical arrangements.
- Develop statements that describe the issue or problem to be addressed in a theoretical framework.
- Plan and use methodological data-collection methods and measurement techniques prior to taking action.
- Avoid domination of the diagnosis and action-planning phases by allowing learning about the subject to improve the idiographic usefulness of any theory.
- Undertake iterative cycles and record repeated planning and action cycles. Report both action successes and failures, as failures may provide insights.
- Make restrained generalizations and use synchronic reliability to achieve consistent observations within each time period.
- Explain what happened in a factual and neutral manner by describing how the project arose, what was intended, the outcomes (intended and unintended, expected and unexpected), and their impact. Support the story by providing evidence of data recorded (e.g., organizational documents, feedback, performance metrics).
- Distinguish facts from value judgements and identify the researcher's inferences and interpretations.
- Make sense of what happened. Provide an analysis of what went on but also describe how it made sense as the story unfolded. Report assumptions and how they were tested, especially if the assumptions were private.
- Explain how the project contributes to theory or usable knowledge. Be able to demonstrate relevance of the project to reader who were not directly involved.

Action research is an accepted but not dominant method in information systems research. Several great example studies can be found (Mathiassen et al., 2012). Action research ideas are also being used in conjunction with other research methods, such as design science—so-called action design research (Mullarkey & Hevner, 2019; Sein et al., 2011), which several people argue is quickly becoming the most popular form of action research.

One of the main advantages of action research is the opportunity to contribute both to academic knowledge and to solving a real-world problem. Thus, this method combines relevance and rigor in research. However, this advantage is also its biggest disadvantage because doing action and research together is a challenging act for anyone, let alone an inexperienced scholar. One of the key related challenges is assuming a position of a value-neutral, independent observer to the extent that it allows for critical reflection and analysis, while at the same time maintaining a role as an influencer and intervener. The most commonly noted barriers to action research include the difficulty in publishing such studies, the required time and other resources necessary, the perception of diminished rigor in comparison to other methods, and the difficulty for novice researchers to learn the method (Avison et al., 2018).

Action research is evaluated based on contributions made to practice (the "action") as well as contributions made to theory (the "research"). These contributions can be demonstrated through statements from an organizational sponsor about the change achieved and by a clear discussion of the study's outcomes and what was learned in light of the theories that are pertinent to the domain.

Types of Qualitative Methods: Grounded Theory

Grounded theory is a type of qualitative research that relies on inductive generation of theory that is grounded in qualitative data about a phenomenon that has been systematically collected and analyzed. The grounded theory approach explores and develops generalized formulations about the basic features of a phenomenon while grounding the account in empirical observations or data. One of the key advantages– and challenges–of the grounded theory approach is that it is applicable to research domains that are new or emergent and may lack substantive theory. It also allows researchers to "take a fresh look," that is, approach a known phenomenon or problem from a new perspective.

Grounded theory originated in sociologists Glaser and Strauss' (1965) study of "Dying" in a California hospital. They found no real theory to test against this subject, so they developed new a methodology to give them a way to develop a theory using only existing data-gathering methods. They wanted a loose, less structured method of developing and testing theory that was not available in traditional, empirical methodologies (particularly quantitative methods). They wanted to develop an alternative to what they called "armchair" theorizing. At the same time, they wanted a method with more structure than existing methods had for data display (e.g., thick descriptions).

Therefore, grounded theory refers to theory that is developed inductively from a corpus of data. If the method is used well, the resulting theory fits at least one dataset perfectly. Grounded theory takes a case rather than a variable perspective, as it focuses on variables that interact as a unit to produce outcomes. As such, grounded theory lends itself well to the study of process/change/other dynamic phenomena.

The grounded theory method has two primary principles. First, theory-building is a highly iterative process during which theory and data undergo <u>constant comparative analysis</u>. Second, grounded theory builds on <u>theoretical sampling</u> as a process of data collection and analysis that is driven by concepts that emerge from the study and appear to be relevant to the nascent theory. Urquhart et al. (2010) identified four main characteristics of grounded theory:

1. The main purpose of the grounded theory method is theory-building, not testing.
2. Prior domain knowledge should not lead to pre-conceived hypotheses or conjectures that the research then seeks to falsify or verify.
3. The research process involves the constant endeavor to collect and compare data and to contrast new data with any emerging concepts and constructs of the theory being built.
4. All kinds of data are applicable and are selected through theoretical sampling.

Grounded theory can be used as a research strategy in itself, with the objective of generating theory, but in practice many scholars draw on grounded theory methods, particularly its guidelines for data analysis and coding, without following the strict goal of developing new theory from the data (Bryant et al., 2004; Matavire & Brown, 2012). One of the main reasons for this reference to grounded theory is that grounded theory methodologists have developed good and clear guidelines for data coding that are also useful in other qualitative research methods, such as case study research.

Grounded theory has two main strands. Glaser and Strauss (1967) first introduced it as a general qualitative research method, which (Strauss & Corbin, 1998) then revised to provide more prescriptive and detailed procedures and techniques for the analysis of data in the "Straussian" approach to grounded theory. Glaser (1992) later disagreed with Strauss about the coding stages and the coding paradigm they proposed. Differences between the two strands of grounded theory include the roles of induction, deduction, and verification, the coding procedures, and the generated theories. Both the "Glaserian" and the "Straussian" approaches are in use today, and several studies have contrasted the relative merits and shortcomings of the two (e.g., Seidel & Urquhart, 2013).

In using grounded theory, the research process typically starts with collecting qualitative data, particularly interviews and participant observations, although originally, Glaser and Strauss (1967) envisaged grounded theory to be agnostic toward data, that is, to be useful in conjunction with both qualitative and quantitative data. Self-reviews, memos and field diaries are also–sometime controversially–used as data in grounded theory studies.

Grounded theory methods emphasize data analysis. Most prevalent is the "Straussian" way, in which the initial stage of data analysis is open coding, which is concerned with identifying, naming, categorizing, and describing phenomena found in the text in the form of emergent codes. The codes that are generated at this stage are descriptive and identify, name, and categorize the phenomena that emerge from the data. Essentially, each line, sentence, paragraph, and so on is read in search of the answer to the questions, "What is this about? What is being referenced here?" Open coding is usually accompanied by constant comparison of codes in search of similarities and differences, and the identification of more abstract and general categories that group individual codes with common properties.

Depending on which version of grounded theory is followed, open coding is typically followed by axial or selective coding. Axial coding relates codes (categories and properties) to each other via a combination of inductive and deductive thinking. To simplify this process, grounded theory emphasizes causal relationships and often (but not always, per Strauss more than Glaser) uses a basic frame of generic relationships. For example, the Straussian axial coding frame contains elements such as phenomena, causal conditions, context, intervening conditions, action strategies, and consequences (Strauss & Corbin, 1994). The objective of this stage is to refine the emerging constructs and develop tentative explanations for the relationships between the descriptive categories and constructs by coding for evidence from the data that suggests the existence, nature, and strength of such relationships.

The third phase, selective coding, describes the process of choosing one category to be the core category and relating all other categories to that one. The idea is to develop a single storyline around which everything is draped and use it to develop a substantive theory that includes inferences, tentative conjectures, or propositions. Causal or correlational links are specified based on the interpretive development of the concepts. This step typically involves examining the data with a focus on some aspect of the theory that is being developed.

Information systems research features a wide range of excellent examples of grounded theory research (Chudoba & Maznevski, 2000; Strong & Volkoff, 2010) and methodological papers about how to do grounded theory (Seidel & Urquhart, 2013; Urquhart & Fernandez, 2013; Urquhart et al., 2010; Wiesche et al., 2019).

While the grounded theory method has an excellent set of guidelines for data analysis and for ensuring rigor of theory-generation procedures, the method describes a process, not an outcome. Successful research is not solely dependent on the faithful application of the method but involves critical and creative thinking. A faithful execution of the grounded theory method does not guarantee a novel theory or a substantial contribution to knowledge.

The advantages of grounded theory certainly include its tight and early immersion into data analysis, unlike, say, quantitative research, where data analysis is typically conducted at a much later stage of the research process. The grounded theory method encourages systematic and detailed data analysis, and the literature provides ample guidelines for conducting these steps. It is also applicable in situations that have little or no theory or when the researcher fundamentally disagrees with the existing theory. Finally, grounded theory allows taking "a fresh look" at phenomena both new and existing.

The main disadvantages of grounded theory also lie in the detailed and systematic bottom-up analysis of data. It is easy to get bogged down in data analysis at a low level of detail, which makes it difficult to integrate the data into higher levels of abstraction. The process and the grounded theory to be developed are dependent on rich data that is typically collected before the researcher knows what to look for, and the researcher's creative and critical thinking ability, which is not easily learned or taught. In fact, a widely held belief is that grounded theory is a particularly challenging method for early-career researchers.

5.3 Design Science Methods

Methods ascribed to design science have attracted interest from the information systems community, especially because of an article published by Hevner et al. Hevner et al. (2004) in *MIS Quarterly*, although earlier work in that tradition has also been done (e.g., March & Smith, 1995; Nunamaker Jr et al., 1991; Walls et al., 1992). The main motivation behind the (re-) emergence of design science as a research paradigm is said to stem from a desire to complement the mainstream behavioral orientation of information systems research with more design-oriented research. Hevner and Chatterjee (2010, p. 5) defined design science research as

> a research paradigm in which a designer answers questions relevant to human problems via the creation of innovative artefacts, thereby contributing new knowledge to the body of scientific evidence. The designed artefacts are both useful and fundamental in understanding that problem.

The fundamental principle of design science research is that knowledge and understanding of a design problem and its solution are acquired in the building, application, and analysis of an artefact. The term "artefact" is central to design science research, in contrast to qualitative or quantitative methods. An artefact is something that is constructed by humans, as opposed to occurring naturally. Simon's *Science of the Artificial* (1996), the intellectual basis of this focus on artefacts, described artefacts as empirical phenomena that are "artificial" rather than "natural." Because the artificial artefacts are human-created, the science of artefacts involves the study of the designs used to perform tasks or fulfill goals and functions with the artefact.

In design science as a research activity, the research interest is on creating or changing such artefacts with the aim of improving on existing solutions to problems or perhaps providing a first solution to a problem. Typically, at least five types of artefacts are differentiated:

- **Constructs** (vocabulary and symbols)
- **Models** (abstractions and representations)
- **Methods** (algorithms and practices)
- **Instantiations** (implemented and prototype systems)
- **Design theories** (improved models of design or design processes)

One characteristic of design science research is that the artefact is this research's main contribution to knowledge an varies by type of project, environment, and

Table 5.6 Types of design science research contributions, with examples

Type of knowledge contribution	Level of contribution	Suitable artefacts	Examples
More abstract, complete, and mature knowledge	Well-developed design theory about embedded phenomena	Design theories (mid-range and grand theories)	Markus et al. (2002), Recker (2016)
	Nascent design theory knowledge in the form of design principles	Constructs, methods, models, design principles, technological rules	Arazy et al. (2010), Seidel et al. (2018)
More specific, more limited, less mature knowledge	Situated implementation of an artefact	Instantiations (software products or implemented processes)	Ketter et al. (2016), Recker (2021)

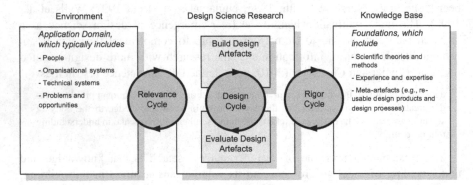

Fig. 5.13 Design science research framework, based on Hevner (2007)

artefact. Gregor and Hevner (2013) suggested at least three types of contributions to knowledge that are made through design science research (Table 5.6):

With the emphasis on design and artefacts, design science research focuses on two research activities at its core (Fig. 5.13), build (constructing the artefact) and evaluate (testing the artefact). In examining how such artefacts can be developed and evaluated, design science research is placed in a broader framework bounded by the practical environment and the available knowledge base at that point in time.

The environment defines the problem space in which the phenomena of interest reside. In information systems research, the environment includes, at minimum, people, organizational structures, and existing digital information or communication technologies and infrastructures. The composition of the environment for a particular artefact should establish why the artefact at the core of the design science research has relevance to stakeholders in that application domain. The knowledge base provides the materials from and through which design science research is accomplished; that is, prior research and results from reference disciplines provide foundational theories, frameworks, instruments, constructs, models, methods, and instantiations that are available for use in the design phase. Therefore, the knowledge base assists design science in achieving rigor. The relevance cycle bridges the research project's contextual environment and the design science activities. The rigor cycle connects the design science activities with the knowledge base of scientific foundations, experience, and expertise that inform the research project. The central design cycle iterates between the core activities of building and evaluating the design artefact and the research processes. Hevner (2007) posited that these three cycles must be present and clearly identifiable in a design science research project.

Design science is still young compared to other modes of inquiry, such as qualitative and quantitative methods. As such, there are many updates of guidelines and procedures for how design science research can be executed or evaluated. For example, guidelines for how to position the design science's contributions have been produced (Gregor & Hevner, 2013), procedural models for how design science research can be carried out have been offered (Peffers et al., 2007), guidelines for how to theorize in design sciences have been offered (Gregor et al., 2020; Gregor & Jones, 2007), and several guidelines and frameworks about how to carry out artefact evaluations are extant (Iivari et al., 2021; Tremblay et al., 2010; Venable et al., 2016).

In recent years, discussions have also emerged about how to apply traditional notions of scientific quality, such as reliability and validity, to design science (Baskerville et al., 2017; Larsen et al., 2020; Lukyanenko et al., 2014). I expect new standards for design science research to keep emerging for some time.

Whatever one's personal views on the topic, I recommend that young academics and scholars consider these and other guidelines using critical reflection. In the end, design science is predominantly focused on the artefact and not on the execution of one or another set of procedural steps. As with any other research method, you may carry out all steps and follow each guideline for design science without ever designing a novel artefact, the goal of design science; and you may design a novel artefact without executing any of these steps.

Indeed, the key evaluation criterion for design science and one of its key challenges is the **demonstrated utility** that the design artefact provides—that is, improved utility beyond the current state of utility. This definition also implies three key criteria that should be met:

(a) that the artefact's demonstrated utility is novel
(b) that the utility of an artefact in comparison to existing work makes a positive difference
(c) that a thorough evaluation provides decisive evidence of the artefact's superior utility

The definition of utility can vary. It can be a performance metric that defines the extent of a novel artefact's improvement over an existing solution, or it may be interpreted by end users or in terms of efficacy, efficiency, effectiveness, or other criteria. It could also be interpreted in terms of humanistic outcomes such as aesthetics or pleasure. The vagueness of the utility concept brings forward issues about defining it adequately and identifying the most appropriate means for evaluation. Typically, at this stage, some sort of empirical study is carried out as a simulation, case study, focus group, survey, or experiment.

Another key challenge of design science research lies in the question: **When does design contribute to knowledge?** One source of confusion to novice design-science researchers in particular is the subtle difference between conducting design as a science versus practicing routine design. The answer lies in the contribution to academic knowledge that is inherent in the design's novelty, both as a process and as an outcome. Another way to examine design science research's potential contribution to knowledge is to differentiate the maturity of the problem and the maturity of the solution (Gregor & Hevner, 2013): New solutions to known problems are improvements, known solutions to known problems are routine (and so do not make major contributions to knowledge), new problems addressed through known solutions are exaptations, and new problems addressed through new solutions are inventions. Exaptations and inventions have significant potential to contribute new knowledge.

A third challenge lies in the **role of theory for design science** (Venable, 2006). The question concerning whether design science needs theory has sparked an ongoing debate in which one side argues that the goal of design science is efficacy and utility, not theory. Others argue that researchers can attempt to define the anatomy of what constitutes good design theory, so an artefact is an instantiation (and, thus, a demonstration) of the theory, which then becomes the fundamental component of the design research.

5.4   Computational Methods

A chapter on research methods in the year 2021 would be incomplete without mentioning digital trace data and computational methods. Although these types of approaches to scholarship have only recently diffused broadly, and considerable ambiguity and confusion remains about their purpose, application, and quality, computational methods still look like an exciting prospect, particularly for information systems scholars. Therefore, I want to at least introduce the main ideas.

Digital Trace Data

Digital trace data describes evidence of activities and events that are logged and stored digitally (Freelon, 2014). Since almost everything people do these days involves or is mediated by digital technologies, digital trace data is quickly becoming a type of research data that information systems scholars and other scholars can use to theorize and analyze phenomena. Information systems scholars have long analyzed various types of digital trace data. Text such as emails, transaction data from enterprise systems, and posts and comments on social media and networking platforms are all forms of trace data. Today, bio health data recorded by wearables, logs produced by digital objects such as toothbrushes and energy meters, and traces generated by digital objects such as electric vehicles are also forms of digital trace data.

Pentland et al. (2021) studied digital trace data in the form of the electronic medical records data of more than 57,000 patient visits to four dermatology clinics. They noticed in the data several sudden changes in record-keeping that occurred simultaneously in all four clinics. When they asked the clinical staffs to explain what had happened, they were unaware that anything had changed at all. Through the analysis of the digital trace data, Pentland et al. (2021) identified a change in policy and the advent of flu season as the two main drivers for the record-keeping process's having changed.

Another example is the study by Vaast et al. (2017) on social media use during British Petroleum's oil spill in the Gulf of Mexico. They analyzed more than 23,000 tweets that carried the hashtags #oilspill or #bpoilspill and determined that individuals engaged in collective action by coproducing and circulating social media content based on an issue of mutual interest.

As these examples demonstrate, digital trace data differs from other forms of research data in several ways.

1. Digital trace data is organic, not designed (Xu et al., 2020): Trace data is a byproduct of activities, not data generated for the purpose of research. For example, in qualitative research, interview transcripts are designed research data because we gather it by asking questions that are developed in light of a research project's goals. By contrast, digital traces of conversations held on Twitter or Facebook are not designed; they appear organically and researchers "find" and collect them. Researchers have less control over the validity of organic data than they do over designed research data because the data-generation process is opaque (or even unknown), and we have little to no control over that process. For example, we do not know why, how, or in what context the Twitter posts in a conversations were made. We also usually have few to no insights into the algorithms that capture the conversations in a set of trace data, so we do not know how the data we capture was generated or whether the technological mechanisms were faithful.
2. Digital trace data can be both heterogeneous and unstructured (Dhar, 2013). For example, they often include text, images, video, or sound. The richness of such data can be a strength because it expands the number of perspectives of a phenomenon (Lindberg, 2020), but it also makes the data more difficult to analyze.
3. Digital trace data can be enormous in volume because it typically records fine-grained events and actions such as individual clicks, posts, and comments. The high volume has advantages because it provides a more precise view of behaviors and occurrences than traditional modes of collection such as observations, interviews, and archival data do (Schensul et al., 1999). However, the sheer size of the data can also quickly become overwhelming for scholars because it brings typical

manual data analysis and theorizing approaches to their limits. For example, it is not feasible to manually code, say, comments made by the 257 million followers of Christiano Ronaldo on Instagram.

4. Digital trace data is inherently event-based. As the name suggests, it "traces"— that is, connects—actions and behaviors that are enabled or mediated by digital technologies as they unfold at various points in time. Digital trace data usually takes the form of time-stamped logs of activities and events that are enacted using digital technologies or platforms. Not all analyses of digital trace data focus on the data's being event-based. For example, analyses of digital trace data from social networks focus on the ties between individuals in a community or group (Howison et al., 2011), and only sometimes do such analyses focus on how these ties change (e.g., form or dissolve) over time. Sentiment analysis of trace data such as social media posts (e.g., Yu et al., 2013) also often focuses more on the emotional connotation of messages than their timing. Still, the event-based nature of digital trace data makes it useful particularly for analyzing and theorizing about behavior, processes, evolution, and change over time (Pentland, 1999; Pettigrew, 1998). Digital trace data's event-based nature also helps in ordering it by, for example, categorizing the data into discrete units of time (e.g., days, weeks, months). Its event-based nature also helps in separating cause from effect and action from consequence because these different elements are temporally connected in that cause precedes effect and consequence succeeds action.

It should be clear by now that digital trace data is unlike the types of data that other research methods typically create or collect. Digital trace data tends to be complex, rich, large-scale, human- or technology-generated behavioral data. Because of these traits, digital trace data provide opportunities for researchers but also bring new methodological challenges in dealing with it. For example, digital traces can easily comprise thousands, if not millions, of data points, making it difficult for qualitative researchers to approach such data using manual coding techniques. Because of its precision, digital trace data can also be opaque, with underlying patterns or mechanisms difficult to discover through human inspection.

With these characteristics, digital trace data also shifts several viewpoints that we have traditionally held about how to perform scientific research. For example, this kind of data challenges the dominance of the hypothetico-deductive approach to science. The ideas about falsifying hypotheses one by one through series of experiments involving samples also stem from the idea that this was the only feasible way to do science, as collecting large samples, such as data from entire populations, was not possible until relatively recently (Glymour, 2004). Therefore, inductively identifying patterns in comparatively small data sets was considered subjective and arbitrary. However, digital trace data can make gathering complete data about certain behaviors possible. Since the samples can be extremely large, inductive theory development can take on a meaning that differs from traditional perspectives on deduction and induction (Berente et al., 2019).

In response, a new strand of methodology has been put forward that allows researchers to deal with the challenges and reap the opportunities of digital trace data. These approaches are called computational methods (Lazer et al., 2009) because they all involve algorithms for augmented or automated data collection, processing, pattern recognition, and/or analysis.

Computational Data Processing and Analysis

Computational methods is an umbrella term that describes a variety of software tools that assist with such research processes as data generation or discovery, data processing or cleansing, and data analysis or interpretation. They have in common that certain steps during data generation, processing, or analysis are carried out through—or with the help of—algorithms that either augment manual work or fully automate an otherwise manual activity. Fig. 5.14 shows several examples of computational methods.

Fig. 5.14 also helps to clarify the difference between computational methods and other software tools that are available to use in research. Fig. 5.14 shows that a

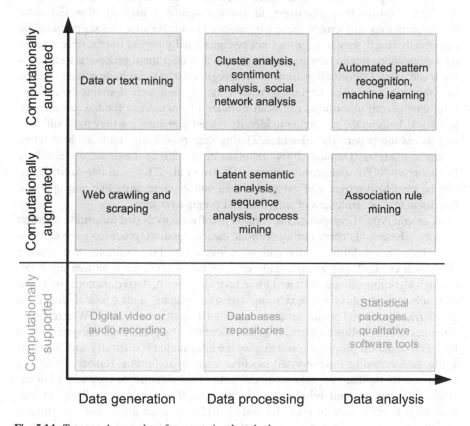

Fig. 5.14 Types and examples of computational methods

common way of **supporting** researchers in carrying out their work is through dedicated research computer software. Examples of statistical packages for quantitative data analysis include R, SPSS, and LISREL, and examples of such packages for qualitative data analysis include NVivo and Atlas.ti. During data generation, video conferencing software such as Skype and Zoom can record video and audio streams digitally, and during data processing, tools such as Excel and Access help in storing and categorizing data. What is common to these examples is that the software tools do not carry out the steps involved in the research but support scholars in carrying them out in the sense that they assist manual activities and make them easier or faster to complete. Therefore, these tools are not really computational methods, as they neither augment nor automate key research activities (which is why I shaded them grey in Fig. 5.14.

In contrast to computational support for research activities, one type of computational method is software tools that **augment** human research activity. Augmentation refers to software that is used to complement and amplify human activity, rather than to supplant it (Glymour, 2004). For example, during quantitative data analysis, statistical software packages such as LISREL automatically make suggestions for (re-)specifying a hypothesized model based on shared correlations between the latent constructs it discovers in the covariance matrix of observed data. Researchers may implement these suggestions or not; because the suggestions are empirically based, they may or may not be conceptually logical or plausible. During data generation, researchers may write scripts that help them process a web document and extract information from it (scraping) or assist them in iteratively finding and fetching web links beginning with a list of seed web domains (crawling). Literature search algorithms can scan millions of documents for the presence of keywords, helping the researcher to identify related literature, but they must still read and assess the papers for relevance. During data processing, tools such as latent semantic analysis (Dumais, 2004; Indulska et al., 2012), Leximancer (Smith & Humphreys, 2006), and process mining (Gaskin et al., 2014; van der Aalst, 2016) can be used to discover and categorize data into discrete units like concepts and themes in text or sequences of activities and events over time.

A second type of computational method is software tools that **automate** research activity. These tools carry out algorithmic data generation, processing, or analysis with little to no human intervention or oversight. For example, text mining (Debortoli et al., 2016) automatically extracts information from written resources through algorithms that extract and parse text, classifies it, derives patterns in it, and evaluates and displays the text using statistics, graphs, and/or visual diagrams. Similarly, cluster and social network analysis (Borgatti et al., 2013; Wierzchoń & Kłopotek, 2018) builds on algorithms that automatically parse data, categorize them based on statistical properties, and display the information statistically and/or graphically. Supervised or unsupervised machine learning algorithms (Gaber, 2010) can automatically produce hypotheses in the form of predictions, or they can automatically find patterns and relationships in the data that would be unlikely to find manually. Process mining (van der Aalst, 2016) automatically constructs models of how processes unfolded from digital trace data and uses algorithms to detect change and drift (e.g., Maaradji et al., 2017; Pentland et al. 2020) and algorithms that yield evidence-based suggestions for redesigning the mined processes (e.g., Cho et al., 2017).

Distinctions between computationally supported, augmented, and automated research are artificial but are used for purposes of clarification. In reality, all research today involves both manual and computational components on a continuum from exclusive choice to inclusive complements (Berente et al., 2019).

Computational methods have several advantages. They can substantially expand the reach and scope of investigation because human limits in terms of time and resource investment in data generation, processing, or analysis can be overcome using algorithms that do not have these limitations. Computational generation, processing, and analysis, can take substantially less time than manual execution of these tasks. Computational methods can also increase the reproducibility of data processing and analysis and help reduce the biases that are common in humans' interpretation and categorization of data.

However, computational methods also carry a number of challenges. At present, few clear and robust methodological guidelines are available that help explain how to use computational analyses in research that is based on hypothetico-deductive, inductive, or abductive intellectual reasoning. The use of computational analyses in such scenarios would involve steps that differ from those of other research methods, from the need to establish good operationalizations in organic data in hypothetico-deductive research to the role of a theoretical lexicon in connecting inductive identification of patterns in digital trace data to the established scientific knowledge in a research community.

Other challenges of computational methods include the difficulty of analyzing complex and messy social phenomena through large digital data archives (Walsham, 2015) and researchers' tendency to oversimplify (naturalize) complex relationships in digital data, which limits their search for meaning (Törnberg & Törnberg, 2018). Computational methods can also make it challenging to focus on and account for the context(s) in which digital trace data are generated (Whelan et al., 2016). These methods also typically rely on organic research data, which produces validity issues (Xu et al., 2020) such as threats from errors in algorithmic outputs, benign errors from relying on probabilistic algorithms such as random search, and lack of generalizability and replicability because digital traces tend to be produced by one digital technology, system, or platform while the behavior or phenomena being studied typically transcends such boundaries.

5.5 Mixed Methods

Mixed methods research is a type of inquiry that features the sequential or concurrent combination of methods for data collection and analysis. Mixed method research emerged in response to the "paradigm wars" between qualitative and quantitative researchers and because it is a pragmatic way to use the strengths of a pluralistic approach to research that combines the strengths of research methods.

Mixed methods designs historically incorporate methods from the quantitative and qualitative research traditions, but mixed methods from other traditions, such as design and quantitative methods or computational and qualitative methods, are also becoming more common. The key to mixed methods in whatever form is always to combine research methods to answer research questions that could not be answered otherwise.

Mixed method research has the **aim** of strengthening inferences, providing a greater diversity of views, and enabling researchers to answer confirmatory and exploratory questions simultaneously while verifying and generating theory at the same time. In other words, mixed method research has the advantages of leveraging the complementary strengths of research methods and mitigating their weaknesses while offering deeper insights into a phenomenon than each of the methods alone could provide. Therefore, mixed methods can lead to better and more accurate inferences from data, often termed meta-inferences: theoretical statements, narratives, concepts, and theoretical logic that are inferred through the integration of findings from the various strands of research that are involved in the mixed method study (e.g., qualitative and qualitative methods).

Conducting mixed method research has five major **purposes** (Greene et al., 1989; Venkatesh et al., 2013)—triangulation, complementarity, initiation, development, and expansion—any of which justify employing a mixed method research design. Triangulation is used to establish convergence of and corroborate results from multiple methods and designs used to study the same phenomenon. Complementarity refers to elaboration, enhancement, illustration, and clarification of the results from one method with results from another method. Initiation finds paradoxes and contradictions that lead to a re-framing of the research questions. Development uses the findings from one method to help inform the other method, such that its use is developmental in nature. Finally, expansion is used to expand the breadth and range of research by using different methods for different components of an inquiry.

Mixed method research carries a number of **design challenges**:

1. Weighing means deciding whether to give the components (e.g., qualitative or quantitative) of a mixed study equal status or to allow one to dominate.
2. Timing concerns the temporal ordering of the phases in which the methods are carried out: sequential (one after another), parallel (both separately but concurrently), conversion (data from one method is transformed to be used with another method), or fully integrated (all at once). Fig. 5.15 illustrates the design choices. QL in these examples denotes qualitative methods, and QN denotes quantitative methods, although the element could be reversed or replaced with another method (e.g., DS for design science or CM for computational methods).
3. Placing refers to deciding in which phase of the research process the "mixing" of methods should occur (in the research questions, methods of data collection, research methods, during data analysis, or data interpretation). For example, this

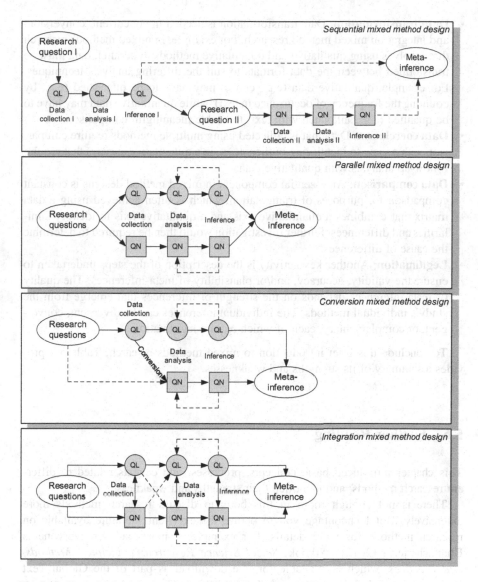

Fig. 5.15 Typical mixed method designs (Tashakkori et al., 2012)

decision must be made in conversion designs (see Fig. 5.15). An example is provided in Mertens and Recker (2020a).

In mixed method research, the processes for data collection, data analysis, and drawing of inferences and conclusions depend on the type of research methods that are used in the mixed design. In addition to the general guidelines for using each of the techniques, a few additional particularities should be considered in mixed method research:

- **Data transformation**: Data transformation is needed in concurrent, conversion, and integration mixed method research. For example, in mixed methods research that involves using qualitative and quantitative methods in parallel, data must be transformed between the data formats to suit the differing analysis techniques. For example, qualitative data (e.g., codes) may have to be quantified (e.g., by counting the frequency of occurrence in text), while quantitative data may have to be qualified (e.g., annotated with text) to enable meaningful comparison.
- **Data correlation**: Data that is collected using multiple methods require comparison with a view to identifying outliers (e.g., in a quantitative survey) that require follow-up analysis with qualitative data.
- **Data comparison**: An essential component in mixed method designs is constant comparison for purposes of triangulation, which is often achieved using a data matrix that combines a quantitative axis and a qualitative axis to identify similarities and differences. Further investigation would then be required to determine the cause of differences.
- **Legitimation**: Another key activity is the description of the steps undertaken to ensure the validity, accuracy, and/or plausibility of meta-inferences. The quality of meta-inferences depends on the strength of inferences that emerge from the study's individual methods. The individual inferences can be divergent, convergent, or complementary, each of which require legitimation.

To conclude this brief introduction to mixed methods research, Table 5.7 provides a summary of its strengths and weaknesses.

5.6   Further Reading

This chapter introduced basic concepts, processes, and caveats related to different research methods, and identified their strengths and weaknesses.

There is not enough room in this book to discuss research methods more extensively. But I encourage you to peruse the excellent literature available on research methods for more details. For example, a must-read for everyone is Bhattacherjee's (2012) textbook, *Social Science Research: Principles, Methods, and Practices*, which is available for free download as part of the Global Text Project (https://scholarcommons.usf.edu/oa_textbooks/3/).

This chapter started with a brief overview of the field's methodological pluralism, but there is an entire stream of literature that deals with this view (Iivari & Lyytinen, 1999; Lyytinen & King, 2004). This stream of literature also features perspectives from those that advocate uniformity (Benbasat & Weber, 1996), to those that address methodological arbitrariness (Gregor, 2018; Treiblmaier, 2018), to those that call for disciplined pluralism (Landry & Banville, 1992; Mingers, 2001; Robey, 1996).

A large variety of excellent resources also deal with quantitative research methods. A starting point for reading about quantitative research is the webpage http://www.janrecker.com/quantitative-research-in-information-systems/. You can

Table 5.7 Strengths and weaknesses of mixed method research

Strengths	Weaknesses
Words, pictures, artefacts, and narrative can be used to add meaning to numbers.	It can be difficult for a single researcher to carry out both qualitative and quantitative research, especially if two or more approaches are to be used concurrently.
Numbers can be used to add precision to words, pictures, artefacts, and narrative.	The researcher must learn about multiple methods and learn to understand how to mix them appropriately.
The research can benefit from the individual strengths of different research methods.	Methodological purists contend that one should always work in either a qualitative or a quantitative paradigm.
The researcher can more easily generate and rigorously test a theory.	Mixed method research is typically more resource-intensive than research that uses a single method and may require a larger research team.
Mixed method research can answer a broader and more complete range of research questions because the researcher is not confined to a single method.	Mixed method research is typically more time-consuming than research that uses a single method.
Mixed method research can be used to provide stronger evidence for a conclusion through convergence and corroboration of findings.	Some of the details of mixed research remain to be worked out fully by research methodologists (e.g., problems of paradigm mixing, how to analyze quantitative data qualitatively, how to interpret conflicting results).
Mixed method research can be used to increase the generalizability of the results.	Mixed method research can be difficult to publish (e.g., because it requires more space).

learn more about the philosophical basis of quantitative research in Popper (1959) and Hempel (1965). Introductions to their ideas and those of relevant others are provided by philosophy of science textbooks (e.g., Chalmers, 1999; Godfrey-Smith, 2003) and articles on how information systems build on these ideas, or not (e.g., Siponen & Klaavuniemi, 2020).

If you are interested in procedural models for developing and assessing measures and measurements, you can read articles that report at some length about their development procedures (Bailey & Pearson, 1983; Davis, 1989; Goodhue, 1998; Moore & Benbasat, 1991; Recker & Rosemann, 2010a).

Good textbooks on survey research include Fowler's (2013) textbook, as well as Babbie (1990), Czaja and Blair (1996). Be sure you check regularly for methodological advances in journal articles, such as those introduced in Baruch and Holtom (2008), Kaplowitz et al. (2004), King and He (2005). I have also co-authored an introductory textbook on quantitative data analysis in accounting and information systems research (Mertens et al., 2017), which can be another entry point for further reading.

A seminal book on experimental research is Shadish et al. (2001), and a wonderful introduction to behavioral experimentation is Slater's (2005) book, *Opening Skinner's Box: Great Psychological Experiments of the Twentieth Century*. I find inspiration on the quantitative side of research from books such as *Freakonomics* (Levitt & Dubner, 2005) and *Fermat's Last Theorem* (Singh, 1997).

Useful additions in terms of the processes and challenges of quantitative methods have been made in, for example, the computer sciences, which has an extensive tradition in discussing quantitative methods, such as threats to validity. Wohlin et al.'s (2000) book on experimental software engineering, for example, discusses many of the most important threats to validity, such as lack of representativeness of independent variables, pre-test sensitivity to treatments, fatigue and learning effects, and dependent variables' lack of sensitivity. Vegas et al. (2016) discuss the advantages and disadvantages of a wider range of experiment designs than has been discussed here, such as independent measures, repeated measures, crossover, matched-pairs, and other kinds of mixed designs.

Another important debate in the realm of quantitative research is that on reflective versus formative measurement. I abstained from this discussion because it could have muddied what I think are more fundamental issues, such as operationalization and measurement. Still, this methodological discussion is an important one that affects all quantitative researchers' efforts. Several viewpoints pertaining to this debate are available (Aguirre-Urreta & Marakas, 2012; Centefelli & Bassellier, 2009; Diamantopoulos, 2001; Diamantopoulos & Siguaw, 2006; Diamantopoulos & Winklhofer, 2001; Kim et al., 2010; Petter et al., 2007). I encourage you to study these and other papers.

Another debate in quantitative research deals with the choice of analysis approaches and toolsets, such as the longstanding debate on the relative merits and limitations of the various approaches to structural equation modelling (Goodhue et al., 2006, 2012; Hair et al., 2011; Marcoulides & Saunders, 2006; Ringle et al., 2012). This debate has resulted in many updates to available guidelines for their application.

Finally, the perennial debate in quantitative research about null hypothesis significance testing (Branch, 2014; Cohen, 1994; Pernet, 2016; Schwab et al., 2011; Szucs & Ioannidis, 2017; Wasserstein & Lazar, 2016; Wasserstein et al., 2019) focuses on the existence and mitigation of problematic practices in the interpretation and use of statistics that involve the well-known p-value. I have also worked on a set of updated guidelines for quantitative researchers for dealing with these issues (Mertens & Recker, 2020b), which I encourage you to read.

Concerning qualitative methods, the webpage http://www.qual.auckland.ac.nz/ is an excellent resource for qualitative researchers in information systems. Myers (2009) is an excellent introductory book about qualitative research in business and management. Other seminal books include (Denzin & Lincoln, 2005; Flick, 2018; Silverman, 2013).

Literature on qualitative research methods is also available. The classic textbook on case study research is Yin's (2009) book, which is filled with guidelines and many examples from social science research. Good resources are available on the techniques involved in case study research, such as interviewing (Fontana & Frey, 2000; Kvale, 1996; Myers & Newman, 2007; Rubin & Rubin, 2004; Schultze & Avital, 2011) and qualitative data analysis (Miles & Huberman, 1994; Saldana, 2016).

An excellent introduction to the action research method is Susman and Evered (1978). For a more in-depth look at the method, the collection of articles in Kemmis and McTaggart (1988) is useful. In information systems research, a good place to start is Baskerville and Wood-Harper (1996, 1998) and *MIS Quarterly*'s 2004 special issue on action research, especially Baskerville and Myers (2004). More recent review and methodological papers on action research include (Aakhus et al., 2014; Avison et al., 2018; Mathiassen et al., 2012; Sein et al., 2011).

The key literature on grounded theory includes the seminal works (Strauss & Corbin, 1994, 1998) and (Glaser & Strauss, 1967). Another excellent book is the *Handbook on Grounded Theory* (Bryant & Charmaz, 2007). The most practical books on grounded theory include (Charmaz, 2006; Urquhart, 2013). *MIS Quarterly* published Wiesche et al.'s (2019) review on grounded theory methodology, which is also useful.

Concerning design science, Hevner and Chatterjee's (2010) edited volume on design science research covers many topics, methodologies, examples, and guidelines in one book. A variety of methodological essays provide guidelines for this type of research (Carlsson, 2005; Gibson & Arnott, 2007; Gregor & Jones, 2007; Hevner, 2007; Hevner et al., 2004; Iivari, 2007; March & Smith, 1995; McKay & Marshall, 2005; Pfeffer et al., 2007; Sein et al., 2011). Excellent examples of good design science research in information systems include (Arazy et al., 2010; Germonprez et al., 2007; Markus et al., 2002; Müller-Wienbergen et al., 2011). The foundations of design science research are covered in Simon's (1996) *The Sciences of the Artificial*.

A number of debates and guidelines have been published that concern the processes of using computational methods (DiMaggio, 2015; Gaskin et al., 2014; Indulska et al., 2012; Levina & Vaast, 2015; Pentland et al., 2021), the relationships of computational methods to other, typically human, approaches to research (Berente et al., 2019; Lindberg, 2020; Whelan et al., 2016), and philosophical and institutional discussions about the nature, implications, and limitations of research carried out using computational methods (Glymour, 2004; Lazer ct al., 2009; Törnberg & Törnberg, 2018).

Finally, for mixed method research, I recommend Creswell's (2009) book on research design as introductory reading. Tashakkori and Teddlie's (2003) seminal *Handbook of Mixed Methods in Social and Behavioral Research* deals extensively with this type of research. Good debates about mixed method methodologies include (Johnson & Onwuegbuzie, 2004; Mingers, 2001; Sale et al., 2002), while examples of mixed method research in information systems research include Gable (1994), Wunderlich et al. (2019), and Crowston and Myers (2004).

References

Aakhus, M., Ågerfalk, P. J., Lyytinen, K., & Te'Eni, D. (2014). Symbolic Action Research in Information Systems: Introduction to the Special Issue. *MIS Quarterly, 38*(4), 1187–1200.

Aguirre-Urreta, M. I., & Marakas, G. M. (2012). Revisiting Bias Due to Construct Misspecification: Different Results from Considering Coefficients in Standardized Form. *MIS Quarterly, 36*(1), 123–138.

Ang, J. S. K., Sum, C.-C., & Yeo, L.-N. (2002). A Multiple-Case Design Methodology for Studying MRP Success and CSFs. *Information & Management, 39*(4), 271–281.

Arazy, O., Kumar, N., & Shapira, B. (2010). A Theory-Driven Design Framework for Social Recommender Systems. *Journal of the Association for Information Systems, 11*(9), 455–490.

Avison, D. E., Davison, R. M., & Malaurent, J. (2018). Information Systems Action Research: Debunking Myths and Overcoming Barriers. *Information & Management, 55*(2), 177–187. https://doi.org/10.1016/j.im.2017.05.004

Avison, D. E., & Myers, M. D. (1995). Information Systems and Anthropology: An Anthropological Perspective on IT and Organizational Culture. *Information Technology & People, 8*(3), 43–56.

Babbie, E. R. (1990). *Survey Research Methods*. Wadsworth.

Bailey, J. E., & Pearson, S. W. (1983). Development of a Tool for Measuring and Analyzing Computer User Satisfaction. *Management Science, 29*(5), 530–545.

Bandara, W., Furtmueller, E., Gorbacheva, E., Miskon, S., & Beekhuyzen, J. (2015). Achieving Rigor in Literature Reviews: Insights from Qualitative Data Analysis and Tool-Support. *Communications of the Association for Information Systems, 37*(8), 154–204.

Bandara, W., Gable, G. G., & Rosemann, M. (2005). Factors and Measures of Business Process Modelling: Model Building Through a Multiple Case Study. *European Journal of Information Systems, 14*(4), 347–360.

Bandara, W., & Rosemann, M. (2005). What Are the Secrets of Successful Process Modeling? Insights From an Australian Case Study. *Systèmes d'Information et Management, 10*(3), 47–68.

Baruch, Y., & Holtom, B. C. (2008). Survey Response Rate Levels and Trends in Organizational Research. *Human Relations, 61*(8), 1139–1160.

Baskerville, R., Kaul, M., & Storey, V. C. (2017). Establishing Reliability in Design Science Research. In *38th International Conference on Information Systems, Seoul, Korea*.

Baskerville, R., & Myers, M. D. (2004). Special Issue on Action Research in Information Systems: Making IS Research Relevant to Practice: Foreword. *MIS Quarterly, 28*(3), 329–335.

Baskerville, R., & Wood-Harper, A. T. (1996). A Critical Perspective on Action Research as a Method for Information Systems Research. *Journal of Information Technology, 11*(3), 235–246.

Baskerville, R., & Wood-Harper, A. T. (1998). Diversity in Information Systems Action Research Methods. *European Journal of Information Systems, 7*(2), 90–107.

Bazeley, P. (2007). *Qualitative Data Analysis with NVivo* (2nd ed.). Sage.

Benbasat, I., & Wang, W. (2005). Trust In and Adoption of Online Recommendation Agents. *Journal of the Association for Information Systems, 6*(3), 72–101. https://doi.org/10.17705/1jais.00065

Benbasat, I., & Weber, R. (1996). Research Commentary: Rethinking "Diversity" in Information Systems Research. *Information Systems Research, 7*(4), 389–399.

Berente, N., Seidel, S., & Safadi, H. (2019). Data-Driven Computationally-Intensive Theory Development. *Information Systems Research, 30*(1), 50–64.

Berente, N., & Yoo, Y. (2012). Institutional Contradictions and Loose Coupling: Postimplementation of NASA's Enterprise Information System. *Information Systems Research, 23*(2), 376–396.

Bhattacherjee, A. (2012). *Social Science Research: Principles, Methods and Practices* (2nd ed.). Global Text Project.

Block, J. (1961). *The Q-Sort Method in Personality Assessment and Psychiatric Research*. Charles C. Thomas Publisher.

Borgatti, S. P., Everett, M. G., & Johnson, J. C. (2013). *Analyzing Social Networks*. Sage.

Bosco, F. A., Uggerslev, K. L., & Steel, P. (2017). MetaBUS as a Vehicle for Facilitating Meta-analysis. *Human Resource Management Review, 27*(1), 237–254.

Boudreau, M.-C., Gefen, D., & Straub, D. W. (2001). Validation in Information Systems Research: A State-of-the-Art Assessment. *MIS Quarterly, 25*(1), 1–16.

Branch, M. (2014). Malignant Side Effects of Null-hypothesis Significance Testing. *Theory & Psychology, 24*(2), 256–277.

Briggs, C. L. (1986). *Learning How to Ask: A Sociolinguistic Appraisal of the Role of the Interview in Social Science Research.* Cambridge University Press.

Bryant, A., & Charmaz, K. C. (Eds.). (2007). *The SAGE Handbook of Grounded Theory.* Sage.

Bryant, T., Hughes, J., Myers, M. D., Trauth, E., & Urquhart, C. (2004). Twenty Years of Applying Grounded Theory in Information Systems: A Coding Method, Useful Theory Generation Method, or an Orthodox Positivist Method of Data Analysis? In B. Kaplan, D. P. Truex, D. G. Wastell, A. T. Wood-Harper, & J. I. DeGross (Eds.), *Information Systems Research: Relevant Theory and Informed Practice* (pp. 649–650). Kluwer Academic Publishing.

Bryman, A., & Cramer, D. (2008). *Quantitative Data Analysis with SPSS 14, 15 & 16: A Guide for Social Scientists.* Routledge.

Burgess, C., & Lund, K. (1997). Modelling Parsing Constraints with High-dimensional Context Space. *Language and Cognitive Processes, 12*(2/3), 177–210.

Burrell, G., & Morgan, G. (1979). *Sociological Paradigms and Organizational Analysis: Elements of the Sociology of Corporate Life.* Ashgate Publishing.

Burton-Jones, A., & Lee, A. S. (2017). Thinking About Measures and Measurement in Positivist Research: A Proposal for Refocusing on Fundamentals. *Information Systems Research, 28*(3), 451–467.

Carlsson, S. A. (2005). Developing Information Systems Design Knowledge: A Critical Realist Perspective. *The Electronic Journal of Business Research Methodology, 3*(2), 93–102.

Centefelli, R. T., & Bassellier, G. (2009). Interpretation of Formative Measurement in Information Systems Research. *MIS Quarterly, 33*(4), 689–708.

Chalmers, A. F. (1999). *What Is This Thing Called Science?* (3rd ed.). Hackett.

Chan, H. C., Kim, H.-W., & Tan, W. C. (2006). Information Systems Citation Patterns from International Conference on Information Systems Articles. *Journal of the American Society for Information Science and Technology, 57*(9), 1263–1274.

Charmaz, K. C. (2006). *Constructing Grounded Theory: A Practical Guide through Qualitative Analysis.* Sage.

Chen, W. S., & Hirschheim, R. (2004). A Paradigmatic and Methodological Examination of Information Systems Research from 1991 to 2001. *Information Systems Journal, 14*(3), 197–235.

Cho, M., Song, M., Comuzzi, M., & Yoo, S. (2017). Evaluating the Effect of Best Practices for Business Process Redesign: An Evidence-based Approach Based on Process Mining Techniques. *Decision Support Systems, 104*, 92–103.

Chudoba, K. M., & Maznevski, M. L. (2000). Bridging Space over Time: Global Virtual Team Dynamics and Effectiveness. *Organization Science, 11*(5), 473–492.

Churchill, G. A., Jr. (1979). A Paradigm for Developing Better Measures of Marketing Constructs. *Journal of Marketing Research, 16*(1), 64–73.

Clark, P. A. (1972). *Action Research and Organizational Change.* Harper and Row.

Cohen, J. (1960). A Coefficient of Agreement for Nominal Scales. *Educational and Psychological Measurement, 20*(1), 37–46.

Cohen, J. (1994). The Earth is Round (p 0.05). *American Psychologist, 49*(12), 997–1003.

Colapinto, J. (2001). *As Nature Made Him: The Boy Who Was Raised As A Girl.* Harper Perennials.

Couper, M. P., Traugott, M. W., & Lamias, M. J. (2001). Web Survey Design & Administration. *Public Opinion Quarterly, 65*(2), 230–253.

Creswell, J. W. (2009). *Research Design: Qualitative, Quantitative, and Mixed Methods Approaches* (3rd ed.). Sage Publications.

Cronbach, L. J. (1951). Coefficient Alpha and the Internal Structure of Tests. *Psychometrika, 16*(3), 291–334.

Cronbach, L. J., & Meehl, P. E. (1955). Construct Validity in Psychological Tests. *Psychological Bulletin, 52*(4), 281–302.

Crowston, K., & Myers, M. D. (2004). Information Technology and the Transformation of Industries: Three Research Perspectives. *Journal of Strategic Information Systems, 13*(1), 5–28.

Czaja, R. F., & Blair, J. (1996). *Designing Surveys: A Guide to Decisions and Procedures*. Pine Forge Press.

Davidson, R., & MacKinnon, J. G. (1993). *Estimation and Inference in Econometrics*. Oxford University Press.

Davis, F. D. (1989). Perceived Usefulness, Perceived Ease of Use, and User Acceptance of Information Technology. *MIS Quarterly, 13*(3), 319–340.

Debortoli, S., Müller, O., Junglas, I., & Vom Brocke, J. (2016). Text Mining For Information Systems Researchers: An Annotated Topic Modeling Tutorial. *Communications of the Association for Information Systems, 39*(7), 110–135.

Denzin, N. K., & Lincoln, Y. S. (Eds.). (2005). *Handbook of Qualitative Research* (3rd ed.). Sage.

Dhar, V. (2013). Data Science and Prediction. *Communications of the ACM, 56*(12), 64–73.

Diamantopoulos, A. (2001). Incorporating Formative Measures into Covariance-Based Structural Equation Models. *MIS Quarterly, 35*(2), 335–358.

Diamantopoulos, A., & Siguaw, J. A. (2006). Formative Versus Reflective Indicators in Organizational Measure Development: A Comparison and Empirical Illustration. *British Journal of Management, 17*(4), 263–282.

Diamantopoulos, A., & Winklhofer, H. M. (2001). Index Construction with Formative Indicators: An Alternative to Scale Development. *Journal of Marketing Research, 38*(2), 259–277.

DiMaggio, P. J. (2015). Adapting Computational Text Analysis to Social Science (and Vice Versa). *Big Data & Society, 2*(2), 1–5. https://doi.org/10.1177/2053951715602908

Doll, W. J., & Torkzadeh, G. (1998). Developing a Multidimensional Measure of System-Use in an Organizational Context. *Information & Management, 33*(4), 171–185.

Dumais, S. (2004). Latent Semantic Analysis. *Annual Review of Information Science and Technology, 38*(1), 188–230.

Dutta, S., Zbaracki, M. J., & Bergen, M. (2003). Pricing Process as a Capability: A Resource-based Perspective. *Strategic Management Journal, 24*(7), 615–630.

Elden, M., & Chisholm, R. F. (1993). Emerging Varieties of Action Research: Introduction to the Special Issue. *Human Relations, 46*(2), 121–142. https://doi.org/10.1177/001872679304600201

Feldman, M. S. (1995). *Strategies for Interpreting Qualitative Data* (Vol. 13). Sage.

Field, A. (2013). *Discovering Statistics using IBM SPSS Statistics*. Sage.

Flick, U. (2018). *An Introduction to Qualitative Research* (6th ed.). Sage.

Fontana, A., & Frey, J. H. (2000). The Interview: From Structured Questions to Negotiated Text. In N. K. Denzin & Y. S. Lincoln (Eds.), *Handbook of Qualitative Research* (2nd ed., pp. 645–672). Sage.

Fowler, F. J. (2013). *Survey Research Methods* (5th ed.). Sage.

Freelon, D. (2014). On the Interpretation of Digital Trace Data in Communication and Social Computing Research. *Journal of Broadcasting & Electronic Media, 58*(1), 59–75.

Freeman, L. (1990). *The Story of Anna O*. Paragon House.

Fromkin, H. L., & Streufert, S. (1976). *Laboratory Experimentation*. Rand McNally College Publishing Company.

Gaber, M. M. (Ed.). (2010). *Scientific Data Mining and Knowledge Discovery*. Springer.

Gable, G. G. (1994). Integrating Case Study and Survey Research Methods: An Example in Information Systems. *European Journal of Information Systems, 3*(2), 112–126.

Gable, G. G., Sedera, D., & Chan, T. (2008). Re-conceptualizing Information System Success: The IS-Impact Measurement Model. *Journal of the Association for Information Systems, 9*(7), 377–408.

Galliers, R. D., & Whitley, E. A. (2007). Vive les Differences? Developing a Profile of European Information Systems Research as a Basis for International Comparisons. *European Journal of Information Systems, 16*(1), 20–35.

Garcia-Pérez, M. A. (2012). Statistical Conclusion Validity: Some Common Threats and Simple Remedies. *Frontiers in Psychology, 3*(325), 1–11. https://doi.org/10.3389/fpsyg.2012.00325

Gaskin, J., Berente, N., Lyytinen, K., & Yoo, Y. (2014). Toward Generalizable Sociomaterial Inquiry: A Computational Approach for Zooming In and Out of Sociomaterial Routines. *MIS Quarterly, 38*(3), 849–871.

Gasson, S. (2004). Rigor in Grounded Theory Research: An Interpretive Perspective on Generating Theory from Qualitative Field Studies. In M. E. Whitman & A. B. Woszczynski (Eds.), *The Handbook of Information Systems Research* (pp. 79–102). Idea Group Publishing.

Germonprez, M., Hovorka, D. S., & Collopy, F. (2007). A Theory of Tailorable Technology Design. *Journal of the Association for Information Systems, 8*(6), 351–367.

Gibson, M., & Arnott, D. (2007). The Use of Focus Groups in Design Science Research. In *18th Australasian Conference on Information Systems, Toowoomba, Australia.*

Glaser, B. G. (1992). *Basics of Grounded Theory Analysis*. Sociology Press.

Glaser, B. G., & Strauss, A. L. (1965). *Awareness of Dying*. Routledge.

Glaser, B. G., & Strauss, A. L. (1967). *The Discovery of Grounded Theory: Strategies for Qualitative Research*. Aldine Publishing Company.

Glymour, C. (2004). The Automation of Discovery. *Daedalus, 133*(1), 69–77.

Godfrey-Smith, P. (2003). *Theory and Reality: An Introduction to the Philosophy of Science*. University of Chicago Press.

Goodhue, D. L. (1998). Development and Measurement Validity of A Task-Technology Fit Instrument for User Evaluations of Information Systems. *Decision Sciences, 29*(1), 105–139.

Goodhue, D. L., Lewis, W., & Thompson, R. L. (2006). PLS, Small Sample Size, and Statistical Power in MIS Research. In *39th Hawaii International Conference on System Sciences, Kauai, Hawaii.*

Goodhue, D. L., Lewis, W., & Thompson, R. L. (2012). Comparing PLS to Regression and LISREL: A Response to Marcoulides, Chin, and Saunders. *MIS Quarterly, 36*(3), 703–716.

Goodwin, L. D. (2001). Interrater Agreement and Reliability. *Measurement in Physical Education and Exercise Science, 5*(1), 13–34.

Greene, J. C., Caracelli, V. J., & Graham, W. F. (1989). Toward a Conceptual Framework for Mixed Method Evaluation Designs. *Educational Evaluation and Policy Analysis, 11*(3), 255–274.

Gregor, S. (2018). The Value of Feyerabend's Anarchic Thinking for Information Systems Research. *ACM SIGMIS Database, 49*(3), 114–120.

Gregor, S., Chandra Kruse, L., & Seidel, S. (2020). The Anatomy of a Design Principle. *Journal of the Association for Information Systems, 21*(6), 1622–1652. https://doi.org/10.17705/1jais.00649

Gregor, S., & Hevner, A. R. (2013). Positioning and Presenting Design Science Research for Maximum Impact. *MIS Quarterly, 37*(2), 337–355.

Gregor, S., & Jones, D. (2007). The Anatomy of a Design Theory. *Journal of the Association for Information Systems, 8*(5), 312–335.

Hair, J. F., Black, W. C., Babin, B. J., & Anderson, R. E. (2010). *Multivariate Data Analysis* (7th ed.). Prentice Hall.

Hair, J. F., Hult, G. T. M., Ringle, C. M., & Sarstedt, M. (2013). *A Primer on Partial Least Squares Structural Equation Modeling (PLS-SEM)*. Sage.

Hair, J. F., Ringle, C. M., & Sarstedt, M. (2011). PLS-SEM: Indeed a Silver Bullet. *The Journal of Marketing Theory and Practice, 19*(2), 139–152.

Hempel, C. G. (1965). *Aspects of Scientific Explanation and other Essays in the Philosophy of Science*. The Free Press.

Henfridsson, O., & Bygstad, B. (2013). The Generative Mechanisms of Digital Infrastructure Evolution. *MIS Quarterly, 37*(3), 907–931.

Hevner, A. R. (2007). A Three Cycle View of Design Science Research. *Scandinavian Journal of Information Systems, 19*(2), 87–92.

Hevner, A. R., & Chatterjee, S. (2010). *Design Research in Information Systems: Theory and Practice* (Vol. 22). Springer.

Hevner, A. R., March, S. T., Park, J., & Ram, S. (2004). Design Science in Information Systems Research. *MIS Quarterly, 28*(1), 75–105.

Hirschheim, R., & Newman, M. (1991). Symbolism and Information Systems Development: Myth, Metaphore and Magic. *Information Systems Research, 2*(1), 29–62.

Hoaglin, D. C., Light, R. J., McPeek, B., Mosteller, F., & Stoto, M. A. (1982). *Data for Decisions: Information Strategies for Policy Makers.* Abt Books.

Howison, J., Wiggins, A., & Crowston, K. (2011). Validity Issues in the Use of Social Network Analysis with Digital Trace Data. *Journal of the Association for Information Systems, 12*(12), 767–797.

Iivari, J. (2007). A Paradigmatic Analysis of Information Systems As a Design Science. *Scandinavian Journal of Information Systems, 19*(2), 39–64.

Iivari, J., Hansen, M. R. P., & Haj-Bolouri, A. (2021). A Proposal for Minimum Reusability Evaluation of Design Principles. *European Journal of Information Systems, 30*(3), 286–303. https://doi.org/10.1080/0960085X.2020.1793697

Iivari, J., & Lyytinen, K. (1999). Research on Information Systems Development in Scandinavia: Unity in Plurality. In W. L. Currie & R. D. Galliers (Eds.), *Rethinking Management Information Systems: An Interdisciplinary Perspective* (pp. 57–102). Oxford University Press.

Indulska, M., Hovorka, D. S., & Recker, J. (2012). Quantitative Approaches to Content Analysis: Identifying Conceptual Drift Across Publication Outlets. *European Journal of Information Systems, 21*(1), 49–69.

Johnson, R. B., & Onwuegbuzie, A. J. (2004). Mixed Methods Research: A Research Paradigm Whose Time Has Come. *Educational Researcher, 33*(7), 14–26.

Jöreskog, K. G., & Sörbom, D. (2001). *LISREL 8: User's Reference Guide.* Scientific Software International.

Kaplan, A. (1998/1964). *The Conduct of Inquiry: Methodology for Behavioral Science.* Transaction Publishers.

Kaplowitz, M. D., Hadlock, T. D., & Levine, R. (2004). A Comparison of Web and Mail Survey Response Rates. *Public Opinion Quarterly, 68*(1), 84–101.

Keil, M. (1995). Pulling the Plug: Software Project Management and the Problem of Project Escalation. *MIS Quarterly, 19*(4), 421–447.

Kemmis, S., & McTaggart, R. (1988). *The Action Research Reader* (3rd ed.). Deakin University.

Ketter, W., Peter, M., Collins, J., & Gupta, A. (2016). A Multiagent Competitive Gaming Platform to Address Societal Challenges. *MIS Quarterly, 40*(2), 447–460.

Kim, G., Shin, B., & Grover, V. (2010). Investigating Two Contradictory Views of Formative Measurement in Information Systems Research. *MIS Quarterly, 34*(2), 345–366.

King, W. R., & He, J. (2005). External Validity in IS Survey Research. *Communications of the Association for Information Systems, 16*(45), 880–894.

Klein, H. K., & Myers, M. D. (1999). A Set of Principles for Conducting and Evaluating Interpretive Field Studies in Information Systems. *MIS Quarterly, 23*(1), 67–94.

Kozinets, R. V. (2002). The Field behind the Screen: Using Netnography for Marketing Research in Online Communities. *Journal of Marketing Research, 39*(1), 61–72. https://doi.org/10.1509/jmkr.39.1.61.18935

Kvale, S. (1996). *InterViews: Introduction to Qualitative Research Interviewing.* Sage.

Landauer, T. K., Foltz, P. W., & Laham, D. (1998). Introduction to Latent Semantic Analysis. *Discourse Processes, 25*(2 & 3), 259–284.

Landry, M., & Banville, C. (1992). A Disciplined Methodological Pluralism for MIS Research. *Accounting, Management and Information Technologies, 2*(2), 77–97.

Lange, M., Mendling, J., & Recker, J. (2016). An Empirical Analysis of the Factors and Measures of Enterprise Architecture Management Success. *European Journal of Information Systems, 25* (5), 411–431.

Larsen, K. R. T., & Bong, C. H. (2016). A Tool for Addressing Construct Identity in Literature Reviews and Meta-Analyses. *MIS Quarterly, 40*(3), 529–551.

Larsen, K. R. T., Lukyanenko, R., Mueller, R. M., Storey, V. C., VanderMeer, D. E., Parsons, J., & Hovorka, D. S. (2020). Validity in Design Science Research. In *15th International Conference on Design Science Research in Information Systems and Technology, Kristiansand, Norway.*

Lazer, D., Pentland, A. P., Adamic, L. A., Aral, S., Barabási, A.-L., Brewer, D., Christakis, N., Contractor, N., Fowler, J., Gutmann, M., Jebara, T., King, G., Macy, M., Roy, D., & Van Alstyne, M. (2009). Computational Social Science. *Science, 323*(5915), 721–723.

Levina, N., & Vaast, E. (2015). Leveraging Archival Data from Online Communities for Grounded Process Theorizing. In K. D. Elsbach & R. M. Kramer (Eds.), *Handbook of Qualitative Organizational Research: Innovative Pathways and Methods* (pp. 215–224). Routledge.

Levitt, S. D., & Dubner, S. J. (2005). *Freakonomics: A Rogue Economist Explores the Hidden Side of Everything.* William Morrow.

Lindberg, A. (2020). Developing Theory through Integrating Human and Machine Pattern Recognition. *Journal of the Association for Information Systems, 21*(1), 90–116.

Lindman, H. R. (1974). *ANOVA in Complex Experimental Designs.* W. H. Freeman.

Liu, F., & Myers, M. D. (2011). An Analysis of the AIS Basket of Top Journals. *Journal of Systems and Information Technology, 13*(1), 5–24.

Liu, M., Hansen, S., & Tu, Q. (2014). The Community Source Approach to Software Development and the Kuali Experience. *Communications of the ACM, 57*(5), 88–96. https://doi.org/10.1145/2593687

Lukyanenko, R., Evermann, J., & Parsons, J. (2014). Instantiation Validity in IS Design Research. In M. C. Tremblay, D. E. VanderMeer, M. A. Rothenberger, A. Gupta, & V. Yoon (Eds.), *Advancing the Impact of Design Science: Moving from Theory to Practice* (Vol. 8463, pp. 321–328). Springer.

Lyytinen, K., & King, J. L. (2004). Nothing At The Center? Academic Legitimacy in the Information Systems Field. *Journal of the Association for Information Systems, 5*(6), 220–246.

Maaradji, A., Dumas, M., La Rosa, M., & Ostovar, A. (2017). Detecting Sudden and Gradual Drifts in Business Processes Based on Event Logs. *IEEE Transactions on Knowledge and Data Engineering, 29*(10), 2140–2154.

MacKenzie, S. B., Podsakoff, P. M., & Podsakoff, N. P. (2011). Construct Measurement and Validation Procedures in MIS and Behavioral Research: Integrating New and Existing Techniques. *MIS Quarterly, 35*(2), 293–334.

March, S. T., & Smith, G. F. (1995). Design and Natural Science Research on Information Technology. *Decision Support Systems, 15*(4), 251–266.

Marcoulides, G. A., & Saunders, C. (2006). Editor's Comments: PLS: A Silver Bullet? *MIS Quarterly, 30*(2), iii–ix.

Markus, M. L. (1983). Power, Politics, and MIS Implementation. *Communications of the ACM, 26* (6), 430–444.

Markus, M. L. (1994). Electronic Mail as the Medium of Managerial Choice. *Organization Science, 5*(4), 502–527.

Markus, M. L., Majchrzak, A., & Gasser, L. (2002). A Design Theory for Systems that Support Emergent Knowledge Processes. *MIS Quarterly, 26*(3), 179–212.

Matavire, R., & Brown, I. (2012). Profiling Grounded Theory Approaches in Information Systems Research. *European Journal of Information Systems, 22*(1), 119–129.

Mathiassen, L., Chiasson, M., & Germonprez, M. (2012). Style Composition in Action Research Publications. *MIS Quarterly, 36*(2), 347–363.

Mazaheri, E., Lagzian, M., & Hemmat, Z. (2020). Research Directions in Information Systems Field, Current Status and Future Trends: A Literature Analysis of AIS Basket of Top Journals. *Australasian Journal of Information Systems, 24.* https://doi.org/10.3127/ajis.v24i0.2045

McKay, J., & Marshall, P. (2005). A Review of Design Science in Information Systems. In *16th Australasian Conference on Information Systems, Sydney, Australia*.

Mertens, W., Pugliese, A., & Recker, J. (2017). *Quantitative Data Analysis: A Companion for Accounting and Information Systems Research*. Springer.

Mertens, W., & Recker, J. (2020a). How Store Managers can Empower their Teams to Engage in Constructive Deviance: Theory Development through a Multiple Case Study. *Journal of Retailing and Consumer Services, 52*, 101937.

Mertens, W., & Recker, J. (2020b). New Guidelines for Null Hypothesis Significance Testing in Hypothetico-Deductive IS Research. *Journal of the Association for Information Systems, 21*(4), 1072–1102. https://doi.org/10.17705/1jais.00629

Miles, M. B., & Huberman, M. (1994). *Qualitative Data Analysis* (2nd ed.). Sage.

Mingers, J. (2001). Combining IS Research Methods: Towards a Pluralist Methodology. *Information Systems Research, 12*(3), 240–259.

Moore, G. C., & Benbasat, I. (1991). Development of an Instrument to Measure the Perceptions of Adopting an Information Technology Innovation. *Information Systems Research, 2*(3), 192–222.

Morgan, D. L. (1997). *Focus Groups as Qualitative Research* (2nd ed.). Sage Publications.

Mullarkey, M. T., & Hevner, A. R. (2019). An Elaborated Action Design Research Process Model. *European Journal of Information Systems, 28*(1), 6–20. https://doi.org/10.1080/0960085X.2018.1451811

Müller-Wienbergen, F., Müller, O., Seidel, S., & Becker, J. (2011). Leaving the Beaten Tracks in Creative Work—A Design Theory for Systems that Support Convergent and Divergent Thinking. *Journal of the Association for Information Systems, 12*(11), 714–740.

Myers, M. D. (2009). *Qualitative Research in Business and Management*. Sage.

Myers, M. D., & Newman, M. (2007). The Qualitative Interview in IS Research: Examining the Craft. *Information and Organization, 17*(1), 2–26.

Nunamaker, J. F., Jr., Chen, M., & Purdin, T. D. M. (1991). Systems Development in Information Systems Research. *Journal of Management Information Systems, 7*(3), 89–106.

Olsen, D. R., Wygant, S. A., & Brown, B. L. (2004). Electronic Survey Administration: Assessment in the Twenty-First Century. *Assessment Update, 16*(3), 1–2.

Orlikowski, W. J. (1993). CASE Tools as Organizational Change: Investigating Incremental and Radical Changes in Systems Development. *MIS Quarterly, 17*(3), 309–340.

Peffers, K., Tuunanen, T., Rothenberger, M. A., & Chatterjee, S. (2007). A Design Science Research Methodology for Information Systems Research. *Journal of Management Information Systems, 24*(3), 45–77.

Pentland, B. T. (1999). Building Process Theory with Narrative: From Description to Explanation. *Academy of Management Review, 24*(4), 711–725.

Pentland, B. T., Recker, J., Ryan Wolf, J., & Wyner, G. (2020). Bringing Context Inside Process Research With Digital Trace Data. *Journal of the Association for Information Systems, 21*(5), 1214–1236. https://doi.org/10.17705/1jais.00635

Pentland, B. T., Vaast, E., & Ryan Wolf, J. (2021). Theorizing Process Dynamics with Directed Graphs: A Diachronic Analysis of Digital Trace Data. *MIS Quarterly, 45*(2), 967–984. https://doi.org/10.25300/MISQ/2021/15360

Perdue, B. C., & Summers, J. O. (1986). Checking the Success of Manipulations in Marketing Experiments. *Journal of Marketing Research, 23*(4), 317–326.

Pernet, C. (2016). Null Hypothesis Significance Testing: A Guide to Commonly Misunderstood Concepts and Recommendations for Good Practice [version 5; peer review: 2 approved, 2 not approved]. *F1000Research, 4*(621). https://doi.org/10.12688/f1000research.6963.5

Peshkin, A. (1986). *God's Choice: The Total World of a Fundamentalist Christian School*. University of Chicago Press.

Petter, S., Straub, D. W., & Rai, A. (2007). Specifying Formative Constructs in IS Research. *MIS Quarterly, 31*(4), 623–656.

Pettigrew, A. M. (1998). Catching Reality in Flight. In A. G. Bedeian (Ed.), *Management Laureates* (Vol. 5, pp. 171–206). JAI Press.

Pfeffer, K., Tuunanen, T., Rothenberger, M. A., & Chatterjee, S. (2007). A Design Science Research Methodology for Information Systems Research. *Journal of Management Information Systems, 24*(3), 45–77.

Popper, K. R. (1959). *The Logic of Scientific Discovery*. Basic Books (Logik der Forschung, Vienna, 1935)

Recker, J. (2007). Why Do We Keep Using A Process Modelling Technique? In *18th Australasian Conference on Information Systems, Toowoomba, Australia*.

Recker, J. (2010). Opportunities and Constraints: The Current Struggle with BPMN. *Business Process Management Journal, 16*(1), 181–201.

Recker, J. (2016). Toward A Design Theory for Green Information Systems. In *49th Hawaiian International Conference on Systems Sciences, Kuaui, Hawaii*.

Recker, J., & Dreiling, A. (2011). The Effects of Content Presentation Format and User Characteristics on Novice Developers' Understanding of Process Models. *Communications of the Association for Information Systems, 28*(6), 65–84.

Recker, J., Holten, R., Hummel, M., & Rosenkranz, C. (2017). How Agile Practices impact Customer Responsiveness and Development Success: A Field Study. *Project Management Journal, 48*(2), 99–121.

Recker, J., Lukyanenko, R., Jabbari, M., Samuel, B. M., & Castellanos, A. (2021). From Representation to Mediation: A New Agenda for Conceptual Modeling Research in a Digital World. *MIS Quarterly, 45*(1), 269–300. https://doi.org/10.25300/MISQ/2020/16207

Recker, J., & Rosemann, M. (2010a). A Measurement Instrument for Process Modeling Research: Development, Test and Procedural Model. *Scandinavian Journal of Information Systems, 22*(2), 3–30.

Recker, J., & Rosemann, M. (2010b). The Measurement of Perceived Ontological Deficiencies of Conceptual Modeling Grammars. *Data & Knowledge Engineering, 69*(5), 516–532.

Recker, J., Rosemann, M., Green, P., & Indulska, M. (2011). Do Ontological Deficiencies in Modeling Grammars Matter? *MIS Quarterly, 35*(1), 57–79.

Reich, B. H., & Benbasat, I. (1990). An Empirical Investigation of Factors Influencing the Success of Customer-Oriented Strategic Systems. *Information Systems Research, 1*(3), 325–347.

Reinhart, A. (2015). *Statistics Done Wrong: The Woefully Complete Guide*. No Starch Press.

Rialp, A., Rialp, J., Urbano, D., & Vaillant, Y. (2005). The Born-Global Phenomenon: A Comparative Case Study Research. *Journal of international Entrepreneurship, 3*(2), 133–171.

Ringle, C. M., Sarstedt, M., & Straub, D. W. (2012). Editor's Comments: A Critical Look at the Use of PLS-SEM in MIS Quarterly. *MIS Quarterly, 36*(1), iii–xiv.

Robey, D. (1996). Research Commentary: Diversity in Information Systems Research: Threat, Promise, and responsibility. *Information Systems Research, 7*(4), 400–408.

Rubin, H. J., & Rubin, I. S. (2004). *Qualitative Interviewing: The Art of Hearing Data* (2nd ed.). Sage.

Saldana, J. (2016). *The Coding Manual for Qualitative Researchers* (3rd ed.). Sage.

Sale, J. E. M., Lohfeld, L. H., & Brazil, K. (2002). Revisiting the Quantitative-Qualitative Debate: Implications for Mixed-Methods Research. *Quality & Quantity, 36*(1), 43–53.

Sarker, S., & Lee, A. S. (2001). Using A Positivist Case Research Methodology To Test Three Competing Theories-In-Use Of Business Process Redesign. *Journal of the Association for Information Systems, 2*(1), 1–72.

Sarker, S., & Lee, A. S. (2002). Using a Case Study to Test the Role of Three Key Social Enablers in ERP Implementation. *Information & Management, 40*(8), 813–829.

Sarker, S., Xiao, X., Beaulieu, T., & Lee, A. S. (2018). Learning from First-Generation Qualitative Approaches in the IS Discipline: An Evolutionary View and Some Implications for Authors and Evaluators (PART 1/2). *Journal of the Association for Information Systems, 19*(8), 752–774.

Schensul, S. L., Schensul, J. J., & LeCompte, M. D. (1999). *Essential Ethnographic Methods: Observations, Interviews, and Questionnaires*. AltaMira Press.

Schlagwein, D., & Bjørn-Andersen, N. (2014). Organizational Learning with Crowdsourcing: The Revelatory Case of LEGO. *Journal of the Association for Information Systems, 15*(11), 754–778.

Schultze, U., & Avital, M. (2011). Designing Interviews to Generate Rich Data for IS Research. *Information and Organization, 21*(1), 1–16.

Schwab, A., Abrahamson, E., Starbuck, W. H., & Fidler, F. (2011). PERSPECTIVE—Researchers Should Make Thoughtful Assessments Instead of Null-Hypothesis Significance Tests. *Organization Science, 22*(4), 1105–1120. https://doi.org/10.1287/orsc.1100.0557

Seidel, S., Chandra Kruse, L., Székely, N., Gau, M., & Stieger, D. (2018). Design Principles for Sensemaking Support Systems in Environmental Sustainability Transformations. *European Journal of Information Systems, 27*(2), 221–247.

Seidel, S., Recker, J., & vom Brocke, J. (2013). Sensemaking and Sustainable Practicing: Functional Affordances of Information Systems in Green Transformations. *MIS Quarterly, 37*(4), 1275–1299.

Seidel, S., & Urquhart, C. (2013). On Emergence and Forcing in Information Systems Grounded Theory Studies: The Case of Strauss and Corbin. *Journal of Information Technology, 28*(3), 237–260.

Sein, M. K., Henfridsson, O., Purao, S., Rossi, M., & Lindgren, R. (2011). Action Design Research. *MIS Quarterly, 35*(2), 37–56.

Shadish, W. R., Cook, T. D., & Campbell, D. T. (2001). *Experimental and Quasi-Experimental Designs for Generalized Causal Inference* (2nd ed.). Houghton Mifflin.

Silva, L., & Hirschheim, R. (2007). Fighting against Windmills: Strategic Information Systems and Organizational Deep Structures. *MIS Quarterly, 31*(2), 327–354.

Silverman, D. (2013). *Doing Qualitative Research* (4th ed.). Sage.

Simon, H. A. (1996). *The Sciences of the Artificial* (3rd ed.). MIT Press.

Singh, S. (1997). *Fermat's Last Theorem: The Story of a Riddle that Confounded the World's Greatest Minds for 358 Years*. Fourth Estate.

Siponen, M. T., & Klaavuniemi, T. (2020). Why is the Hypothetico-Deductive (H-D) Method in Information Systems not an H-D Method? *Information and Organization, 30*(1), 100287. https://doi.org/10.1016/j.infoandorg.2020.100287

Sivo, S. A., Saunders, C., Chang, Q., & Jiang, J. J. (2006). How Low Should You Go? Low Response Rates and the Validity of Inference in IS Questionnaire Research. *Journal of the Association for Information Systems, 7*(6), 351–414.

Slater, L. (2005). *Opening Skinner's Box: Great Psychological Experiments of the Twentieth Century*. Norton & Company.

Smith, A. E., & Humphreys, M. S. (2006). Evaluation of Unsupervised Semantic Mapping of Natural Language with Leximancer Concept Mapping. *Behavior Research Methods, Instruments, and Computers, 38*(2), 262–279.

Stevens, J. P. (2001). *Applied Multivariate Statistics for the Social Sciences* (4th ed.). Lawrence Erlbaum Associates.

Straub, D. W., Boudreau, M.-C., & Gefen, D. (2004). Validation Guidelines for IS Positivist Research. *Communications of the Association for Information Systems, 13*(24), 380–427.

Strauss, A. L., & Corbin, J. (1994). Grounded Theory Methodology: An Overview. In N. K. Denzin & Y. S. Lincoln (Eds.), *Handbook of Qualitative Research* (pp. 273–285). Sage.

Strauss, A. L., & Corbin, J. (1998). *Basics of Qualitative Research: Techniques and Procedures for Developing Grounded Theory* (2nd ed.). Sage.

Streiner, D. L. (2003). Starting at the Beginning: An Introduction to Coefficient Alpha and Internal Consistency. *Journal of Personality Assessment, 80*(1), 99–103.

Strong, D. M., & Volkoff, O. (2010). Understanding Organization-Enterprise System Fit: A Path to Theorizing the Information Technology Artifact. *MIS Quarterly, 34*(4), 731–756.

Susman, G. I., & Evered, R. D. (1978). An Assessment of the Science Merits of Action Research. *Administrative Science Quarterly, 23*(4), 582–603.

Szucs, D., & Ioannidis, J. P. A. (2017). When Null Hypothesis Significance Testing Is Unsuitable for Research: A Reassessment. *Frontiers in Human Neuroscience, 11*(390), 1–21. https://doi.org/10.3389/fnhum.2017.00390

Tabachnick, B. G., & Fidell, L. S. (2001). *Using Multivariate Statistics* (4th ed.). Allyn & Bacon.

Tashakkori, A., & Teddlie, C. (Eds.). (2003). *Handbook of Mixed Methods in Social and Behavioral Research*. Sage Publications.

Tashakkori, A., Teddlie, C., & Sines, M. C. (2012). Utilizing Mixed Methods in Psychological Research. In J. A. Schinka & W. F. Velicer (Eds.), *Research Methods in Psychology* (Vol. 2, 2nd ed., pp. 428–450). Wiley.

Thomas, D. M., & Watson, R. T. (2002). Q-Sorting and MIS Research: A Primer. *Communications of the Association for Information Systems, 8*(9), 141–156.

Törnberg, P., & Törnberg, A. (2018). The Limits of Computation: A Philosophical Critique of Contemporary Big Data Research. *Big Data & Society, 5*(2), 1–12. https://doi.org/10.1177/2053951718811843

Treiblmaier, H. (2018). Paul Feyerabend and the Art of Epistemological Anarchy—A Discussion of the Basic Tenets of Against Method and an Assessment of Their Potential Usefulness for the Information Systems Field. *ACM SIGMIS Database, 49*(2), 93–101. https://doi.org/10.1145/3229335.3229342

Tremblay, M. C., Hevner, A. R., & Berndt, D. J. (2010). Focus Groups for Artifact Refinement and Evaluation in Design Research. *Communications of the Association for Information Systems, 26*(27), 599–618.

Trochim, W. M. K., Donnelly, J. P., & Arora, K. (2016). *Research Methods: The Essential Knowledge Base* (2nd ed.). Cengage Learning.

Tsang, E. W. K., & Williams, J. N. (2012). Generalization and Induction: Misconceptions, Clarifications, and a Classification of Induction. *MIS Quarterly, 36*(3), 729–748.

Urquhart, C. (2013). *Grounded Theory for Qualitative Research: A Practical Guide*. Sage.

Urquhart, C., & Fernandez, W. D. (2013). Using Grounded Theory Method in Information Systems: The Researcher as Blank Slate and Other Myths. *Journal of Information Technology, 28*(3), 224–236.

Urquhart, C., Lehmann, H., & Myers, M. D. (2010). Putting the Theory Back Into Grounded Theory: Guidelines for Grounded Theory Studies in Information Systems. *Information Systems Journal, 20*(4), 357–381.

Vaast, E., Safadi, H., Lapointe, L., & Negoita, B. (2017). Social Media Affordances for Connective Action: An Examination of Microblogging Use During the Gulf of Mexico Oil Spill. *MIS Quarterly, 41*(4), 1179–1205.

van der Aalst, W. M. P. (2016). *Process Mining: Data Science in Action*. Springer.

Vegas, S., Apa, C., & Juristo, N. (2016). Crossover Designs in Software Engineering Experiments: Benefits and Perils. *IEEE Transactions on Software Engineering, 42*(2), 120–135. https://doi.org/10.1109/TSE.2015.2467378

Venable, J. R. (2006). The Role of Theory and Theorising in Design Science Research. In *1st International Conference on Design Science in Information Systems and Technology, Claremont, California*.

Venable, J. R., Pries-Heje, J., & Baskerville, R. (2016). FEDS: A Framework for Evaluation in Design Science Research. *European Journal of Information Systems, 25*(1), 77–89.

Venkatesh, V., Brown, S. A., & Bala, H. (2013). Bridging the Qualitative-Quantitative Divide: Guidelines for Conducting Mixed Methods Research in Information Systems. *MIS Quarterly, 37*(1), 21–54.

Walls, J. G., Widmeyer, G. R., & El Sawy, O. A. (1992). Building an Information Systems Design Theory for Vigilant EIS. *Information Systems Research, 3*(1), 36–59.

Walsham, G. (1995). Interpretive Case Studies in IS Research: Nature and Method. *European Journal of Information Systems, 4*, 74–81.

Walsham, G. (2015). Using Quantitative Data in Mixed-Design Grounded Theory Studies: An Enhanced Path to Formal Grounded Theory in Information Systems. *European Journal of Information Systems, 24*, 531–557.

Wassermann, S., & Faust, K. (1994). *Social Network Analysis: Methods and Applications*. Cambridge University Press.

Wasserstein, R. L., & Lazar, N. A. (2016). The ASA's Statement on P-values: Context, Process, and Purpose. *The American Statistician, 70*(2), 129–133.

Wasserstein, R. L., Schirm, A. L., & Lazar, N. A. (2019). Moving to a World Beyond "p < 0.05". *The American Statistician, 73*(Suppl 1), 1–19.

Whelan, E., Teigland, R., Vaast, E., & Butler, B. S. (2016). Expanding the Horizons of Digital Social Networks: Mixing Big Trace Datasets with Qualitative Approaches. *Information and Organization, 26*(1–2), 1–12.

Wierzchoń, S., & Kłopotek, M. (2018). *Modern Algorithms of Cluster Analysis*. Springer.

Wiesche, M., Jurisch, M., Yetton, P., & Krcmar, H. (2019). Grounded Theory Methodology in Information Systems Research. *MIS Quarterly, 41*(3), 685–701.

Wohlin, C., Runeson, P., Höst, M., Ohlsson, M. C., Regnell, B., & Wesslén, A. (2000). *Experimentation in Software Engineering: An Introduction*. Kluwer Academic Publishers.

Wunderlich, P., Veit, D. J., & Sarker, S. (2019). Adoption of Sustainable Technologies: A Mixed-Methods Study of German Households. *MIS Quarterly, 43*(2), 673–691. https://doi.org/10.25300/MISQ/2019/12112

Xu, H., Zhang, N., & Zhou, L. (2020). Validity Concerns in Research Using Organic Data. *Journal of Management, 46*(7), 1257–1274. https://doi.org/10.1177/0149206319862027

Yin, R. K. (2009). *Case Study Research: Design and Methods* (Vol. 5, 4th ed.). Sage Publications.

Yu, Y., Duan, W., & Cao, Q. (2013). The Impact of Social and Conventional Media on Firm Equity Value: A Sentiment Analysis Approach. *Decision Support Systems, 55*(4), 919–926.

Part III
Publishing Research

Chapter 6
Writing IS Research Articles

6.1 Why Publishing Is Important

Published research is a scholar's main vehicle by which to add to the body of knowledge. When we write about our research, we add to the stock of writings that make up the library of knowledge. Publications have traditionally been an accepted form of ensuring that knowledge persists, as opposed to oral dissemination of knowledge passed on from generation to generation.

Publications are also typically the only way we can build a manifestation of a research process–or of ourselves as scholars. Papers describe "the study," "the outcome," and in some sense also "the scholar." Over the course of your career, you are likely to meet scholars whose papers you have read. I have always found such meetings to be stimulating experiences—to identify the person behind a paper, to associate an idea with a face.

Before we continue with advice on publishing research, we should note some important characteristics that relate to this process. First, at the writing stage of research, we have typically completed the research itself, that is, we examined a phenomenon of interest, theorized about it, collected and analyzed data to test our ideas, and established a research outcome.

This comment is important. Research reports disclose information about research outcomes and the related processes when the research has uncovered findings that are worth reporting. One of the unfortunate characteristics of virtually all fields of research—and information systems research is no exception—is that we see only reports of successful research, that is, outcomes of research processes that have led to novel findings and contributions to knowledge and where the research reports have been peer-reviewed and accepted by the community for publication. We typically do not see research endeavors that were not successful because unsuccessful research is virtually never published. From my own experience, the number of such studies and research projects is, to say the least, high.

© Springer Nature Switzerland AG 2021
J. Recker, *Scientific Research in Information Systems*, Progress in IS,
https://doi.org/10.1007/978-3-030-85436-2_6

I have seen many attempts to produce research reports about projects that were not sufficiently successful to warrant publication. A common misapprehension is that "we have done this study so it should be published." Researchers perform case studies, surveys, and experiments that, for a variety of reasons, do not yield good findings or valid results, but the researchers involved still push to get a paper on the research published.

Why is this situation a problem? Publishing is about reporting findings, which requires telling "what you have found" rather than "what you have done." The results of research, whether a new theory, new empirical results, or a new artefact, are what is worth publishing. But not all results of research are findings that are worth telling. Some findings are not relevant to anyone. Others are well-established already.

There is, of course, also a flipside to this argument: In her book, *Research Confidential*, Hargittai (2009) suggests that scholars in the social sciences (such as information systems) may be unaware of certain problems in part because academics do not (or cannot) share stories of what did not work in their projects and how to deal with the associated challenges, especially in empirical research projects.

Either way, writing a good research article is challenging and consumes a great deal of time and dedication, so with all of our other commitments as academics, we should only write papers that are worth writing. Papers about "unsuccessful" research are simply too difficult to publish. Virtually none appear in most publication outlets. There are exceptions, of course (for example, the *Journal of Trial and Error* is dedicated to making the struggles of research public), but one is much better off not trying to publish unsuccessful research just for the sake of publishing. For example, many a time I have completed a study, examined the results, found them not to be strong or convincing enough, and still spent a great deal of time and effort trying to get a report on the study published. I failed in most cases to get the paper published. The point of my story is that I needed a lot of time to learn to "let go" of research projects and realize that you simply cannot get it right every time and not every study is "successful" enough to warrant the effort required for publishing it.

Despite all these problems related to writing, publishing is probably the key performance metric for any academic—students, early career researchers, and tenured faculty members alike.

Recall that an academic must produce **and** disseminate research results. Your publications advertise your skills, areas of interest, and expertise. They are a demonstration of how well you conduct research. Therefore, the **number** and **quality** of your publications will determine, at least to some degree, the level of success you will enjoy in your career. Your publications could influence your reputation, your ability to work at institutions where you want to work, and your salary, as most universities pay higher salaries to successful researchers with many excellent publications than they do to academics who are excellent in other areas of academic work, such as teaching or service, but not research.

As an example, when you finish your Ph.D. and perhaps a post-doctoral appointment and start your first academic position—typically, as an assistant professor, junior professor, or lecturer—you will be evaluated based on the number of scientific journals in which you have been published or for which you are writing. For example, to achieve tenure in some of the top information systems research schools, eight or more papers published in top journals are expected within five to six years of graduation (Dean et al., 2011). Whilst a range of criteria can affect who is hired as a young faculty member, such as the focus of their research, their experiences in teaching, and their success in obtaining grants or other funding, the one criterion that is almost always dominant is the list of publications and research in progress.

Publications are also a way to compare the success and productivity of individuals and institutions. Publicly available rankings track the publication performance of scholars and universities (e.g., https://www.aisresearchrankings.org/). Tools like as Harzing's (2010) *Publish or Perish* (https://harzing.com/resources/publish-or-perish) compare the publication productivity of scholars in all fields. Databases of the most successful scientists are available across all fields of science (Ioannidis et al., 2019).

While having many publications may be important, the quality of publications is much more important. While all publications are relevant to an academic's success, few really matter in terms of how they impact a field. Look at how citations of papers in the social sciences are dispersed (Larivière et al., 2009): More than 30% of papers are never cited, while 28% of papers attract 80% of the citations.

The number of <u>citations</u> is a typical metric by which to measure a paper's academic impact. Citations track papers referenced by other papers. Citations indicate how many scholars have used an article in their own lines of argumentation in a paper. Typically, it is assumed that papers that are cited often are "good" papers, else other scholars would not refer to them. There are exceptions to this rule, of course, such as when a paper contains flaws that other scholars attempt to address and overcome in their papers. In the publishing field, as in any other field, the top is sparsely populated and difficult to reach.

Citations are also an important metric for publication outlets. For example, the so-called journal impact factor is a scientometric index that reflects the yearly average number of citations that articles published in a given journal received. It is one of the key quality metrics of a scientific journal and is used with other criteria, such as the reputation and composition of its editorial board, to determine its ranking among academic journals. Journal ranking is a crucial tool academics use to compare the prestige and quality of publication outlets and to evaluate the papers published in the journal. The analogy is "if this paper was accepted for publication in that journal, it must be good because the journal is highly ranked."

Finally, citations also matter to individual scholars. Aside from the total number of papers published, citations in published papers is the second most important key performance indicator used to evaluate and compare academics. For example, Google Scholar (my own profile is at https://scholar.google.com/citations?user=HQcik5oAAAAJ) tracks citations not only by paper or journal but also by individual or institution. It is often used to rank individuals in a university or in a defined topic area.

In closing, it should be evident by now that publications and their impact are important to academics. But publications are also important for aspiring research students. Students' publications are indications of successful research training and are often a good indicator of the quality of a student's thesis. A thesis that builds on a set of successful publications is difficult for a thesis examiner to reject because some or all of the individual studies reported in the thesis have already been subjected to the peer review process and deemed acceptable.

Publication also advertises the strengths and areas of interest of the student, the research group, or even the university as a whole. Published research can also generate direct income from the federal government that the university uses to support its researchers' and students' research. An academic's life is often summarized in the saying that lends the name to Harzing's citation-tracking tool: "Publish or perish!"

6.2   How Publishing Works

Because of the importance of publishing research to scientists, scientific writing should be considered a strategic activity and should receive at least the same dedicated attention, training, and management that other parts of research receive.

In simple terms, the main message is that it is important to **publish high-impact papers** (as measured by citations, amongst other criteria) in **high-quality outlets**. Scientific publication outlets include books, book chapters, papers in conference proceedings, edited volumes, and journal articles. Each category has many options in terms of, for example, book publishers, conferences, and journals. It is a large jungle of publishing options, but publication outlets differ widely in terms of quality. Amongst journals alone are many hundreds of scientific journals published by a wide range of publishers that are principally interested in information systems scholarship. Some of these are considered "good" and some are not.

In most scientific fields, the highest-quality outlets are a set of **highly ranked journals**. To assist scholars in deciding which journals to target with their work, ranking lists have been developed that evaluate journals based on metrics such as impact factor, readership, editorial board composition, and other criteria. In information systems, for example, the College of Senior Scholars, a consortium of reputable scholars that have certain credentials, has jointly defined a set of eight elite journals, called the "Senior Scholars' Basket of Journals":

- Management Information Systems Quarterly
- Information Systems Research
- Journal of the Association for Information Systems
- European Journal of Information Systems
- Journal of Management Information Systems

- Information Systems Journal
- Journal of Information Technology
- Journal of Strategic Information Systems

Of course, many other journals not featuring on that list are good as well, and schools, universities, domain areas, and countries typically have their own ranking lists (e.g., as A-level, B-level, or C-level journals). In Australia, for example, a ranking exercise was conducted in 2010 as part of the "Excellence in Research in Australia" initiative (http://lamp.infosys.deakin.edu.au/era/?page=fordet10& selfor=0806). In Germany, the German Association for Business School Professors ranks a list of journals (https://vhbonline.org/en/vhb4you/vhb-jourqual/vhb-jourqual-3/complete-list) that are relevant to business school researchers (including information systems) in five tiers (A+, A, B, C, D). The listed journals for information systems in 2020 comprised 2 A+ journals, 10 A journals, 27 B journals, 42 C journals, and 8 D journals. Although widely disputed and certain to be changed over time, such ranking lists can be useful for learning about the outlets most highly esteemed and a journal's ranking on such a list gives some indication of how challenging it is to publish in that journal.

It is also important to note that not all research appears in journals. Scholars write entire books, for example (such as this one) and sometimes research is published as a refereed book chapter in an edited book. Scholars typically write fewer chapters than journal articles because book chapters are not considered as important, and some universities do not count them at all as publications as part of promotion or tenure decisions. Of course, this does by no means imply that the quality of these writings is worse (or better) than that of a journal article.

A third outlet for information systems researchers is conference proceedings, which contain copies of papers that were presented at the conference. They are usually shorter than journal articles and often describe research that is ongoing. Some universities recognize papers in conference proceedings in tenure or promotion decisions, but by and large they do not usually play a role as publications per se. In most countries, and certainly in the best universities, conference proceedings cannot be used to build an argument about a scholar's publication production or success because the review process at most conferences is significantly shortened and far less rigorous than it is for a good journal. In addition, the purpose of conferences is often to give academics an opportunity to present their ongoing research to the community so they can harvest opinions and feedback and new ideas about how they perform their research in the best possible way. Therefore, papers presented at conferences are usually meant to be a stepping-stone in the research and publication process, not the end goal.

Therefore, a good rule for any academic in Information systems is that you need to publish in journals, not conferences. In fact, publishing too many papers at conferences may even count against you. I know of the case of a colleague who was rejected for tenure because of a high ratio of conference papers to journal papers published. Because my colleague had published around fifty conference papers and

Table 6.1 Qualities of papers and research

Good research...	Good papers...
...is purposive.	...are purposive.
...has clearly defined goals.	...have clearly defined goals.
...follows a replicable procedure.	...contain reporting of procedures (including flaws) that is complete and honest.
...uses appropriate analytical techniques.	...describe the use of appropriate analytical techniques.
...provides conclusions that are limited to those clearly justified by the data or facts.	...present conclusions that are limited to those clearly justified by the data or facts.

five or so (good) journal papers, the committee felt that the researcher had a tendency "not to see studies through to the end."

So, how do we get to publishing in high-quality outlets? The most important rule when strategizing about publishing is that good papers build on good research (Table 6.1), and good publication outlets such as highly ranked journals only publish selected good research.

The first rule of publishing is that **you can write good papers only when you do good research so you can have good research outcomes**. If your research does not meet the quality criteria established and accepted for your type of inquiry (such as validity and reliability in quantitative methods), you will not be able to publish the research in a good journal, and even the most carefully executed experiment will not result in a good paper if you did not get good (that is, valid, reliable, and significant) results.

We can also apply this universal principle to a second key rule of publishing: **You can waste good research by not writing about it well enough**. As Bem (2003, p. 205) observed,

> the difference between the manuscripts accepted and the top 15 to 20% of those rejected is frequently the difference between good and less good writing. Moral: Do not expect journal reviewers to discern your brilliance through the smog of polluted writing. Revise your manuscript. Polish it. Proofread it. Then submit it.

A third key rule of publishing is that **journals are selective in what they publish**; they only look for certain types of contributions, so you need to submit papers only to journals that want to publish the type of contribution your research makes. Journals have different audiences and different aims, and only if your writing speaks to these aims and these audiences will the journal be interested in whether your work meets the first two criteria of good research written well.

6.3   Preparing Publications

With the importance of good research, good writing, and finding the right audience established, let us look at the publication process itself.

The Publishing Process

Scholarly publications "count" as scientific publications only if they are <u>peer-reviewed</u>. Peer review (also known as refereeing) means subjecting a scholarly work to the scrutiny of experts in the same field before a paper will be published. Peer review is the standard way of assuring quality in scientific work: Papers are evaluated by a set of knowledgeable peers who advise the journal whether the work can be accepted, considered again after revisions, or rejected outright.

Review by "knowledgeable peers" requires a community of experts in a narrowly defined field who are qualified to perform impartial review. Being impartial means that the reviewers are free of conflicts of interests, such as when authors and reviewers work together, work in the same institution, share the same advisor or mentor, or are otherwise professionally related. Because such situations could (but not necessarily) bias a reviewer's evaluation (positively or negatively), peer review demands that such conflicts of interests be avoided, as confirmed by both the authors and the reviewers.

As a safeguard against conflicts of interests, the most common mode of peer review is **double-blind**, where the authors and reviewers do not know each other's identity. Only editors in charge of the review process know the respective identities, and it is their responsibility to guarantee a review process that is free of potential conflicts of interest.

With this design, you will realize that peer review is a social process: authors submit their work for review, reviewers comment on their perception of the work's quality, and both sides engage in a social process of argumentation and negotiation.

The publication process through peer review typically works as follows: On submission of a paper for publication, the journal's or book's **editor** sends advance copies of the author's work to researchers who are experts in the field (known as "referees" or "reviewers") by e-mail or through a web-based manuscript processing system. Two or three referees usually review an article, although sometimes more. (I once received comments from six reviewers on a manuscript.)

These **referees** each return an evaluation of the work to the editor, noting weaknesses, problems, and suggestions for improvement. This evaluation is usually in the form of free text and can vary in length from a few lines to several pages.

The author usually sees most of the referees' comments after they pass through the editor—typically a successful senior scientist who is familiar with the field of the manuscript. The editor evaluates the reviewers' comment, forms his or her own opinion about the manuscript in light of the journal's or book's context, readership, and scope and decides whether the paper should be accepted, revised and resubmitted, or rejected outright. The editor then passes this decision to the author, along with the referees' comments.

An accepted manuscript will be published without changes other than, perhaps, copyediting, proofreading, and layout. While this outcome is what academics hope for, it also means the paper's content and its messages are frozen and can no longer be changed. A rejected manuscript will not be considered for publication by that outlet now or in the future; once rejected, always rejected. A revise-and-resubmit decision lies between acceptance and rejection, as the editor has decided not to publish the paper in its current form but also does not want to reject it outright. The request to revise the paper and resubmit it often occurs because the study or its outcomes are not as well described as the editors and reviewers would like or the paper contains insufficient data or evidence to substantiate the conclusions it offers. Editors might ask you to collect and/or analyze more data to substantiate your findings before making a final decision about whether to publish it. A revise-and-resubmit decision can form a loop—you revise the paper based on the comments you received, and the revision is evaluated again, resulting again in acceptance, rejection, or even another revise-and-resubmit decision.

During this process, the decisions to accept or reject a paper lies with the editor while the role of the referees is advisory. Editors are under no formal obligation to accept the reviewers' opinion although most times they follow the reviewers' advice. Furthermore, in scientific publication, the referees do not act as a group, do not communicate with one another, and are usually unaware of each other's identities or evaluations.

This process is common across various kinds of outlets, be they journals, conference proceedings, or scholarly books. The outlets usually provide information about their editorial and review processes to inform prospective authors about how they handle incoming manuscripts and how they make decisions about them.

Key Publishing Decisions

When selecting a suitable target outlet for an academic paper, keep several things in mind: First, the academic publishing process is a "one shot option": once you have published a result, you cannot publish it again in a better outlet or write another paper on the same finding and publish it elsewhere. This (mal-)practice is called double-dipping or self-plagiarism (a topic we return to in Chap. 7).

Second, the academic publishing process is an open publishing process: Once you publish an idea, it is out there with your name attached to it. This can be good or bad for a reputation, depending on the idea and the quality of the research conducted. (Believe me, I can name one or two papers I wish I had never written.)

Third, remember also that scientific writing is a skill that is typically not part of the curriculum for your doctoral degree (or any other degree you might have pursued). Good research writing takes time and practice. I give students several pieces of advice:

1. Write early and write often. Publish papers from your honors or masters-level research, or identify some areas of your work that are completed, and start writing. Target a conference (initially), then a reasonably good journal, and over time aim higher and higher. At the end of your studies, you will need to produce a thesis that documents your work, your research, and its outcomes.

Table 6.2 Paper-based research and research-based papers

Paper-based research	Research-based papers
You want to write a paper, so you start doing some research.	You did some research, and you seek to publish a paper about your findings.
Often deadline-driven.	Often results-driven.
Works relatively well for conference papers.	Often "too much to write about" for a conference paper.
Typically does not work well for publication in (good) journals.	Works well for publications in journals.
Rarely works for a thesis.	Works well for a thesis.

Theses range from 100 to more than 400 pages–essentially the length of a book. Writing papers is the best practice for writing a good thesis.

2. Read before you write. Get the "voice" of studies published in the journals you want to submit to in your head by reading as many of these studies—whether they are in your field or not—as possible.

3. Third, hire a professional editor if you have been told (or you already know) your writing is poor. A perfectly good study can be rejected outright if the editor cannot make himself or herself read bad writing. Like employers who read resumes all day, editors read and can choose from many studies; do not give them an excuse to toss yours aside and move to the next. I have published hundreds of papers, but I still pass on my manuscripts to a trusted professional editor from time to time to improve my writing.

Fourth, remember the difference between research-based papers and paper-based research. I often find, especially with young academics, that they plan to write because a deadline for a particular conference or journal issue submission is approaching, and they think, "Let's produce something for this outlet." I call this "paper-based research" and differentiate it from "research-based papers" (Table 6.2).

Paper-based research can be problematic because it is typically deadline-driven. From a call for papers to submission, we typically have only six to eighteen months to conduct research, produce an outcome, and write about it. Most substantial research consumes much more time than that. If you give yourself, say, twelve months to execute a study, your choices about what you do are constrained. For example, the research pretty automatically will not be longitudinal, as you cannot measure changes over years if you have only one year. In essence, paper-based research often boils down to the questions "which problem can I solve in timeframe X?", and "which methods will I use that will be acceptable for publishing this paper?" Applying acceptable methods is different from applying the best possible methods to solve a problem. Too many academics present their research and justify their choices because "we believe this approach will be accepted by reviewers." This approach is typical of papers-based research; it is not problem-driven research where the choice of an approach to use depends on its effectiveness for solving the problem, not by expectations about the least one can do to be published.

In summing up, publication is the final outcome of a study. The decision to present a study for publication should be driven by novel and insightful outcomes that should be communicated. In other words, the best reason for writing a paper is that the research is finished and successful in terms of useful results. This approach typically leads to much stronger papers because their contributions are better developed without catering to submission deadlines.

Managing Co-Authorship

Co-authored papers are the norm, not the exception, in scholarly publications because collaboration is a key element of scientific work. Collaboration might mean working with your supervisor or other junior or senior academics on topics of mutual interest.

Co-authoring papers is a preferred strategy for several reasons. Working by yourself requires that you not only to do all the work yourself but also that you be strong in all aspects of the research lifecycle, from problem identification to idea generation, theorizing, research methods, data analysis, and writing. Because of the amount of work required, you will also not be able to progress on as many projects and papers concurrently as colleagues who collaborate extensively. Collaborations offer the possibilities for synergizing based on mutual domain expertise, complementing the strengths you have with those of others, or simply sharing the workload.

A successful collaboration depends on with whom you work. There is a good reason that several well-known scholars co-author so many papers: They are good at what they do, which makes them attractive candidates for others to co-author papers with. One rule in co-authoring publications is work with people who are good at some aspect of scholarship—ideally, better than you are, because then you will have the opportunity to learn. I had the fortune to work with people who are better than I am in such aspects of research as theory development, data collection and analysis, and (importantly) writing, which has helped me to learn and get better at these things as well.

Aside from searching for and working with good people, look for complementarity of skills and alignment in working styles. Complementarity refers to the benefits of synergy that stem from working with people who provide strengths that are not the same as your own. If you are an expert in some area (say, quantitative data analyses), you may be a perfect collaborator for someone who needs such expertise. As for alignment, successful collaboration is likely to come from work with people who have similar work styles and with whom you enjoy working.

Many tasks are involved in the research lifecycle that can be shared:

- Developing an original idea
- Designing a study
- Organizing data collection
- Collecting data
- Analyzing data
- Writing and revising a paper

When these tasks are not only and solely performed by you, that is, when others were involved in some or all of these tasks, you should consider co-authorship. Making co-authorship decisions is important because on the one hand co-authorship confers credit to individuals for their contribution to academic tasks, which can have academic, social, and financial implications; but on the other hand, co-authorship also implies responsibility and accountability for published works.

My rule of thumb for deciding whether someone should be a co-author concerns whether he or she has:

1. made substantial contributions to the conception or design of the research or the acquisition, analysis, or interpretation of data for the research; and
2. made substantial contributions to drafting the publication or revising it critically for important intellectual content; and
3. given final approval of the version to be published; and
4. agreed to be accountable for all aspects of the work, including being accountable for the parts of the work he or she has done, being able to identify which co-authors are responsible for other parts of the work, and having integrity about the contributions of other co-authors.

These are my criteria; they may or may not be yours. They are also not entirely consistent with public or official regulations. For example, these four points are formulated more narrowly than the guidelines for good scientific practice published by the German central research funding body (DFG), which speak primarily of "participation" in acts of researching or writing. I speak of "contributions" because I have seen many scholars who are passive in their participation. In my view, co-authorship should demand more than attending meetings.

Similarly, in my view, authorship credit should not be claimed where contribution to a study consisted solely of acquiring funding or collecting data. Similarly, in my view, general supervision of a research group or management of a research project does not automatically constitute authorship. Many institutions follow other practices.

In determining your role in co-authorship, remember that good papers build on good research. Examine honestly your individual strengths and capabilities to determine your role:

- Are you an original thinker? Are you capable of extending the thinking in your field? Do you have new theoretical ideas?

- Are you an expert in conducting research? Do you know a great deal about methods? Approaches? Analysis techniques?
- Are you good at writing?

In most collaborations, different people have different, dedicated roles. This approach works much better than, for instance, having four expert analysts but no one who is a skilled writer.

One of the key decisions in publishing with co-authors is the order in which the authors will appear because credit for papers is usually ascribed to the first author, who receives most of the reputational credit for the publication. While every co-author is entitled to claim the paper as part of his or her publication record, co-authorship credit is more than the sum of its parts; everyone benefits, but the first author usually gets most of the credit because readers assume the first author took the lead.

Therefore, typical practices when it comes to putting the authors' names on a paper include ensuring that the name of the principal contributor appears first and that subsequent names appear in decreasing order of contribution. Some institutions include project leaders, and in some areas of social science, scholars place the authors' names in alphabetical order, regardless of the amount of effort they contributed. In information systems research, authors are usually named in order of their contribution.

In most collaborations, it is advantageous to identify one person as the driver of the project. He or she pushes the project forward, takes over critical tasks, consolidates and reviews contributions from the collaborators, resolves differences in opinion by making decisions, and overall ensuring that the project and/or paper stays on track. The driver is likely to be (and should be) the leading author on the paper. When there is no such driver, co-authorship and collaboration roles are best discussed up front: Who will "own" the research? Who will own the data? Who will drive its publication(s)? The collaboration process is likely to be more efficient if one person is in a position to make these and other decisions if needed. Truly equal collaborations sound nice but tend to be slow because every decision requires building a consensus, and the reality is that one author will inevitably end up as the first author, just as one author will have to be named last.

Maintaining open lines of communication throughout the research process means talking openly and frankly as a team and taking responsibility for creating a communication environment that is without fear of reprisal, demotion, or other punishment. The most important parts of the communication process are:

- making one's investment in and contribution to the project clear
- creating transparency about publication strategies
- recognizing each other's goals and contributions
- being flexible, and
- establishing the criteria for making decisions

The Pre-Submission Lifecycle

There are several aspects to consider long before you submit a manuscript to a publication. First, you must decide on your **target outlet**, that is, where you want to publish.

Choose a format or a journal based on whether it targets your audience and to gives your work the highest possible impact. However, be realistic in doing so; do not waste time and effort submitting to journals that you know will not publish your work because has never shown interest in your topic or never publishes students' or junior scholars' papers. This decision is often difficult to make, so consult with your supervisor, mentor, or other senior academic whom you may know and who has experience with various outlets. You may be constrained to lower-tier venues because of the size of your manuscript—some outlets have word or page limits— the speed of publication—some journals' publishing processes take years, which will not work for you if your topic is topical or in a highly dynamic area, or the availability of special volumes or proceedings.

In deciding on a target outlet, consider five questions:

1. What journals did you consult most when doing the research? Typically, journals have more or less explicit favorite domains about which they often publish papers. You can typically tell from your own reference list which journals tend to favor the work that your work builds on. If you cite, say, twenty papers from *MIS Quarterly*, then that is likely to be an audience that will care about your work.
2. How well do you know the outlet? Check the written descriptions of target areas on the conference's or journal's website and read any editors' introductions, which often contain advice about what the journal looks for in papers. Look at other articles published in the outlet and identify their type and style of work. If in doubt about the appropriateness, email your abstract to the editor and ask whether it is appropriate for that journal/conference.
3. Do you meet the outlet's requirements for submissions? All outlets provide submission guidelines or requirements. Follow format requirements closely, adhere to the word or page limit, and follow their advice for structuring the sections of your paper. Many manuscripts are rejected straightaway for failing to meet these simple requirements.
4. What is the audience and pool of reviewers? Who reads the journal and who publishes in it? Who will decide on your submission and how? Typically, outlets provide information about their editors and referees and will list the members of their editorial and/or review boards. You can look for their areas of expertise, favored theories, and methods. Identify authors who appear regularly in the journal, and journals often recruit referees from among contributors.
5. How low should you go? Since academic publishing is a one-shot opportunity, aim as high as possible without wasting time on too-prestigious outlets you know will not accept your work (yet). If your manuscript is rejected at one outlet, you can try another—perhaps a less highly ranked one with more relaxed require- ments for rigor or contribution (but never two at the same time). If you aim too

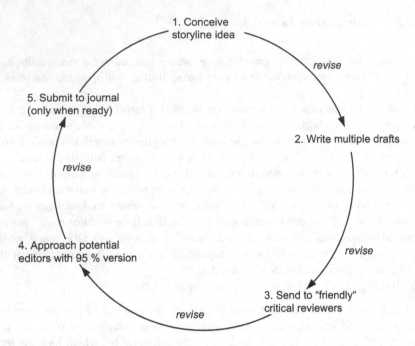

Fig. 6.1 Manuscript pre-submission lifecycle

low, you will never know whether you had a chance at a better journal. Moreover, because the *quality* of journal publications is more important than the quantity of journal publications, aiming too low can backfire on your career.

Second, once you have identified a suitable target, the next phase consists of working your way through the **pre-submission lifecycle** shown in Fig. 6.1.

As Fig. 6.1 indicates, the pre-publication is process is all about revising, honing the writing, and doing it again and again. Good writing alone will never be enough for a paper to be accepted, but it is more than enough reason for one to be rejected! A paper that is ungrammatical, filled with sloppy errors, badly organized, and awkwardly phrased puts editors off.

Fig. 6.1 also shows that research can be written about differently. Identifying what the storyline or "narrative" will be is affects how you construct the paper, how you build its sections, and who the audience is: no storyline will interest everyone; your paper's audience is determined by its narrative.

Finding and building this storyline usually takes many iterations of writing and revising, the latter of which can be difficult. You may not notice ambiguities and logical gaps because you know what you meant to say, and you understand what has been omitted. One way to address this difficulty is to put your manuscript aside for a while and return to it later when it has become less familiar (step 2 in Fig. 6.1).

You should also approach a friendly colleague who is willing to be critical as the paper matures (step 3 in Fig. 6.1). The best readers are those who have published in the journals you target but who are unfamiliar with the subject of your article. Such a reader could be someone from a different disciplinary field or someone from your own field but not familiar with the method, problem, or theory that you focus on. Such readers give you an outsider's view similar to those that the editors and reviewers will have.

If your colleagues—or anyone else, really—find that something is unclear, do not argue. They are right: If they do not get your meaning, you did not convey it. Their suggestions for revisions in these areas may be wrong, but that may be because you were not clear. It does no good to explain the point to your colleague until he or she understands it; it must be clear on the page. Change the paper in response to the feedback, do not verbally rebut the colleague.

An optional (but helpful) step is to obtain pre-submission feedback from the outlet you plan to target. Most journal editors will give you early feedback before you formally submit your manuscript and will comment on coarse flaws and the manuscript's suitability for the journal. They will not tell you whether they are likely to publish it, so do not ask.

It can take up to a year after the research work is finished for a manuscript to be ready for submission. It does not have to take this long, but a polished manuscript is critical and requires considerable effort. Avoid "hot off the press" manuscript submissions because you have only one chance to interest an editor, and writing quickly without reflection and external input increases the likelihood of errors in presenting your research work. Having a paper rejected not because the research was not good but because of how it was represented in the manuscript is disheartening and completely avoidable.

Once all the iterations of the pre-submission lifecycle are complete, you may at last have a version that has the best of chances of traversing the review process successfully.

6.4 Writing a Paper

Concerning how to actually develop a manuscript, let us start by re-iterating a few general principles about writing:

1. Writing is a process that takes time. Dedicate resources to this task. Include it in your time and project management and make it a priority.
2. Writing is a skill that must be developed and honed. Spend time on learning how to write better. Read before you write, learn from professionals, editors, and of course engage in learning by doing.
3. Review other authors' papers. While you can learn a great deal from reading papers that have been published, you can often learn even more from manuscripts that were written and submitted but may never be published–and understanding why.

4. Write, revise, give it to someone to read, put in the drawer for a month, and then revise, polish, and edit over and over.

In learning how to write, there are many helpful tips available. For example, one way I like to learn about writing is to find a good published paper that documents research similar to that that I am doing and use it as a template to help me structure my own paper. Reviewers, editors, and readers alike value familiarity in the "plot" of a paper, just as novels, films, and other stories tend to follow a similar structure.

Structuring Your Paper

The type of structure your manuscript requires will vary depending on the field (information systems versus computer science versus management, for example) and on the type of research (case study versus experiment versus design science). Regardless, the general writing process should look as follows:

1. Develop a structure for your paper.
2. Consider alternative structures, get feedback on the structure, and revise the structure if necessary.
3. Start populating the sections composing the structure.
   Populating the sections need not be sequential. For example, the first paragraph of the introduction is often the hardest part of a paper to write (Rai, 2018), while the "methods" section is usually straightforward and can sometimes even be started before the research is finished.
4. Re-read each section, get feedback on the sections, be prepared to edit and revise the section.
5. Once you have all sections complete and a first complete paper draft, re-read the paper, edit the paper, get feedback on the paper, and be prepared to revise the entire paper.
6. Put the paper in a drawer, take it out, read it again, revise it again.
7. Give it to a friendly reviewer, pre-submit to an editor, and only after the polishing or revising the paper based on their feedback submit the paper.

While the structure of papers varies across methodologies and fields (e.g., some fields may use different headings or sections), most papers in information systems research adhere to a reasonably standard generic structure (Tams & Straub, 2010), which is shown in the leftmost column in Table 6.3. I included two examples from some of my papers (one quantitative, one qualitative) to show how this generic structure can be instantiated in papers. When developing or revising the structure for your own paper, remember that a good option is always to follow as closely as possible the standard paper structure instead of inventing new structures. Innovative structures are not always well received in the academic community because the novel structure makes reading the paper more difficult. Because reviewers and readers are accustomed to a certain way of reading an article, which is called an

Table 6.3 Paper structure with examples

Generic paper structure	Example I Recker et al. (2011), quantitative study published in *MIS Quarterly*	Example II Seidel et al. (2013), qualitative study published in *MIS Quarterly*
1. Introduction	1. Introduction	1. Introduction
2. Theoretical background/ Literature review	2. Theory	2. Theoretical background
3. Research model/ Hypothesis or theory development (where appropriate)	3. Proposition development	
4. Procedure/Approach/ Methodology/Research Design	4. Research method	3. Research method
5. Results/Findings/ Outcomes	5. Scale validation 6. Results	4. Interpretation and analysis of the case 5. An integrated model of functional affordances in the sustainability transformation process 6. Two vignettes of sensemaking and sustainable practicing
6. Discussion	7. Discussion (includes subsections for limitations and implications)	7. Discussion and Implications
7. Limitations and implications for research and practice		8. Limitations
8. Conclusion	8. Conclusion	9. Conclusion

epistemic script (Grover & Lyytinen, 2015), a new structure distracts from the content contained in the structure. When reviewers and readers encounter a structure that differs from the one they are used to, they feel they have to learn how the different, new storyline will end up in an argument. They will have to focus on structure, which gives them less capacity to focus on content. Think about your research as new science in an old format.

Writing an Introduction

The introduction is an incredibly important part of your paper. Often, this is part of the paper where you either lose or win your readers' interest (including that of editors and reviewers), so it determines whether they will read on. You should spend a lot of time on writing, revising, and optimizing your introduction, especially the first page (Rai, 2018).

Your introduction spells out the study's motivation, justification, and approach, all elements of the research design. Avoid going into so much detail here that the rest of your paper becomes repetitive, but do not skip this step either.

The introduction is difficult to write because it must convey a great deal of information concisely. It is not the quantity but the quality of an introduction that matters. It should contain only three parts:

1. **Motivation**: <u>What</u> is your problem? <u>Why</u> is it a problem? For <u>whom</u> is it a problem?
2. **Specification**: What is your research question/research outcome? What is your research approach to answering the question (in general terms)?
3. **Outline**: <u>How</u> will the paper tell us about what you did?

Thus, the introduction defines the problem the research will address, establishes why the research question is important, and explains the value proposition (the contribution) the research offers. The introduction entails identifying "what" a reader should care about, "who" should care about it," and "why" they should care about it. In addition, you should tell us about the main thesis or idea (the value proposition) and why, what, and to whom it will contribute.

Fig. 6.2 shows an example of the motivation, specification, and outline (highlighted in red) from one of my papers (Seidel et al., 2013). Independent from what the paper is about, note how we use one or two paragraphs with one or two key phrases to achieve four objectives: present our problem, distinguish our value proposition from other works in the field, explain how the general approach to the study was carried out, and describe how the paper unfolds.

The key to writing a persuasive introduction like the one presented in this example is to motivate your research with a "hook," not a "gap" (Grant & Pollock, 2011). A gap usually boils down to the argument that something has not been done yet, so the motivation strategy centers on the incompleteness of the body of knowledge. This way of motivating a paper is restrictive. What if there is a body of knowledge that is available about a problem (so there is no gap) but the knowledge is inadequate, inconsistent, or outright false? Moreover, there might be valid reasons for the body of knowledge's being incomplete: not every gap needs filling, as not every unsolved problem is worth looking at. Yes, X has been determined to be true in 190 countries, although not in Uruguay, but is that really a gap worth filling?

In contrast, the "hook" is a problematization strategy (Alvesson & Sandberg, 2011). Problematization means finding a problem with the body of knowledge, not just gaps. A gap might be a problem but only if the problem is worthy of our attention. Problems other than also exist: Assumptions made in the literature on which findings are based might be wrong or outdated. Findings might be conflicting or inconclusive. All these are problems that additional research can address to correct what might need correcting in the body of knowledge.

The hook strategy identifies such a problem, who cares about the problem, where the problem is, what we know about the problem, and what we will learn about the problem. Thinking this way can be an effective strategy for introducing a paper, although gap-spotting is practiced far more often than problematizing or hooking (Chatterjee & Davison, 2021; Sandberg & Alvesson, 2011).

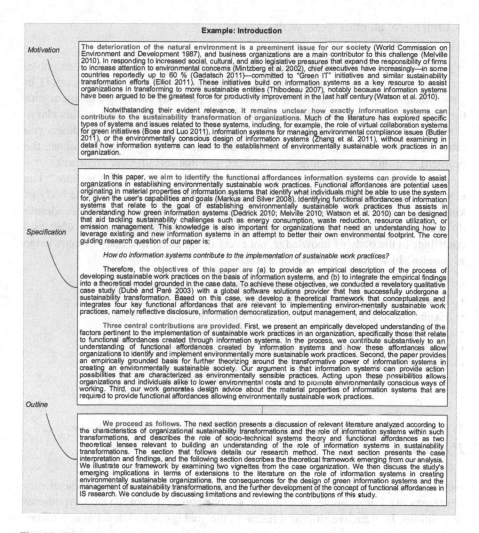

Fig. 6.2 Example of an introduction (Seidel et al., 2013, p. 1276), with annotations

Writing a Background Section

The background section provides what is required for your reader to understand your research processes and findings. That is, it discusses the theories that are the foundation for your study, the concepts or terms that you will use, and possibly methods/algorithms/findings/arguments on which your work builds.

Scholars make common mistakes when they write background sections. First, let us look at what a background section is not:

• A recap or listing of all other works in the area
• Every paper that you have read about the area

- Criticism of all other works in the area, or
- A collection of term definitions

Instead, the background section sets the scene for what is to come. For example, we might introduce the context or setting of our study, such as IT in healthcare, IT in government, or IT in sports. If you motivate your paper by claiming a problem with the literature, the background section is often the place to substantiate this claim. When you plan to use a particular theory in your research approach or findings, you introduce it here. In sum, you present the literature that led you to investigate the problem, that puts your findings into context, and that sets up your argument.

A good rule of thumb for writing a background section is that "less is more." The key is finding a balance between demonstrating that you really know the body of knowledge as it relates to your work and not boring the reader with meandering discussions of others' work. Most readers have an interest in learning what you contribute to the body of knowledge, not every detail about that body of knowledge as it exists. In writing the background section:

- Organize the section according to topics, not as a list of studies.
- Discuss related work, rather than just listing it.
- Explain how your work complements others' work.
- Explain how your work contradicts previous work.
- Highlight areas in which your work builds on others' work.
- Keep it concise.

Writing About Your Research Model, Your Theory, or Your Hypotheses

Not every paper features a section on the research model (or hypothesis/theory development). For example, most design science papers do not develop hypotheses or positions. In inductive empirical research, the goal is often to develop new theory as the outcome of empirical field work; in this case, the theory or propositions often follow the findings section (as in example II in Table 6.3). However, in many other empirical (and usually quantitative) papers, the theoretical expectations/hypotheses/proposals are presented before empirics are used to evaluate/test/corroborate/falsify these expectations.

The section on your research model provides an overview of the factors being studied in an empirical setting, such as the independent and dependent factors in an experiment, the important theoretical constructs and their relationships in a survey, or the set of hypotheses or propositions to be tested, explored, or falsified in a case study.

The section should be organized by first providing an overview of the concepts, constructs, or factors that are relevant to your study. This section contains a research model that describes all relevant elements and their relationships. This description can be graphic, such as the research model in example I in Table 6.3, or it can be textual or tabular. Both tables and visualizations are helpful in presenting theoretical ideas, as tables present the reader with a structure for discussing concepts in terms of, for example, their definitions, explanations, examples, and related work, while visualizations help you position concepts in comparison to each other, which helps the reader identify associations, relationships, importance (e.g., core versus ancillary), and boundary conditions.

Another organizing principle is to follow a disciplined structure that moves from concepts to associations to laws to boundaries. (See Chap. 4.) After introducing the concepts, you can turn to building propositions or hypotheses that relate to how the concepts or constructs relate to one another and why. Here, the key point is to develop each association on its own (e.g., each in its own sub-section) and to precede each proposition or hypothesis with a strong argument as to why it should hold (to build a justificatory mechanism for the theory, as explained in Chap. 4). A proposition or hypothesis must always be preceded by a logical and persuasive argument for why you expect it to hold. Hypotheses need the explanations because no hypothesis should be self-evident or without purpose.

Keep your propositions or hypotheses simple and precise. They should specify two (or more, but usually only two) key concepts or constructs and the relationships between them. When working with hypotheses, identify dependent and independent variables and the direction of the expected relationships. Operationalize the variables in a hypothesis in such a way that they can clearly be mapped to measurement variables (and values) that you will discuss in the "research method" section that follows. Do not use words such as "prove." Instead, use words such as "suggest" or "support" (because hypotheses in the social sciences can never be proven, only supported). The excerpt shown in Fig. 6.3 gives you an example of the reasoning that led to a hypothesis I developed in one of my papers (Recker, 2013).

A third organizing principle is to connect your arguments in this section to existing research. Include references to key literature in building your argument (as shown in the example in Fig. 6.3), remembering that the literature you use here should have been introduced in your background section. However, pointing to (empirical) support for a hypothesis in the literature is not sufficient justification for why you expect the relationship to manifest in a particular way. Demonstrating that the relationship exists by referencing prior studies that obtained the same result is different from hypothesizing why or how it manifests.

Writing About Your Procedures, Your Research Approach, Your Methods, or Your Research Design

In this section, you describe how your research was carried out in such a way that another research can repeat your work based on your description (to meet the requirement of replicability). Key elements in this section explain and justify the

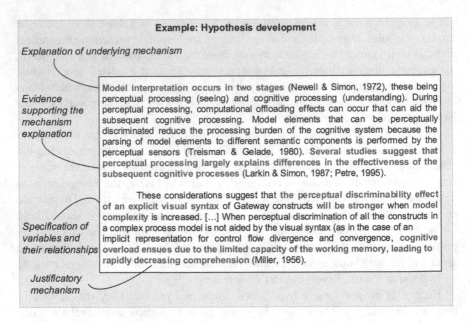

Fig. 6.3 Example of a hypothesis development section (Recker, 2013, p. 677), with annotations

selection of a research strategy, materials, case sites, the scope of data collection, sampling, participant selection, and any other decision that is pertinent to your research design. Other key elements include a detailed description of the analytical measurements and data collection techniques employed as well as the data analysis techniques used.

This section is, relatively speaking, easy to write for most quantitative studies because instrument development, measurement validation, and sampling choices typically follow established guidelines and criteria, so you can write this section easily by following a favorite example. Try not to be too creative in writing up this section, as most reviewers are accustomed to a particular style and expect certain content and structure. For example, in experiments, the typical script involves specifying the experimental design, variables and measures, materials, tasks, procedures, and participants, typically each in a separate subsection. Similarly, in survey research, we describe design, measures, sampling strategy, procedures, and validation of measures.

Qualitative studies, too, typically follow a particular script: The methods section often discusses the empirical setting, modes of data collection, and processes and techniques employed in data analysis. Design science studies typically follow a script that includes an overview of the research process, the development of meta-requirements or design principles, the description of the artefact, and the means chosen for evaluation.

Writing About Results, Findings, or Outcomes

This section depends on the nature of your research and your chosen methodology, so it is difficult to give general advice. Check published papers that use an approach that is similar to yours and use their description as a template.

The results/findings/outcomes section typically "drives" a paper in that it describes the evidence gathered to test or evaluate hypotheses or propositions or presents new data that spawns new ideas, theory, or propositions. In design-oriented work, this section presents the artefact in all its facets, so it creates the basis on which all your claimed contributions will be judged.

This section is descriptive: We describe findings, we report results from statistical tests, we offer our interpretation of a case, or we display an artefact. All these tasks are descriptive in that they report something and are not speculative or predictive.

Finally, try to describe your outcomes and findings as simply as possible. Use tables and figures to structure this part of the paper, and avoid unnecessarily long passages of free text. Do not present irrelevant data or outcomes to which the discussion that follows does not refer. Do not include passages that are labelled "other findings" or "other results." Such sections have no place. Report the results/findings/outcomes that fit your narrative, not every little thing you found.

Writing the Discussion Section

This section is where a paper becomes interesting. In fact, most readers tend to skim through the introduction and glimpse at some graphs and tables in the results section, but they read the discussion section in detail. In this section, we interpret the data, the findings, and the outcomes we reported in the previous section. This is where we make sense of the research outcomes by exploring what they indicate, how they relate to our theoretical expectations, and how they inform our future thinking.

The discussion section should begin by summarizing the main findings in one, or at most two, sentences. Then, interpret the findings: What do the results mean? Why did you get the results that you obtained? What do they tell you in light of the theory you set out to evaluate? Thus, you are explaining the results, abstracting the results, and theorizing about the results.

Two problems often occur in discussion sections. One occurs when the discussion goes beyond the data to discuss things that were not presented in the results/findings/outcomes section. Consequently, interpretation and explanation are replaced by speculation without substantiation or evidence, which renders the contribution arbitrary and subjective. Another problem occurs when the discussion section introduces new findings or outcomes that should have been introduced in the preceding section, not here.

A good discussion section provides a sense of **reflection**, as it relates the findings back to the initial problem the paper set out to address. A good discussion section should also help **sensemaking**: What do the findings mean? Why did you get the outcomes that you obtained? You should also **abstract** your findings or outcomes by relating them back to the literature that was your point of departure.

Do your results confirm existing theories? Falsify them? Do they serve as supporting or contrarian arguments to claims or arguments made in the literature? This step shows how your research adds to, complements, or clarifies the current body of knowledge, and you may be able to explain inconsistencies in prior work or improve a theoretical explanation of some phenomenon based on your results.

Finally, be realistic and cautious and do not over-interpret you results. Findings are often tentative and suggestive rather than conclusive because of limitations in the data collection or analysis.

Writing About Implications

Research should inform future studies and current practice in the domain that is being studied, so good journals demand specific and explicit implications of your findings for ongoing research and practice. Fig. 6.4 gives three examples for writing implications sections: (i) an excerpt from the "Implications for Research" section in Recker (2013), which describes some future research opportunities, (ii) an excerpt from the "Implications for Research" section in Recker et al. (2021), which discusses how extant foci by researchers should change, and an excerpt from the "Implications for Practice" section in Recker (2013), which discusses options that managers might take in overseeing practical work.

Implications for practice detail how the study's findings may impact how stakeholders work in practice. A study's findings often inform a set of guidelines for practices related to those findings. It is good practice to identify the type of stakeholders who are the primary addressees of the implications. Are your implications addressed to managers, executive, end users, or customers? How are their practices implicated by your research? Should they change what they do? How?

Implications for research often take one or both of two forms. One type of implications for research discusses future research opportunities that can address the limitations of your study or otherwise extend or replicate it. For example, papers often focus on a set of independent and dependent variables that could be extended or replaced with others. Papers may include a new measurement instrument that was developed for the study and is now available for other researchers to use in future studies. A paper might develop a new theory that is now awaiting further exploration, application, or evaluation. Another set of implications could relate to extensions of the study that explore, for example, the boundary conditions of a theory being developed or investigate inconsistencies uncovered in the data.

A second way of constructing implications for research involves asking scholars to think differently about phenomena, methods, or theories and to go about their research in that domain differently. Such would be the case, for example, if an empirical study disconfirms a theory or falsifies it, when a new way of

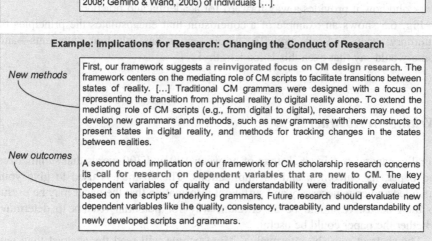

Example: Implications for Research: Future Research Opportunities

Different independent variables

We chose one semantic characteristic, construct excess as a manifestation of ontological non-clarity, and one syntactic characteristic, perceptual discriminability. Thus, opportunities exist for fellow scholars to examine different semantic and syntactic characteristics of process models, and the impact these characteristics may have on the ability of individuals to understand the models.

Different measurements

Other research could extend our approach to measuring process model interpretability. [...] We focused on individuals' understanding of grammatical elements and their meaning in a process model (surface understanding), which is fundamental to being able to faithfully and efficiently interpret a process model. Future work could now extend this work and examine the problem solving performance (which is indicative of deep understanding, see Burton-Jones & Meso, 2008; Gemino & Wand, 2005) of individuals [...].

Example: Implications for Research: Changing the Conduct of Research

New methods

First, our framework suggests a reinvigorated focus on CM design research. The framework centers on the mediating role of CM scripts to facilitate transitions between states of reality. [...] Traditional CM grammars were designed with a focus on representing the transition from physical reality to digital reality alone. To extend the mediating role of CM scripts (e.g., from digital to digital), researchers may need to develop new grammars and methods, such as new grammars with new constructs to present states in digital reality, and methods for tracking changes in the states between realities.

New outcomes

A second broad implication of our framework for CM scholarship research concerns its call for research on dependent variables that are new to CM. The key dependent variables of quality and understandability were traditionally evaluated based on the scripts' underlying grammars. Future research should evaluate new dependent variables like the quality, consistency, traceability, and understandability of newly developed scripts and grammars.

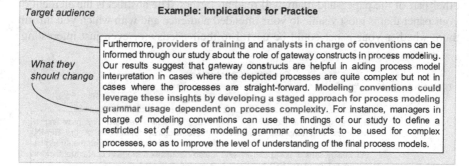

Target audience

Example: Implications for Practice

What they should change

Furthermore, providers of training and analysts in charge of conventions can be informed through our study about the role of gateway constructs in process modeling. Our results suggest that gateway constructs are helpful in aiding process model interpretation in cases where the depicted processes are quite complex but not in cases where the processes are straight-forward. Modeling conventions could leverage these insights by developing a staged approach for process modeling grammar usage dependent on process complexity. For instance, managers in charge of modeling conventions can use the findings of our study to define a restricted set of process modeling grammar constructs to be used for complex processes, so as to improve the level of understanding of the final process models.

Fig. 6.4 Examples of implications for research and practice, with annotations

conceptualizing or measuring some phenomenon demonstrably outperforms the classical way, or when new theory opens up avenues to consider new types of research methods (such as computational methods or neuroscientific measurements).

Writing a Conclusion

The conclusion section provides the closing frame to a paper. This section should be short! It briefly recaps the key contributions of the paper, without going into detail. It provides a reflection of the research presented in the paper without introducing new material, findings, or implications. In fact, you will find some papers offer no conclusion at all.

Should you write a conclusion, identify the key findings of your paper and relate them back to the introduction. If you find that doing so is not possible, you will have to rewrite either the introduction or the conclusions. Highlight the significance of the work and how it provides a way forward for academia and practice.

Fig. 6.5 shows an example of a conclusion that encapsulates the principles of summary, recap, and reflection. The whole section has only four statements—and some would say that even this is too lengthy!

Writing an Abstract

Finally, papers contain an abstract of between 100 and 300 words that summarizes the paper, its outcomes, and its implications. The abstract is used to give your intended audience necessary and sufficient information that the paper may be useful to their needs. It should be an efficient way for potential readers to determine whether the paper could be useful.

The abstract must be informative. More people will read the abstract than any other part of the paper, and many will read no farther. The abstract is the element of your paper that is most visible to your intended audience and with which you inform them whether your paper could be useful to their needs—or even just interesting.

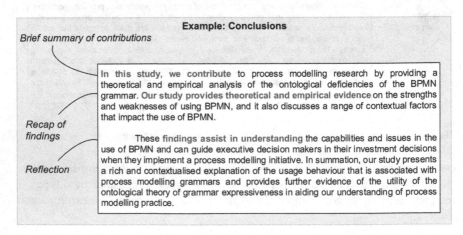

Fig. 6.5 Example of a conclusions section, from (Recker et al., 2010), with annotations

The title is also a way to influence your reviewers: Reviewers typically see only the title and abstract when they are invited to review a paper, and the "first impression" they get from these elements can bias them against your paper if they are poorly written, or, when they are well written, you may already a have a fan on your side.

The short length of an abstract requires that you write clearly and concisely. The abstract should contain a statement of the problem being addressed, a statement about the approach/methods, a brief summary of the results, your key interpretations of the results, and the major implications of the results and conclusions. Avoid jargon, complex concepts with which readers may not be familiar, and complicated measures of outcomes (such as statistics). Spend the most effort on explaining the paper's contributions and implications. Do not write "these findings have important implications": tell us what they are!

6.5   Revising a Paper

Understanding Reviews

The peer review is an important process in academia. It ensures that certain quality standards are met, and that the quality of research and publication work being done in the profession is of a high standard. When that standard is not met, reviewers and editors are entitled to reject the work outright or to ask for further research or work on its presentation before they make a decision. Such a request usually means a second version (a revision) will be reviewed again. This process helps to ensure that only strong research and strong manuscripts make it through to publication. If weak work were accepted, standards would slip, and the profession as a whole would suffer.

How does this process of review work? Submissions are commonly made by electronic upload. Then an editor pre-screens the submission to gauge the general suitability of the manuscript for the outlet and its likely viability for surviving the review process. If a paper is in obvious misalignment with the outlet's focus or the research is of poor quality, the editor can **desk-reject** a paper, without sending it out for review, to reduce reviewers' significant workload, whose work is often voluntary and requires a significant commitment of time and effort. Desk rejects are hard for authors to take, but they benefit from them too, as they get quick feedback on their work and, if it is simply a matter of choosing the wrong outlet, they can try another outlet without having to wait for reviewers to state the inevitable. If the research or presentation is poor, authors can avoid wasting time submitting to other outlets before making improvements.

Manuscripts that survive the screening stage are usually sent to two or more reviewers who comment on various (and varying) characteristics of the manuscript, such as the significance of its contributions; the quality of its methods, data analysis, reasoning, results, and conclusions; and whether it is up-to-date with the literature, well written, and so on.

The time until a review is received varies from outlet to outlet. Good journals tend to provide reviews and decisions within two to four months of submission. Lower-ranked journals not only have lower expectations about a paper's contributions but also often have review processes that are not so efficient (or effective) as those of high-quality journals. I have received reviews as quickly as a couple of weeks, all the way up to fourteen months. I have received reviews of two lines and reviews that extend ten or more pages. I have waited for a year or more to learn that a paper was accepted and have also received a rejection after waiting for more than a year. Fortunately, most outlets now employ digital manuscript submission systems such as ScholarOne that allow authors, reviewers, and editors to monitor and inquire about the status of a paper.

Submitting a paper for review leads to one of three outcomes:

1. **Rejection**: The outlet will not consider this manuscript or any reworked version of it. This is the most disappointing outcome–and a final one at that.
2. **Request to revise and resubmit**. The manuscript is denied publication in its current state, but the editors and reviewers feel that a reworked manuscript may be accepted if submitted to the journal again for new evaluation, typically by the same editor and reviewers. These revise-and-resubmit decisions are often further differentiated into major versus minor revisions. Major revisions are often requested when the editors and reviewers see potential in the research, but it cannot be published as presented in the manuscript with substantial and extensive changes. These revisions can relate to writing (the manuscript's structure, writing, clarity, completeness) or to the research itself (requests for different kinds of analyses, collection of additional data, (re-)consideration of theory). However, major revisions and the time they require also involve some risk, as you have no guarantee that the revised paper will be accepted. A request for minor revisions indicates that the editors and reviewers see the manuscript as strong but have some comments, issues, and suggestions for improving it. Typically, a manuscript that needs only minor revisions is well one the way to publication; while acceptance is not guaranteed, it is often likely.
3. **Acceptance or conditional acceptance**: This outcome is good news, as it indicates that the editor has decided that the paper can be published as is, or with changes so minor that it does not require further review.

These outcomes are ordered not only from worst to best but also by frequency of occurrence. Paper acceptance rates are low; only around 10% of submissions to most journals are accepted. Virtually all initial reviews ("first-round" reviews) demand major revisions or resubmission if they are not rejected out of hand. In fact, your expectation should be (a) no acceptance in the first round, and (b) major revisions will be required.

I find that the best attitude in handling reviews is the "we are in the game unless they kick us out" position. An opportunity to revise and resubmit is good news, as you are still in the game, and they have not decided to kick you out. With this attitude, reviews that may seem harsh (and requests for major revisions are harsh) are much easier to handle. You are in control: It is up to you to improve the manuscript so it can be published.

One of the common myths in the publishing process is that reviewers want to reject your paper. This is simply not true. Good journals are good because they use good reviewers. Good reviewers write reviews that contain clear and precise criticism, along with constructive suggestions. Such reviewers want to see their advice taken seriously, and rejections based on good reviews give you the best opportunity to improve the paper so it can be published.

Revising a Paper Based on Reviews

At some stage after you submitted your paper for peer review, you will receive a decision, typically via email. This moment tends to be very emotional for academics. Nervous excitement and anxiety mingles; and often, the first impression can in fact be disappointment. This is because in next to all cases, you will not receive the news you really hoped for (acceptance as is) but likely a rejection or a letter asking for revisions.

The first rule to handling reviews is not to let pride or arrogance get in your way. Your objective is to get the paper published. If reviewers and editors find flaws in your work, then there are flaws in your work that you need to rectify. It is not their fault; it is yours. I hear many comments along the line of "the reviewer didn't understand what I was doing." That may be true, but it is your fault, not theirs. You did not communicate well enough for others to understand.

The second rule to handling reviews is to manage your emotions. Learn to be self-reflective so you can avoid reacting emotionally, rather than rationally, to review comments. Remind yourself of the reality that most papers are rejected, most (if not all) reviews of an initial version of a manuscript will ask for major revisions, and acceptances are rare. Your paper is not finished just because you submitted it; there is always room for improvement and many ideas or actions that could be communicated better.

If you do receive a rejection, focus on why. The editor and reviewers will give you plenty of reasons that are in your power to address. Fix the flaws identified by the rejection rather than submitting the same flawed manuscript somewhere else, which will be a waste of time and effort or, at best, result in a weak publication. If the research has flaws, good reviewers will spot them. It is selfish and arrogant to consume reviewers' time and then not listen to them.

Being asked for revisions (major or minor) is good news. The editors believe there is potential for the paper to be published. If they did not think so, they would have rejected it. You are still in the game!

However, handling revisions can be even harder than the writing the initial manuscript. You may get upward of tens of pages of detailed comments from editors and several reviewers. (My high so far, I think, was twenty-seven single-spaced pages of comments in a first round. The revision took me ten months and led to two more rounds of reviews and revisions, but the paper was published!) The sheer volume of comments can make it difficult to address all of them in a consistent manner, as reviewers may give opposing suggestions.

While handling many review comments in a revision can be challenging, at least you have specific suggestions for what to work on. In the best possible case, the reviewers suggest changes and you implement them. Sometimes implementing them takes months of re-analyzing data, collecting more data, updating the literature you cite, and so on, but at least you have a roadmap. That is a much easier decision to take than deciding entirely free about what to include, and where, in a paper. So, reviews give you directions. They might be hard to follow, but the space of options is much smaller than initially

In managing revisions, I suggest the following procedure:

First, **put the review aside for a while**. Given that virtually all first-round reviews are critical (you will rarely be accepted straightaway–it has happened to me only once), you will probably have some strong negative reactions. The comments sound unfairly harsh, the suggestions virtually impossible to achieve, and it is a mountain of work to be done. In this state of mind, your revision will be affected by your emotions, so put the reviews aside and read them again after several days have passed. the suggestions will suddenly look more manageable, the revision more doable, and the reviews either understandable (in case of a reject decision) or addressable (in case of a revise and resubmit decision).

Second, **tabulate the reviews**. Make sure that you fully understand each and every comment. Do not start revising, editing, or responding before you have a firm grasp on each comment as well as the overall direction that the reviews provide. Only in this way can you develop a strategy that allows you to handle each comment but also the message that all the comments together send.

A simple but effective tool is to create a **table** for each of the editors and reviewers and copy and paste each review comment into a separate row. Have three columns, one for the comment, one for the response, and one for notes and discussions within the research team. I start tabulating early because it forces me to read consciously so I can summarize and dissect the issues. After several rounds of reading the reviews, I jot down thoughts and strategies about the comments. For example, I often mark some issues as "quick fixes" (easy to handle) and "major work" and indicate the type of revision required: (a) change the research, (b) change the presentation of research, or (c) reject the suggestion because it cannot be handled given the research conducted. Over time, the responses column will be populated, and the table will be complete.

Third, **revise the paper**. At some stage or another, changes will have to be made to the document. It may (and should) take a while before you can start revising the paper; for example, you may need to collect and analyze new data first.

Depending on the type of revision (minor or major), the changes will be more or less voluminous, ranging from changing, inserting, or deleting paragraphs/figures/ tables of some sections, to writing a completely new manuscript. Do not be afraid to make big changes; a major revision should look like a major revision. Re-writing a paper from scratch for major revisions can often be more effective than making changes to an existing manuscript. Several of my published papers look vastly different from the manuscript that was initially submitted.

Fourth, **write a response letter**. You must respond to all review comments in a separate document. Editors and reviewers typically demand point-by-point responses to all their comments because then it is easier for them to trace the changes, especially if they asked for many revisions. Start with a pre-amble that expresses your gratitude for the reviewers' and editor's investing their time in giving you feedback and assisting you in improving your work. Then outline the strategy you pursued in your revision by summarizing the main changes. Then respond to each reviewer separately, rather than clumping comments from different reviewers together. Respond to all comments, one by one, be they positive (simply write "Thank you!") or negative. Do not skip any.

Response letters serve as a frame of reference to the review team when they look at the revision. It has usually been months since they read the initial paper, and they will want a reminder, as well as to know what you changed and where they will find the change in the paper. Because the response letter is an auxiliary document, it should be as short as possible but as precise as necessary. A good practice is to mention for each point whether you agree with the comment or not, what you did in response to the comment, and where reviewers can find the change (with reference to page numbers, or figures or tables).

In concluding this section, remember that considerable effort is required to revise your paper successfully, and success in the way of acceptance for publication is not guaranteed. A major (or even a minor) revision does not guarantee acceptance. Like many of my colleagues, I have had papers finally rejected after four or five rounds of reviews.

The first round of reviews is the one that matters most, the "first revision" is key (Rai, 2019). Reviewers and editors either see promise in your paper or they do not, so the first attempt at revising a paper can determine whether it moves toward publication. Reviewers and editors tend to give authors the benefit of the doubt: The initial manuscript may have issues in research design, methods, theory, or ideas, or the paper may not be professionally written, yet still they see the possibility that the authors can overcome these challenges. When they look at the first revision, then, they seek to eliminate the uncertainty, and if the paper has not made strong progress in addressing the key issues, they are likely to end the review process. Moreover, with every revision, new issues may arise. Because everyone wants to finish the review process in a reasonable time, editors are not likely to offer unlimited opportunities to revise and resubmit to "see if it can be done better," so the first revision is crucial. Attend to it carefully and make it a priority over all other projects, including new papers.

As a final piece of advice, ensure that your tone in the response letter is always polite. No one is attacking or criticizing you personally, and firing arguments at the reviewers will not change their views or their impression of your work. You may disagree with the reviewer (which is fine), or the reviewer's suggested changes may be impossible (which is also fine), but just state why you will not pursue the change requested without arrogance or veiled insults ("you may not have the knowledge to understand. . .").

Still, with all the hurdles and challenges of reviews and revisions, when you realize that your manuscript is improving over the rounds of reviews, it will be a gratifying and exciting experience. The final versions of all my published papers were much better than the initial manuscripts. Moreover, the gratification is not limited to the authors alone. Reviewers and editors who are involved in shepherding a paper through to publication often share the joy of authors, in part because they helped but also because they, too, are authors.

6.6   Further Reading

Many articles give useful advice about how to write academic papers. Below are some sources that address the elements of academic writing that I have found helpful.

Venkatesh (2011) dedicated chapter four of his book on academic success to paper-writing. It makes for a valuable read. (No wonder, given how prolific Venkatesh has been in terms of paper publishing.) Another good source is Wilkinson's (1991) guide to scientific writing, as is Lagendijk's (2008) book, especially in terms of suggestions for developing statements that show strong and clear argumentation.

With the increasing emphasis on publication in academia, several resources can help you manage your writing and increase your ability to write effectively and efficiently. For example, in *How to write a Lot*, Silvia (2018) suggests time-management principles for scheduling time to write. Other similar principles for staying focused on writing and methods for organizing your work are included in such works as Allen's (2015) *Getting Things Done*. Books that are specifically about writing a doctoral dissertation include Davis and Parker (1997), Evans et al. (2011).

Finally, an enormous number of articles offer advice about the challenges of academic writing. Tips on writing and publishing can often be found in the editorial section of major journals. They focus on topics such as:

- Advice on writing about empirical research: (Bem, 2003; Wolcott, 2001)
- Guidelines for writing with a scientific style: (American Psychological Association, 2020; Starbuck, 1999)
- Tips about reviewing papers: (Daft, 1995; Lee, 1995; Saunders, 2005; Straub, 2009b)
- Publishing tips from an editor's perspective: (Bergh, 2003; Feldman, 2004; Rai, 2017; Rynes, 2002; Schminke, 2004; Straub, 2009a, 2009c)
- Guidelines for writing specific parts of a paper, such as the introduction or theory development: (Cornelissen, 2017; Grant & Pollock, 2011)

References

Allen, D. (2015). *Getting Things Done: The Art of Stress-Free Productivity.* Penguin Books.

Alvesson, M., & Sandberg, J. (2011). Generating Research Questions Through Problematization. *Academy of Management Review, 36*(2), 247–271.

American Psychological Association. (2020). *The Publication Manual of the American Psychological Association* (7th ed.). APA Press.

Bem, D. J. (2003). Writing the Empirical Journal Article. In J. M. Darley, M. P. Zanna, & H. L. Roediger III (Eds.), *The Compleat Academic: A Practical Guide for the Beginning Social Scientist* (2nd ed., pp. 185–219). American Psychological Association.

Bergh, D. D. (2003). From the Editors: Thinking Strategically about Contribution. *Academy of Management Journal, 46*(2), 135–136.

Chatterjee, S., & Davison, R. M. (2021). The Need for Compelling Problematisation in Research: The Prevalence of the Gap-spotting Approach and its Limitations. *Information Systems Journal, 31*(2), 227–230. https://doi.org/10.1111/isj.12316

Cornelissen, J. P. (2017). Editor's Comments: Developing Propositions, a Process Model, or a Typology? Addressing the Challenges of Writing Theory Without a Boilerplate. *Academy of Management Review, 42*(1), 1–9.

Daft, R. L. (1995). Why I Recommended That Your Manuscript Be Rejected and What You Can Do About It. In L. L. Cummings & P. J. Frost (Eds.), *Publishing in the Organizational Sciences* (2nd ed., pp. 164–182). Sage.

Davis, G. B., & Parker, C. A. (1997). *Writing the Doctoral Dissertation: A Systematic Approach* (2nd ed.). Barron's Educational Series.

Dean, D. L., Lowry, P. B., & Humpherys, S. L. (2011). Profiling the Research Productivity of Tenured Information Systems Faculty at U.S. Institutions. *MIS Quarterly, 35*(1), 1–15.

Evans, D., Zobel, J., & Gruba, P. (2011). *How To Write A Better Thesis* (3rd ed.). Melbourne University Press.

Feldman, D. C. (2004). The Devil is in the Details: Converting Good Research into Publishable Articles. *Journal of Management, 30*(1), 1–6.

Grant, A. M., & Pollock, T. G. (2011). Publishing in AMJ—Part 3: Setting the Hook. *Academy of Management Journal, 54*(5), 873–879.

Grover, V., & Lyytinen, K. (2015). New State of Play in Information Systems Research: The Push to the Edges. *MIS Quarterly, 39*(2), 271–296.

Hargittai, E. (2009). *Research Confidential: Solutions to Problems Most Social Scientists Pretend They Never Have.* University of Michigan Press.

Harzing, A.-W. (2010). *The Publish Or Perish Book: Your Guide to Effective and Responsible Citation Analysis.* Tarma Software Research Pty Limited.

Ioannidis, J. P. A., Baas, J., Klavans, R., & Boyack, K. W. (2019). A Standardized Citation Metrics Author Database Annotated for Scientific Field. *PLoS Biology, 17*(8), e3000384. https://doi.org/10.1371/journal.pbio.3000384

Lagendijk, A. (2008). *Survival Guide for Scientists: Writing—Presentation—Email* (3rd ed.). Amsterdam University Press.

Larivière, V., Gingras, Y., & Archambault, É. (2009). The Decline in the Concentration of Citations, 1900–2007. *Journal of the American Society for Information Science and Technology, 60*(4), 858–862. https://doi.org/10.1002/asi.21011

Lee, A. S. (1995). Reviewing a Manuscript for Publication. *Journal of Operations Management, 13*(1), 87–92.

Rai, A. (2017). Editor's Comments: Avoiding Type III Errors: Formulating IS Research Problems that Matter. *MIS Quarterly, 41*(2), iii–vii.

Rai, A. (2018). Editor's Comments: The First Few Pages. *MIS Quarterly, 42*(2), iii–vi.

Rai, A. (2019). Editor's Comments: The First Revision. *MIS Quarterly, 43*(3), iii–viii.

Recker, J. (2013). Empirical Investigation of the Usefulness of Gateway Constructs in Process Models. *European Journal of Information Systems, 22*(6), 673–689.

Recker, J., Indulska, M., Rosemann, M., & Green, P. (2010). The Ontological Deficiencies of Process Modeling in Practice. *European Journal of Information Systems, 19*(5), 501–525.

Recker, J., Lukyanenko, R., Jabbari, M., Samuel, B. M., & Castellanos, A. (2021). From Representation to Mediation: A New Agenda for Conceptual Modeling Research in a Digital World. *MIS Quarterly, 45*(1), 269–300. https://doi.org/10.25300/MISQ/2020/16207

Recker, J., Rosemann, M., Green, P., & Indulska, M. (2011). Do Ontological Deficiencies in Modeling Grammars Matter? *MIS Quarterly, 35*(1), 57–79.

Rynes, S. (2002). From the Editors: Some Reflections on Contribution. *Academy of Management Journal, 45*(2), 311–313.

Sandberg, J., & Alvesson, M. (2011). Ways of Constructing Research Questions: Gap-spotting or Problematization? *Organization, 18*(1), 23–44. https://doi.org/10.1177/1350508410372151

Saunders, C. (2005). Editor's Comments: Looking for Diamond Cutters. *MIS Quarterly, 29*(1), iii–viii.

Schminke, M. (2004). From the Editors: Raising the Bamboo Curtain. *Academy of Management Journal, 17*(3), 310–314.

Seidel, S., Recker, J., & vom Brocke, J. (2013). Sensemaking and Sustainable Practicing: Functional Affordances of Information Systems in Green Transformations. *MIS Quarterly, 37*(4), 1275–1299.

Silvia, P. J. (2018). *How to Write a Lot: A Practical Guide to Productive Academic Writing* (2nd ed.). APA Press.

Starbuck, W. H. (1999). *Fussy Professor Starbuck's Cookbook of Handy-Dandy Prescriptions for Ambitious Academic Authors or Why I Hate Passive Verbs and Love My Word Processor*. http://people.stern.nyu.edu/wstarbuc/Writing/Fussy.htm

Straub, D. W. (2009a). Editor's Comments: Creating Blue Oceans of Thought Via Highly Citable Articles. *MIS Quarterly, 33*(4), iii–vii.

Straub, D. W. (2009b). Editor's Comments: Diamond Mining or Coal Mining? Which Reviewing Industry Are We In? *MIS Quarterly, 33*(2), iii–viii.

Straub, D. W. (2009c). Editor's Comments: Why Top Journals Accept Your Paper. *MIS Quarterly, 33*(3), iii–x.

Tams, S., & Straub, D. W. (2010). The Effect of an IS Article's Structure on Its Impact. *Communications of the Association for Information Systems, 27*(10), 149–172.

Venkatesh, V. (2011). *Road to Success: A Guide for Doctoral Students and Junior Faculty Members in the Behavioral and Social Sciences*. Dog Ear Publishing.

Wilkinson, A. M. (1991). *The Scientist's Handbook for Writing Papers and Dissertations*. Prentice Hall.

Wolcott, H. F. (2001). *Writing up Qualitative Research* (2nd ed.). Sage.

Chapter 7
Ethical Considerations in Research

7.1 The Role of Ethics in Research

In this part of the book, I want to draw your attention to ethical considerations as they pertain to research in information systems (IS). Ethics is a branch of philosophy that addresses questions about morality, that is, concepts like good and bad, right and wrong, justice and injustice, and virtue and evil. Ethics define the principles of right and wrong conduct in a community or profession, and they can be used by individuals acting as free agents to guide their choices and behaviour. For example, doctors in many countries take the Hippocratic Oath, which, among other things, states that they will do no harm to their patients and preserve their privacy. Engineers follow ethical guides that tell them to "hold paramount the safety, health, and welfare of the public." Such ethical principles are deeply ingrained in these professions, and it is no different in science, as ethics are part of how we practice research. Scientific ethics describe **norms for conduct** that distinguish between acceptable and unacceptable behaviour in scientific work and reflect the chief concerns and goals of science (Resnik, 2016).

Ethical behaviour describes a set of actions that abide by rules of responsibility, accountability, liability, and due diligence:

- *Responsibility* means accepting the potential costs, duties, and obligations of one's decisions.
- *Accountability* means being answerable to others for decisions made and actions taken.
- *Liability* means accepting responsibility and accountability so individuals can recover damages done to them through breaches of responsibility.
- *Due diligence* means investigating or exercising care to ensure individuals can examine or appeal how responsibility, accountability, and liability are applied.

Like all other professional communities, science follows ethical standards that specify what is acceptable and unacceptable behaviour in the conduct of research in

© Springer Nature Switzerland AG 2021
J. Recker, *Scientific Research in Information Systems*, Progress in IS,
https://doi.org/10.1007/978-3-030-85436-2_7

relation to responsibility, accountability, liability, and due diligence. The main principles of science stipulate "honesty and integrity" in all stages of scientific conduct, which includes all aspects of scientific activity, such as experimentation, testing, education, data collection, data analysis, data storage, data sharing, peer review, government funding, staffing of research teams, and other activities that have a direct bearing on science. The following synthesis by Resnik (2016) lists six fundamental ethical principles for scientific research:

1. **Scientific honesty**: scientists should not commit scientific fraud by, for example, fabricating, "fudging," trimming, "cooking," destroying, or misrepresenting data.
2. **Carefulness**: scientists should avoid careless errors and sloppiness in all aspects of scientific work.
3. **Intellectual freedom**: scientists should be free to pursue new ideas and criticise old ones and conduct research on anything they find interesting.
4. **Openness**: whenever possible, scientists should share data, results, methods, theories, equipment, and so on; allow people to see their work; and be open to criticism.
5. **Attribution of credit**: scientists should not plagiarise the work of other scientists. They should give credit where credit is due but not where it is not due.
6. **Public responsibility**: scientists should report research in the public media when the research has an important and direct bearing on human happiness and when the research has been sufficiently validated by scientific peers.

Problems with Scientific Ethics in Research Practice

You may think that these principles are clear and easy to follow, but they are not. The principles are abstract and general so they can be applicable to all varieties and contexts of scientific work. As such, they do not fully reflect the contexts that we encounter in daily scientific practice. The principles provide general guidance for situations that scientists encounter, but they are not an algorithmic blueprint for carrying out scientific work.

One problem is that acceptable versus unacceptable behaviour can sometimes be hard to distinguish. Consider, for example, whether credit should be attributed to an advisor or mentor by naming him or her as co-author on a paper. If the mentor has contributed little to the writing of the paper but funded the research and your involvement in it, organised access to the data, and discussed ideas with you several times, should he or she be listed as co-author? Arguments can be made either way.

A second example involves the principle of *public responsibility*, which stipulates that scientists should present their research findings to the general public only after the findings have been validated through peer review. Concretely, this means you should not publish a newspaper article or even tweet about your findings from a study until the scientific outcome has been accepted for publication. The problem is that this process of validation can take months or years. During the Covid-19 pandemic, which started in 2020, the general public had a vested interest in learning about the virus and its consequences as quickly as possible: citizens, decision-makers, and politicians did not want to wait years for scientific research to be peer reviewed and published, so many scientific findings were shared publicly in the form of **preprint articles** in open repositories like ArXiv, SocArXiv, medRxiv, and others. This move made emergent knowledge available to the public faster, even though these findings have typically not yet been validated through peer review. (Remember, most articles are typically rejected during that process.) The task of evaluating and interpreting research findings was left to scientists and the general public, most of whom have not received training in discerning quality scientific work from less rigorous studies. Science journalists had to evaluate whether to report some preprint findings, a decision that can be complicated (Makri, 2021).

Another problem is that ethical principles can be in conflict with one another as sometimes the same action can be guided by different ethical rules that endorse or prohibit certain actions. In medicine, for example, doctors vow to do no harm and to respect the autonomy of patients' decisions, but what if a patient chooses to pursue a medical treatment that is likely to cause harm? Which principle should a doctor follow?

Since scientists, like all humans, do not always abide by the rules, ethical misconduct can result. To illustrate, consider a case that became known as the Schön scandal.

The Schön scandal concerned German physicist Jan Hendrik Schön, who rose to prominence in 2001 after a series of apparent breakthroughs in the area of electronics and nanotechnology. Schön's field of research was condensed matter physics and nanotechnology, and he rose to prominence upon reaching spectacular findings on the use of organic materials in lasers or for the display of superconductivity. Schön published widely and extensively (at one stage, authoring a new publication every eight days) in top journals like *Nature and Science* and gained worldwide attention.

However, no research group succeeded in reproducing the results Schön claimed. Moreover, scholars who attempted to replicate the experiments noted anomalies. For instance, several papers described the exact same "data noise" in experiments that supposedly used different parameters and settings. Later, investigations found examples of Schön having used the same data graphs in papers that supposedly reported on different experiments. As a result of these anomalies, an investigation revealed that Schön had erased the computer's raw data files from the experiments because, according to Schön, the computer had limited hard drive space. In addition, all of the experiments' samples had been discarded or damaged beyond repair.

The investigative report eventually identified at least 16 cases of scientific misconduct, and the journals that had published the studies retracted 21 of Schön's papers.

After the investigation, Schön acknowledged that the data were incorrect in many of these papers and claimed that the substitutions could have been honest mistakes. Schön admitted to having falsified some data to show more convincing evidence for the behaviours the experiments revealed. Subsequent experiments failed to obtain results similar to Schön's findings.

Schön did not work alone but collaborated with others who co-authored the papers. During the ethics investigation, the co-authors were relieved of the ethical allegations. This decision sparked widespread debate in the scientific community concerning how blame for misconduct should be shared among co-authors, particularly when they shared a significant part of the credit.

You may think that this story is long in the past and that cases of ethically unacceptable research behaviour are rare or occur only in distant fields, but you would be wrong. Science has had many encounters with ethical dilemmas, including in the present, and these cases occur in our field, not just in other disciplines. Here are more examples:

- The Piltdown man case, where scientists reported finding hominid remains in Sussex in 1912, which were later proven to be the skull of a modern man to which researchers had added a jawbone from an orangutan.
- The Nazi experiments on prisoners during World War II, especially concerning twins, matter transplantation, and the modelling of battlefield wounds.
- The Stanford prison experiment in 1971, in which volunteers were randomly assigned roles as guards or inmates and which led to outbreaks of sadism and psychological terror.
- The case of William Summerlin, who researched tissue rejection and performed experiments in 1974 that included transplanting fur from a black mouse onto a white mouse, where the black fur was actually drawn on with a black marker.
- The 1978 case of Vijay Soman and Philip Felig, who copied sections of a paper sent to them for review into a "new" submission of their own, together with additional material later shown to have been invented.
- The case of German minister Karl-Theodor zu Guttenberg, whose doctoral thesis contained a significant use of plagiarism.
- The case of Harvard University psychologist Marc Hauser, who fabricated and falsified data and made false statements about experimental methods in six federally funded studies.
- The case of Ulrich Lichtenthaler, who rose to fame in Germany because of his success in publishing research on open innovation. In 2012, several controversies arose around undeclared, multiple submissions that resulted in the parallel publication of similar papers, misrepresentation of the statistical significance of findings, and removal of variables in some papers despite their having been being reported as significant in his other papers using the same data. By 2014, 16 published papers were retracted.

These cases are only a few examples; there are many others. For example, *The New York Times* published a story about the case of Diederik Stapel, a Dutch social psychologist who made up studies that told the world what it wanted to hear about human nature (Bhattacharjee, 2013). All these cases point to a common narrative: research, as a profession, is susceptible to misbehaviour and misconduct in the same way as any other community of practice. Arguably, the cases above are severe, and some you might even find funny, but most of these and other cases resulted in legal actions, such as revoking of degrees, stripping of prestigious positions, cancellation of research funding, and even imprisonment. Other cases of ethical issues may not lead to legal action yet still bear consequences in terms of professional reputation, standing, or job security. Scientists can make honest mistakes, but they do not have to engage in ethical misconduct. Some of the well-known cases mentioned above have led to digital platforms that work to create more transparency about ethical mistakes and misconduct. Retraction Watch, for example, is a blog that reports on retractions of scientific papers and related topics. Launched in August 2010, the blog provides a window into the self-correcting nature of science and information about cases of scientific misconduct and fraud.

7.2   Ethical Considerations for Scientific Conduct

All behaviours involved in the research process, such as developing a theory, collecting data, and testing hypotheses, are subject to ethical considerations, codified and uncodified, particularly ethics related to empirical data collection and human subjects. For example, most universities, especially in the United States, Europe, and Australia, demand that research projects that involve human subjects undergo formal approval by an institutional review board prior to the research. This process is called **ethical clearance**. In Australia, research that requires the participation of humans must be undertaken in accordance with the National Statement on Ethical Conduct in Human Research. The purpose of the Statement is to promote ethical conduct in all aspects of research involving humans. Since information systems research typically involves humans, a research proposal must be submitted to an appropriate level of a university for ethical review, and the researcher must receive approval before commencing the research. Germany has similar guidelines that require ethical clearance prior to even submitting a grant application to receive funding for a research project. Ethical clearances must be applied for and approved *prior to starting* any research activities (e.g., primary data collection) that involve humans.

Regarding primary empirical **data collection involving humans**, while information systems research does not usually present the potential for harm to participants in the same way that biological or medical studies may, an ethics review board still considers the extent to which participation in a study is voluntary, does not exert physical or psychological stress, and does not cause other kinds of damage to participants, as well as whether participants must give consent regarding how their data will be used or reported or how the data will be protected in terms of anonymity or confidentiality and whether they have the right to withdraw from participation at any time.

Since information systems research is a social science, an ethical principle in conducting research is that the researcher must be responsible for securing the permission and attending to the interests of all individuals involved in the study. We should not misuse any of the information we compile, and we have a duty to protect the rights, privacy, confidentiality, and anonymity of people who participate in the study.

In some cases, the principle of **anonymity**, which means that individuals cannot be identified even by the researcher, may run against the data-collection method. For example, anonymity is difficult to preserve in in-person interviews. In such cases, appropriate actions must be taken to ensure that, while full anonymity cannot be guaranteed, the **confidentiality** of the data will be maintained such that no participant's identity can be revealed from any form of research disclosure, including reports, papers, and presentations.

Typically, information systems studies involve **voluntary participation** by human subjects, where people are free to choose whether to participate in a study without suffering negative consequences. For example, a study in which we promise students bonus marks as a reward for participating in an experiment is not ethical because it coerces students to participate since otherwise, their grades will suffer in comparison to those of other students. An ethical solution would be to offer those students who choose not to participate an alternative way to receiving bonus marks (e.g., through an alternative task).

Voluntary participation also means clarifying participants' right to withdraw from a study prior to its conclusion. Participants must also be given information about the **potential risks** of participation. All these details about a study are typically summarised in an **information consent form** that all participants sign. An example is shown in Fig. 7.1.

Ethical considerations related to conducting research also involve standards for the **storage and analysis of research data** so cases like the Schön scandal can be reviewed expeditiously. Generally speaking, all research data, including primary materials and raw data, such as survey questionnaires, measurements, recordings, and computer results, must be stored in secure and durable storage facilities. The minimum recommended period for the retention of research data and primary materials is five years from the date of publication, but this period may vary based on the nature of the research. Elements to consider regarding storage typically include ownership (especially in cross-institutional collaboration), storage and backup, privacy, confidentiality, access, and reuse.

Ethical obligations regarding data analysis refer to honest and complete reporting of how data are analysed and reported. Negative or undesired results still require full disclosure unless you abandon that part of the research, even if they run against the premise of the paper or the research design. Other unethical behaviours related to data analysis include evaluating hypotheses based on partial, incomplete, or improper data analysis; segmenting data for analysis to increase support for hypotheses; and fabricating, changing, or deleting data to achieve better results. Some of these practices have become known under labels like p-Hacking (manipulating, transforming, testing, and analysing data until some statistically significant result emerges) and HARKing (hypothesising after results are known). P-Hacking involves subjecting data to many calculations or manipulations in search of a statistical result that yields the desired patterns. HARKing involves presenting a post hoc hypothesis in a paper as if it were an a priori hypothesis (e.g., in the introduction) (Kerr, 1998). HARKing treads a fine line between being ethical or not depending on whether hypotheses were anticipated and/or plausible and whether the

Consent to participate in research

Project title: _____
Lead investigator: _____
Ethical clearance: _____

> Add project details and a unique reference to the ethical clearance provided by an independent ethics review board

- I, ..., voluntarily agree to participate in this research study.
- I understand that even if I agree to participate now, I can withdraw at any time or refuse to answer any question without any consequences of any kind.
- I understand that I can withdraw permission to use data from my participation within two weeks after the participation, in which case the material will be deleted.

> Here you typically insert specifics about what participation actually means (e.g., being interviewed or completing a survey)

- I have had the purpose and nature of the study explained to me and I have had the opportunity to ask questions about the study.
- I understand that participation involves at least **one semi-structured in-depth interview (follow-up interviews and observations are optional)**.
- I understand that I will not benefit directly from participating in this research.
- I agree to my interview being audio-recorded, transcribed and analysed.

> Here you specify who will be able to access the research data

- I understand that the access to the interview transcript will be limited to **Prof Dr Jan Recker**.
- I understand that all information I provide for this study will be treated confidentially and that I have been informed about being able to sign a non-disclosure agreement in addition.
- I understand that in the report on the results of this research my identity will remain anonymous. This will be done by changing my name and disguising any details of my interview that may reveal my identity or the identity of people I speak about.
- I understand that disguised extracts from my interview may be quoted (directly and indirectly) in reports about this research. With regards to being quoted, please make an 'x' next to any of the statements that you agree with:

  ☐ I wish to review the notes, transcripts, or other data collected during the research pertaining to my participation.

  ☐ I agree to be quoted directly if my name is not published and a made-up name (pseudonym) is used.

  ☐ I wish to review any report/paper pertaining to my participation prior to submission.

> Here you can list choices a participant has about his data will be used

- I understand that if I inform the researcher that myself or someone else is at risk of harm they may have to report this to the relevant authorities - they will discuss this with me first but may be required to report with or without my permission.
- I understand that signed consent forms and original audio recordings will be retained by the research team for a period of time in accordance with research data management regulations.
- I understand that under freedom of information legalisation I am entitled to access the information I have provided at any time while it is in storage as specified above.
- I understand that I am free to contact any of the people involved in the research or **the independent ethics committee at ...** to seek further clarification and information.

> Here you specify an independent third party that could be involved in the matter

Signature of research participant

------------------------------   ------------------------------
Signature of participant   *City, Date*

Signature of researcher

I believe the participant is giving informed consent to participate in this study.

------------------------------   ------------------------------
Signature of researcher   *City, Date*

Fig. 7.1 Sample information consent form for empirical research

reasoning mode was hypothetico-deductive or inductive. You can read about some of these and other practices that may be associated with ethical issues in articles like Mertens & Recker (2020) and O'Boyle Jr. et al. (2017).

Examples I Have Encountered

Ethical considerations in information systems research are not some kind of semantic or ephemeral concern. You will, as I have, encounter them in your work. To make the material palpable, I present three cases I have encountered. All involve *potential* ethical conflict rather than an ethical violation. These examples are not black or white: different parties had different viewpoints on the matter, which is common in ethical dilemmas. I encourage you to consider for yourself whether these cases involve strong ethical misconduct, some ethical misconduct, or none at all.

The first case occurred with a study on how novice analysts would conceptualise business processes if we did not train them to use a particular language, notation, or tool for doing so. Process analysts' work is usually done using certain standards and tools, and we wanted to know whether these methods align with how those who carry out this work would intuitively describe business processes if they did not have to follow these standards.

At that time, we taught process analysis as an introductory university course for first-semester bachelor's degree students. They came straight out of high school, so they had received no training that could have influenced or biased them.

Our experiment consisted of giving each student in the class a single blank sheet of paper and a pencil on the first morning of their first semester. We told them the story of a business process involving a person who had to catch a flight to Sydney and asked them to capture this process on their paper in any way they saw fit. We later collected the papers, which contained drawings and/or text, and analysed them for the quality of the information they contained about the business process.

We had not applied for ethical clearance as I did not see the need. At that time, I honestly was not really well trained in ethics. It did not feature as a course in my PhD education. But admittedly, at that time, I had already undertaken other empirical studies that involved ethical clearance, so I was aware of this process and had completed it before.

As in any class, we gave students a blank piece of paper, asked them to perform a task, and collected their responses. We did not manipulate them. We did not experiment on them. They did not have to solve a problem where they were scored in any sense. The activity had nothing to do with the grades they would eventually receive in the course.

As it happened, though, one student notified the ethics committee, which found that we did not have ethical clearance and did not ask for informed consent, so the committee did not allow us to analyse the collected data or to report it. We had to wait one more year to repeat the study with a new cohort of first-year students. Of course, we obtained ethical clearance in advance, all students signed the information and consent form they had to sign, and so forth, and we published the study a year later (Recker et al., 2012). Nowhere in the paper will you read that we had originally worked on the same idea with different data one year earlier but without due ethical diligence. In hindsight, I admit to my mistake even though at that time I was angry that I had to wait one more year before I could proceed with my research. But it was important: the difference between what we asked these students to do and any other assignment was that we intended to use the data we collected to analyse their responses for the purposes of research and publication.

The second example involves research I carried out in collaboration with a large retail organisation in Australia. We had a collaboration agreement under which we agreed to carry out a variety of studies. As part of this collaboration, the organisation provided us with access to certain data, for which several legal contracts were in place to govern this access. In one situation, they gave us access to their enterprise social networking platform, a type of organisational internal social network that was not unlike Facebook. We received a data file that contained the entire log of that network—all posts and comments made by all members of the organisation on that platform over almost two years.

This access presented us with an ethical dilemma as the data were not anonymous or confidential: we could see who posted what to whom and when. Ethical guidelines would stipulate that we needed written consent from some 180,000 staff who worked in that organisation, which was not really feasible with any reasonable amount of time and effort. In the end, we had to liaise between the organisation in the form of an information technology (IT) staff member who was responsible for hosting the data and making it available to us, the ethics board at our university (which stipulated the conditions by which we could use the data), and our own research team, which had certain requirements for the data to be useful to our research. Through multiple rounds of discussions, we settled on the organisation's anonymising the data prior to giving us access—details like names were omitted, staff IDs were replaced with scrambled codes, and so forth—while still yielding access to data like the posters' role in the organisation and the location of work in terms of a particular retail store (because this information was relevant to our research question). As a result, we received not the raw data but an amended data set that was agreeable to the independent review board and that was both sufficiently confidential and sufficiently descriptive for our research purposes. You can imagine that this process of finding the right balance took several months, but we were eventually able to carry out our research and publish it (Recker & Lekse, 2016).

The third example concerns a situation that was not an ethical mistake or an ethical challenge but perhaps more an example of ethical harm. I once collaborated with researchers from another institution to do some interesting research that we published. We were excited about the outcome and planned to do more research together, so I presented an idea for a study that I had at that time, my thoughts on theory and hypothesis development, and my thoughts about a research design for testing the idea.

We never started that collaboration as we were all busy with other things, but some years later, I stumbled across a paper that was co-authored by one of the collaborators with whom I had shared the idea. That paper reported on research in progress and contained my idea, theory, and suggested research design, plus some initial results they had obtained.

You may imagine I was furious. I felt they had stolen my idea without involving me. The opportunity to collaborate with me was there as I was still collaborating with them in other ways and in other projects. I brought the matter up, and they decided not to pursue the project further (as far as I know).

This example shows how difficult ethical cases can be. I felt credit was mis-attributed, but I also realise that one can also look at the situation differently: I had shared an idea, but I had not pursued it. I had not written about it. In a way, I exposed intellectual property, but I did not secure it. One view might be that other people have the right to develop an idea further, but the question is at what point would such a behaviour stop being okay and be unethical instead? One good outcome from this case was that we discussed the situation and how we felt about it, and it has not significantly affected our collaboration since.

7.3 Ethical Considerations for Scientific Writing

One subset of ethical issues in scientific conduct relates only to the reporting of research. The example of the student reporting our study to the university's ethics committee being an exception, it is typically only through reported research that an ethical issue is revealed as we typically cannot learn about data fabrication or amendment until those data are disclosed. We cannot identify a lack of attribution of credit until an unnamed contributor sees it in writing. However, as my examples show, scientific reporting alone does not necessarily fully disclose all ethical issues that might have occurred.

Here I discuss four ethical considerations that relate to scientific writing, these being plagiarism, recognition of co-author contributions, honest reporting, and the appropriate use of language.

Plagiarism is the wrongful appropriation, close imitation, or purloining and publication of another author's language, thoughts, ideas, or expressions and their representation as one's own work. It is, essentially, the misattribution of credit. It is also the most common form of scientific misconduct.

While plagiarism is often intentional, it may also be unintentional because of confusion regarding the definition of plagiarism. Several varieties of plagiarism exist, some of which skirt the line between ethical and unethical behaviour.

Intentional plagiarism occurs when a writer knowingly lifts text directly from other authors' work without giving appropriate credit. *Self-plagiarism* occurs when a writer copies large parts of an earlier manuscript word for word into a new manuscript. This kind of plagiarism can occur, especially when individuals pursue large programs of research over many years on the same topic, so they are constantly building on their own work and in their own language. *Duplicate publication* occurs when an author submits for publication a previously published work as if it were original.

Institutions like universities and scientific publishers often use plagiarism-detection software, which compares the text of a manuscript with a database of published scholarly work. It typically provides a similarity index, often expressed in terms of the percentage of a manuscript's text that is similar (from somewhat similar to closely similar) to some other text.

I feel it is very important to state the obvious: plagiarism can destroy a reputation and a career, and you are unlikely to get away with it. The simple rule is this: do not plagiarise in any form. Instead, do the following:

1. Always acknowledge the sources of and contributions to your ideas.
2. Enclose in quotation marks any passage of text that is directly taken from another author's work and acknowledge that author in an in-text citation.
3. Acknowledge every source you use in writing, whether you paraphrase it, summarise it, or quote it directly.
4. When paraphrasing or summarising other authors' work, reproduce the meaning of the original author's ideas or facts as closely as possible using your own words and sentence composition.
5. Do not copy sections of your previously published work into a new manuscript without citing the publication and using quotation marks.

Next, the **recognition of co-author contributions** concerns appropriately acknowledging collaborators' substantial contributions to a scholarly work. The appropriate recognition of co-author contributions (not too much or too little) is an ethical issue that appears frequently in scientific work. It is difficult to deal with because the correct attribution of credit sounds easy but is hard to identify in practice. In Chap. 6, we discussed guidelines for identifying co-authorship situations. You can use these guidelines to avoid four kinds of ethical issues that relate to authorship:

1. *Coercion authorship* occurs when intimidation is used to gain authorship credit, such as when a senior person pressures a more junior person to include the senior person's name on a paper to which he or she has not contributed enough to qualify for authorship. Such situations often occur when a department head or director of an institution asks to be named on papers that are produced in their labs or groups or when researchers who secured funding ask to be named on the papers whose research benefited from the funding but who were not sufficiently involved in the research.
2. *Gift authorship* describes situations in which individuals are given recognition as co-authors without having made substantial contributions, often for reasons like acknowledging friendship, gaining favour, or giving the paper more legitimacy by adding well-known senior researchers to the list of authors.
3. *Mutual support authorship* occurs when two or more authors (or author groups) agree to place their names on each other's papers to enhance their perceived productivity. The "authors" can count both publications towards their own list of papers, receive citations for both papers, and so forth.
4. *Ghost authorship* occurs when papers are written by people who are not included as authors or are not acknowledged. A typical form of ghost authorship involves using or hiring professional scientific writers, perhaps because the researchers feel they cannot write "well" or "scientifically."

Honest reporting is a third ethical consideration in scientific writing. It is an ethical standard that demands that research publications comply with expectations for transparency, openness, and reproducibility, which are principles recognised as vital features of science. Honest reporting can become an ethical issue because of publication bias (a systematic suppression of a certain type of research results in published papers, such as negative hypothesis tests) or because of skewed incentive systems (such as demanding innovative and novel findings rather than replications and confirmation of known findings). For example, it is well established that many journals, including information systems journals, tend to publish studies in which statistically significant support for hypotheses is reported rather than not (Mertens & Recker, 2020; Starbuck, 2016).

Since about 2015, hundreds of journals have started to implement a set of eight standards for honest reporting called TOP (transparency and openness promotion) (McNutt, 2016; Nosek et al., 2015):

1. The *citation standard* stipulates that all data, program code, and other methods be appropriately cited using persistent identifiers, except for truly special situations, such as non-disclosure agreements about sensitive data, which should be discussed with editors during the review process.
2. The *data standard* stipulates that it must be possible to make the research data used in a paper available to other researchers for the purpose of reproducing or extending the paper's analysis. Exceptions should be discussed with editors during the review process.
3. *Analytic methods transparency* stipulates that the methods/code/scripts used in data analysis be made available to other researchers for the purpose of reproducing the paper's analysis where needed. Exceptions should be discussed with editors during the review process.
4. *Research materials transparency* stipulates that the materials used in an analysis be made available to other researchers for the purpose of directly replicating the procedure where needed. Authors are also expected to honour reasonable requests for research materials so other research groups can extend and advance the results. Any restrictions on the availability of materials should be discussed with editors during the review process.
5. *Design and analysis transparency* stipulates that authors adhere to reporting standards in their field that relate to how key aspects of the research design and analysis should be carried out and reported.
6. The *pre-registration of studies* stipulates that, where possible, a research design, including materials, measurements, and hypotheses, be pre-registered (Warren, 2018) and made available prior to data collection.
7. The *pre-registration of analysis plans* stipulates that, where possible, analysis plans be pre-registered and made available prior to the analysis of data.
8. The *replication standard* stipulates that academic journals hold replication studies to the same standards as other content submitted to the journal. There are also guidelines for reporting research data, such as statistics, in such a way that they

contain all information that would be required to replicate the analyses (e.g., Wasserstein & Lazar, 2016).

These standards were put forward only recently, and not all stakeholders involved in publishing (authors, editors, reviewers, publishers) have accepted them in all outlets and fields. It is not easy for all fields to adopt them (McNutt, 2016), but a shift in the research culture, often called the open science culture, is underway (Molloy, 2011; Nosek et al., 2015). Increasing numbers of journals have published editorials to promote a shift in authoring and reviewing work in light of these standards. (e.g., Bettis et al., 2016; Wasserstein et al., 2019).

The field of information systems has not, in my view, been an early adopter of the new ethical standards for transparency, openness, and reproducibility, but I hope we will see changes in how we report our research. For example, a dedicated replication project initiative was carried out in information systems research (Dennis et al., 2020), which can be interpreted as an attempt to follow the replication standard. Or, with a colleague, I developed new guidelines for reporting quantitative information systems studies that include suggestions for data sharing, pre-registration, and a declaration regarding whether the data were analysed inductively (without a priori hypotheses) or deductively (with hypotheses and a statement that identifies which were supported or rejected by data) (Mertens & Recker, 2020).

There are also ways in which authors themselves can shift the research culture. For example, I have made my research data sets openly available in several papers (e.g., Recker & Mendling, 2016; Zelt et al., 2018), I have pre-registered several of my hypotheses a priori on open science repositories (https://osf.io/ecwsj), and I have made transparent how a paper evolved in several versions through the review process (https://doi.org/10.31235/osf.io/5qr7v).

Finally, the **appropriate use of language** refers to the wording of reports so they are not biased in terms of gender, race, orientation, culture, or any other character-istics. Several guidelines exist about the appropriate use of language. One such guideline demands specificity, such as describing behaviours as dominant and opinionated instead of "typically male"; labelling, such as referring to countries' populations—Mexicans or Chinese—instead of classes like "Hispanics" or "Asians"; and professional acknowledgments, like "medical practitioner" or "doc-tor" instead of "female doctor." The appropriate use of language also involves using gender-responsible, ethnicity-responsible, and inclusive language.

Examples I Have Encountered

Again, I want to give a few examples of ethical dilemmas I have faced over the years in academic publishing. My first example occurred while I was working in Australia. A research group from another country had secured some travel grant money to send doctoral students to our research group. A senior researcher secured the grant and managed the process of sending students over to us in Brisbane for about a year each.

While they were with us, I collaborated with some of these students, including a student who worked with a postdoctoral researcher and me on a project related to digital innovation. We spent about a year collecting data, analysed that data, and wrote a paper that we first presented at a conference and later prepared for journal submission.

As the three of us had just about finished writing the initial conference paper (about ten pages long), the senior researcher from the student's home institution asked to be included as a co-author. The senior researcher had not actively or otherwise substantially been involved in the research process, but we were working against a hard deadline, time was running out, the student told me that the practice was the norm in their institution, and I did not want to engage in what would be an awkward debate, so while I principally disagreed with the request, we added the name to the paper.

Afterwards, as we worked towards the journal version of the paper (about 25 pages long), the situation recurred. This time, I expressed my discontent with granting the senior researcher co-authorship credit for what appeared to me an insufficient intellectual contribution to the paper. We offered an opportunity for the researcher to become more actively involved and to contribute substantially by writing a section of the paper, but the person did not accept the opportunity while still requesting to be included as an author. We made an appointment to discuss the issue with the entire team. The other researcher continued to claim authorship for making the research possible by securing the grant and managing the exchange, but as the most senior researcher on the research team, I did not compromise. In the end, we did not include the person on the paper. As a result, in my perception, my relationship with that person soured.

Such situations occur frequently and are not easy to resolve, even if you think the ethical guidelines are clear, as there are always other factors to consider. Social relationships, power relationships, and dependencies also have effects, such as when one person has financial authority over the contracts of another person or when one person has the authority to decide on the conferral of a research degree.

Because of the experiences I have made, I have formulated my own ethical principle that I will allow myself to be included on papers only when I have substantially contributed to the research and publication process. In situations where I am not sure whether my contributions, in my own view, are substantial, I ask not to be included as a co-author. In situations that involve others, I am usually more lenient regarding their requests to be included, if only to preserve relationships or to avoid putting other researchers, particularly students, at risk because of power dependencies. I am not sure I am holding a strong ethical position here, but I can look at myself in the mirror.

A second example occurred recently. I was asked to handle the review process for a paper as a senior editor for a journal and asked an associate editor to help. During the review process, we found that the paper was a resubmission from the same author on the same topic with the same data that, as a previous submission, the author had sent us four of five times before. It was rejected each time, but every time by a different editor. It was only by chance that the associate editor I asked to help had been involved with a prior submission of the same research. We investigated and found the trail of submissions in the manuscript-handling system. We confronted the author with this information because authors who submit papers have to declare adherence to the AIS Code of Research Conduct and the journal's provenance declaration, and the author's submission breached these requirements.

Through follow-up conversations between editors and authors, it became apparent the author believed that a rejected paper that is rewritten can be resubmitted as a new paper, although such is not the case.

This example shows that not all authors are aware of or trained in the extant ethical standards. Institutions are increasingly including ethics in their formal research training curricula (Resnik & Dinse, 2012), but their numbers remain small. The case also shows that while scientific journals typically require authors to confirm their adherence to ethical standards, it is not a safeguard against ethical violations. The paper was reviewed using voluntary resources at least four times before the problem was discovered and addressed.

7.4 Further Reading

Three key resources can give you more information about ethics in information systems research. The first is the **set of ethical standards set by the Association for Information Systems**, the professional community of academics in the information systems field. This professional body has a research conduct committee that acts as an independent review board when cases of potential ethical misconduct occur in our field.

Their standard for ethical behaviour in information systems research, the AIS Code of Conduct, can be found at https://aisnet.org/general/custom.asp?page=AdmBullCResearchCond. A journal article that explains the process of developing the code of conduct was published in *MIS Quarterly* (Kock & Davison, 2003). This article also examines reasons for engaging in ethically controversial research behaviours. The AIS Code of Conduct has four primary objectives:

1. To provide guidance for people who are entering or are currently in the profession of information systems research regarding what plagiarism is and how to avoid it
2. To provide a reference point for members of the profession of information systems research, including guidance on how to evaluate whether a particular act or omission constitutes plagiarism and how serious an instance of plagiarism is
3. To provide a basis for consideration by the AIS Research Conduct Committee of instances of possible scholarly misconduct by members in relation to research and publication activities
4. To provide a benchmark with which organisations like courts, tribunals, employers, and publishers can consider instances of possible scholarly

Category One
Code items in this category must _ALWAYS_ be adhered to and disregard for them constitutes a serious ethical breach. Serious breaches can result in your expulsion from academic associations, dismissal from your employment, legal action against you, and potentially fatal damage to your academic reputation.

✓ Do not plagiarize.
✓ Do not fabricate or falsify data, research procedures, or data analysis.
✓ Do not use other people's unpublished writings, information, ideas, concepts or data that you may see as a result of processes such as peer review without permission of the author.
✓ Do not make misrepresentations to editors and conference program chairs about the originality of papers you submit to them.

Category Two
Items in this category are _RECOMMENDED_ ethical behaviour. Flagrant disregard of these or other kinds of professional etiquette, while less serious than violations in category one, can result in damage to your reputation, editorial sanctions, professional embarrassment, legal action, and the ill will of your colleagues. While individual scholars may disagree about the most appropriate action to take in a particular situation, a broad consensus exists that violation of any of the rules in this category constitutes a breach of professional ethics.

✓ Give priority to the public interest, particularly when designing or implementing new information systems or other designed artefacts.
✓ Respect the rights of research subjects, particularly their rights to information privacy, and to being informed about the nature of the research and the types of activities in which they will be asked to engage.
✓ Do not abuse the authority and responsibility you have been given as an editor, reviewer or supervisor, and ensure that personal relationships do not interfere with your judgment.
✓ Do not take or use published data of others without acknowledgement; do not take or use unpublished data without both permission and acknowledgement.
✓ Declare any material conflict of interest that might interfere with your ability to be objective and impartial when reviewing submissions, grant applications, software, or undertaking work from outside sources.
✓ Acknowledge the substantive contributions of all research participants, whether colleagues or students, according to their intellectual contribution.
✓ Use archival material only in accordance with the rules of the archival source.

Advice
Items in this category are considered _SUGGESTIONS_ on how to protect yourself from authorship disputes, missteps, mistakes, and potential legal action.

✓ Keep the documentation and data necessary to validate your original authorship for each scholarly work with which you are connected.
✓ Do not republish old ideas of your own as if they were a new intellectual contribution.
✓ Settle data set ownership issues before data compilation.
✓ Consult appropriate colleagues if in doubt.

Fig. 7.2 AIS Code of Conduct for information systems researchers

misconduct by information systems professionals in relation to research and publication activities

As Fig. 7.2 shows, the Code of Conduct differentiates mandatory codes that must always be adhered to (**category one**) from recommended codes that should be followed (**category two**) and optional **advice** about how to protect yourself from authorship disputes, missteps, mistakes, and legal action.

The debate about the role, content, and impact of these standards is ongoing, and the association reviews and updates the code annually.

The second resource is the available set of **explanations of scientific ethics and standards for ethical conduct of science in general**, beyond the information systems field. Resnik's (2020) excellent introduction to scientific ethics features several illustrative cases, including the Schön scandal. The blog also features references to several codes and policies for research ethics that are published by government agencies, professional associations, and other public institutions that are related to scientific work, such as the Australian Research Council, the German Research Foundation, and the (United States) National Science Foundation. The United States also has a program that issues certifications in ethics training (CITI Program, 2010) that you can obtain and which many institutions require before a researcher can even apply for ethical clearances or grants. Finally, the article, "Ethical Consideration in Scientific Writing" (Carver et al., 2011) is also useful.

Studies and papers on ethics in information systems research and related fields constitute a third category of resources. Allen et al. (2011) investigated IS researchers' adherence to the AIS ethical standards. Finding that the focus and stage of career influenced individual judgments, they developed a set of recommendations regarding the role of ethical norms. Kock's (2001) "A Case of Academic Plagiarism" described a case in which the author was the victim of scientific misconduct. *Communications of the Association for Information Systems* published a special issue about the ethical issues relating to self-citation practices in journals (Gray, 2009). Another view on this topic was offered in Clarke (2006), an analysis of plagiarism in academic research settings. Clarke's useful web page related to ethics and information systems can be accessed at http://www.rogerclarke.com/SOS/ #ISEthics.

Literature on *questionable research practices* (Bedeian et al., 2010; O'Boyle Jr. et al., 2017) has addressed issues that skirt the line between ethical and unethical behaviours, which are prevalent in academia (Kerr, 1998; Starbuck, 2016). It makes sense to learn about the ethics of certain practices so you can make informed decisions about whether to engage in them.

References

Allen, G. N., Ball, N. L., & Smith, H. J. (2011). Information Systems Research Behaviors: What Are the Normative Standards? *MIS Quarterly, 35*(3), 533–551.

Bedeian, A. G., Taylor, S. G., & Miller, A. N. (2010). Management Science on the Credibility Bubble: Cardinal Sins and Various Misdemeanors. *Academy of Management Learning & Education, 9*(4), 715–725.

Bettis, R. A., Ethiraj, S., Gambardella, A., Helfat, C., & Mitchell, W. (2016). Creating Repeatable Cumulative Knowledge in Strategic Management. *Strategic Management Journal, 37*(2), 257–261.

Bhattacharjee, Y. (2013). The Mind of a Con Man. *The New York Times Magazine.* Retrieved February 8, from https://www.nytimes.com/2013/04/28/magazine/diederik-stapels-audacious-academic-fraud.html

Carver, J. D., Dellva, B., Emmanuel, P. J., & Parchure, R. (2011). Ethical Considerations in Scientific Writing. *Indian Journal of Sexually Transmitted Diseases and AIDS, 32*(2), 124–128.

CITI Program. (2010). *The Trusted Standard in Research, Ethics, and Compliance Training.* CITI Program. Retrieved February 8, 2021 from https://about.citiprogram.org/en/homepage/

Clarke, R. (2006). Plagiarism by Academics: More Complex Than It Seems. *Journal of the Association for Information Systems, 7*(5), 91–121.

Dennis, A. R., Brown, S. A., Wells, T. M., & Rai, A. (2020). Editor's Comments: Replication Crisis or Replication Reassurance: Results of the IS Replication Project. *MIS Quarterly, 44*(3), iii–vii.

Gray, P. (2009). Journal Self-Citation I: Overview of the Journal Self-Citation Papers—The Wisdom of the IS Crowd. *Communications of the Association for Information Systems, 25*(1), 1–10.

Kerr, N. L. (1998). HARKing: Hypothesizing After the Results are Known. *Personality and Social Psychology Review, 2*(3), 196–217.

Kock, N. (2001). A Case of Academic Plagiarism. *Communications of the ACM, 42*(7), 96–104.

Kock, N., & Davison, R. (2003). Dealing with Plagiarism in the Information Systems Research Community: A Look at Factors that Drive Plagiarism and Ways to Address Them. *MIS Quarterly, 27*(4), 511–532.

Makri, A. (2021). What do Journalists say About Covering Science During the COVID-19 Pandemic? *Nature Medicine, 27*, 17–20. https://doi.org/10.1038/s41591-020-01207-3

McNutt, M. (2016). Taking Up TOP. *Science, 352*(6290), 1147.

Mertens, W., & Recker, J. (2020). New Guidelines for Null Hypothesis Significance Testing in Hypothetico-Deductive IS Research. *Journal of the Association for Information Systems, 21*(4), 1072–1102. https://doi.org/10.17705/1jais.00629

Molloy, J. C. (2011). The Open Knowledge Foundation: Open Data Means Better Science. *PLoS Biology, 9*(12), e1001195.

Nosek, B. A., Alter, G., Banks, G. C., Borsboom, D., Bowman, S. D., Breckler, S. J., Buck, S., Chambers, C. D., Chin, G., Christensen, G., Contestabile, M., Dafoe, A., Eich, E., Freese, J., Glennerster, R., Goroff, D., Green, D. P., Hesse, B., Humphreys, M., et al. (2015). Promoting an Open Research Culture. *Science, 348*(6242), 1422–1425.

O'Boyle, E. H., Jr., Banks, G. C., & Gonzalez-Mulé, E. (2017). The Chrysalis Effect: How Ugly Initial Results Metamorphosize Into Beautiful Articles. *Journal of Management, 43*(2), 376–399.

Recker, J., & Lekse, D. (2016). A Field Study of Spatial Preferences in Enterprise Microblogging. *Journal of Information Technology, 31*(2), 115–129.

Recker, J., & Mendling, J. (2016). The State-of-the-Art of Business Process Management Research as Published in the BPM Conference: Recommendations for Progressing the Field. *Business & Information Systems Engineering, 58*(1), 55–72.

Recker, J., Safrudin, N., & Rosemann, M. (2012). How Novices Design Business Processes. *Information Systems, 37*(6), 557–573.

Resnik, D. B. (2016). Ethics in Science. In P. Humphreys (Ed.), *The Oxford Handbook of Philosophy of Science* (pp. 252–273). Oxford University Press.

Resnik, D. B. (2020). *What Is Ethics in Research & Why Is It Important?* National Institute of Environmental Health Sciences. Retrieved February 3, 2021 from https://www.niehs.nih.gov/research/resources/bioethics/whatis/index.cfm

Resnik, D. B., & Dinse, G. E. (2012). Do U.S. Research Institutions Meet or Exceed Federal Mandates for Instruction in Responsible Conduct of Research? A National Survey. *Academic Medicine, 87*(9), 1237–1242. https://doi.org/10.1097/ACM.0b013e318260fe5c

Starbuck, W. H. (2016). 60th Anniversary Essay: How Journals Could Improve Research Practices in Social Science. *Administrative Science Quarterly, 61*(2), 165–183.

Warren, M. (2018). First Analysis of 'Pre-registered' Studies Shows Sharp Rise in Null Findings. *Nature*, October 24. d41586-41018-07118-41581.

Wasserstein, R. L., & Lazar, N. A. (2016). The ASA's Statement on P-values: Context, Process, and Purpose. *The American Statistician, 70*(2), 129–133.

Wasserstein, R. L., Schirm, A. L., & Lazar, N. A. (2019). Moving to a World Beyond "p < 0.05". *The American Statistician, 73*(Suppl 1), 1–19.

Zelt, S., Recker, J., Schmiedel, T., & vom Brocke, J. (2018). Development and Validation of an Instrument to Measure and Manage Organizational Process Variety. *Plos ONE, 13*(10), e0206198.

Chapter 8
Concluding Remarks

In reflecting on the second edition of this book, I feel joy and relief but also a bit of trepidation. The thought of updating my experiences, lessons learned, and personal values and beliefs related to research has been with me for several years now, and I am grateful that this book presents the opportunity to share these thoughts with others. I am also happy that I finally took to the task of writing a second edition of the book that is more voluminous and, I think, significantly better, than the first. It is also much more personal, as I not only curate others' advice and guidelines but also express my own opinions and views on many matters. These are my views based on my years of experience, but they are not necessarily held by everyone, and they do not have to be yours.

I hope that my observations, ideas, and advice offer you sound guidance and that they make your adventure on the strenuous path toward becoming an accomplished researcher easier. I also hope that it increases your excitement about growing into what I find a gratifying, exciting, and honorable profession.

The aim of the book was to lay a foundation for students and young scholars on which to build their professional academic work. I hope it serves you well by painting a comprehensive picture of the life of a researcher and inspires you to pursue this profession with enthusiasm, creativity, and dedication.

If there is just one thing I hope you gain from reading this book, it is a desire to learn more about and do more research on what interests you and can benefit science and practice. Scientific work is challenging, and because it is challenging, it is rewarding. It is a profession of lifelong learning and constant personal development. I hope this book provides a gateway to expanding your interests and searching for more knowledge.

While you are on this path, remember that the time you spend learning and doing research–especially during your doctoral studies–is likely to be the most stimulating of your life. You are about to develop knowledge that humankind has been lacking to date! How exciting is that?

Also remember that science is a social process. It is done by a community of scientists, a small, eclectic, and sometimes weird group of people that largely

© Springer Nature Switzerland AG 2021
J. Recker, *Scientific Research in Information Systems*, Progress in IS,
https://doi.org/10.1007/978-3-030-85436-2_8

governs itself without much interference from the outside world. Thus, we have the freedom to pursue our own interests. We also review and publish our own work, jointly create and enforce standards, develop norms, and forge our own culture. Becoming a scientist means engaging in this social community, where what we do is not driven by mandate or financial incentive but by a desire or an obligation to contribute to the community and the world at large.

The good news about our own little community, the information systems field, is that it is full of smart, warm people. Go out and meet these people, shake their hands (or bump elbows), and talk to them. In most situations, they will be happy to talk to you and will gladly share their experiences and give advice. They will be interested in what you want to do and what you have to say. It is wonderful that we have such a friendly community, and it fills me with the aspiration to give back to this community, whether through voluntary reviews, committee work, or other acts of help. I hope you will have the same aspiration.

Let me end this book with some notes of caution. This book is colored by my own experiences as a scholar and is an attempt to convey my own lessons and knowledge about research and how best to conduct it. But the journey towards becoming a better researcher—including my own journey—is never finished. The knowledge and experiences conveyed in this book are the results of my own interpretations of my work and that of others, and any errors I have made are my own and no one else's. I simply hope that sharing experiences from my journey will help to ease your own.

One saying in our discipline is "read before you write!" Now that you have read the final lines of this book, start writing—start practicing research and tell others about your work. And should you be tired of reading but still not ready to start writing, perhaps you want to listen first. In such a case, take out your headphones and tune into our podcast "this IS research", available on all major podcasting platforms, where we discuss all sorts of topics related to information systems scholarship. Just Google "this IS research" and you will find it.

Most importantly, make sure you enjoy what you do, and do your best to do it well. That is always the main ingredient to a happy and fulfilling life.

Jan Recker

Hamburg, Germany, May 2021

Index

Findings, 185
Focal constructs, 62
Formative measurement, 148
Formatively-measured, 95

G
Gap, 37, 180
Generalisability, 49, 79
Ghost authorship, 207
Gift authorship, 207
Grounded theory, 115, 132, 149
Grounded theory research, 116

H
HARKing, 202
Holistic, 126, 127
Honest reporting, 208
Honesty, 198
Hook, 180
Hypotheses, 182–183
Hypothesis, 27, 28
Hypothetico-deductive model of science, 89

I
Idiographic, 60, 114
Iependent, 66
Impact, 165
Implications, 80, 186, 187
    for practice, 186
    for research, 186
Independence, 23
Independent, 66
Independent variable, 66
Induction, 40–42, 72
Inductive research, 64
Inferential analysis, 111
Information and communication technologies,
    3, 4, 13, 19
Information systems, 3
Information systems research, 3
Initiation, 144
Integrity, 198
Intellectual reasoning, 40–42
Internal validity, 95, 107, 110
Inter-Nomological Network (INN), 98
Interpretive, 116
Interpretivism, 117, 126
Interrater reliability, 97
Interviewing, 117, 148
Interview protocols, 128
Investigative question, 38

J
Journal impact factor, 165

K
Key informants, 117
Knowledge base, 136

L
Lab experiment, 107
Laboratory, 45
Latent semantic analysis, 121, 142
Laws of interactions, 63
Legitimation, 146
Leximancer, 142
Liability, 197
LISREL, 142
Literature, 52
Literature reviews, 55
Longitudinal, 45

M
Machine learning, 142
Mail surveys, 102
MAN(C)OVA, 113
Managerial question, 38
Manipulation checks, 113
Manipulation validity, 96
Measure, 92
Measurements, 22, 91, 92
    development, 100
    error, 18
    instrument development, 98
    model, 105
    testing, 100
    validation, 98
Mechanisms, 61–65, 75, 107
Mediating, 66
Mediating variable, 66
Memoing, 120
MetaBUS, 98
Meta-inferences, 144
Metaphorising, 79
Methodologies, 54
Methods, 21, 183, 184
Mid-range theory, 74
Mixed methods, 48, 51, 143, 149
    designs, 145
Moderating variables, 66
Motivation, 180
Multidimensional constructs, 28, 97
Multiple-case, 127

Printed in the United States
by Baker & Taylor Publisher Services